Teach Yourself the Astrology of Human

Mavis Klein

Teach Yourself the Psychology & Astrology of Human Relationships

©Copyright Mavis Klein 2007

ISBN 186163 283 5

ALL RIGHTS RESERVED

No part of this publication may be reproduced, stored in a retrieval system or transmitted in any form or by any means, electronic, mechanical, photocopying, scanning, recording or otherwise without the prior written permission of the author and the publisher.

Cover design by Paul Mason

Published by:

    Capall Bann Publishing
    Auton Farm
    Milverton
    Somerset
    TA4 1NE

To the Reader

While this course assumes that you are already familiar with the basic vocabulary and grammar of astrology and are able to calculate and draw up horoscopes (with or without the aid of a computer program), the early lessons contain brief summaries of all the concepts needed to speak the language of astrology. These lessons will serve to consolidate your previous knowledge and increase your confidence and fluency in your use of the technical terms as well as providing you with a comprehensive dictionary of terms for you to refer to whenever you feel the need.

From Chapter 5 onwards, the fun really begins, when your patience will be rewarded with a step-by-step guide to interpreting individual horoscopes and many different types of relationship. By the time you have finished this course you will be a very competent and increasingly confident practising natal and relationship astrologer.

I have done my best to make all the questions and exercises set as enjoyable as possible. Answers to questions that have particular correct answers will be found at the end of the book.

Wishing you great joy,
Mavis Klein, London, January 2005

By the same author

Lives People Live
How to Choose a Mate
Discover Your Real Self
Understanding Your Child
Pain & Joy in Intimate Relationships
Live Issues
(with Kerry Howard and Julia Hampshire) The Book of Love & Happiness
The Psychodynamic Counselling Primer

Contents

Chapter 1	What We Are Talking About	1
Chapter 2	Elements, Modes, Planets and Nodes	19
Chapter 3	Signs and Houses	33
Chapter 4	Planetary Aspects	46
Chapter 5	The Science, Art, and Profession of Astrology	71
Chapter 6	Pain and Joy in Intimate Relationships	101
Chapter 7	Synastry	140
Chapter 8	Love and Marriage Relationships	163
Chapter 9	Family Relationships	196
Chapter 10	Friendship and Work Relationships	240
Chapter 11	Relationships and Life Cycles	267
Answers to Questions		292
Index		296

List of Charts

	Page
1. Daniel	76
2. Michael	82
3. A Gentle Murderer	85
4.-10. (See answers p. 293)	293
11. Ruth	124
12. Bill Clinton	128
13. Monica Lewinsky	130
14. Composite Bill Clinton and Monica Lewinsky	132
15. Bi-wheel Bill Clinton and Monica Lewinsky	134
16. Yoko Ono	158
17. John Lennon	159
18. Composite Yoko Ono and John Lennon	160
19. Bi-wheel Yoko Ono and John Lennon	161
20. Elizabeth Taylor	144
21. Richard Burton	146
22. Composite Elizabeth Taylor and Richard Burton	148
23. Bi-wheel Elizabeth Taylor and Richard Burton	150
24. Esther	166
25. Mark	168
26. Tony	172
27. Miriam	174
28. Composite Tony and Miriam	176
29. Bi-wheel Tony and Miriam	178
30. Prince Charles	182
31. Composite Prince Charles and Princess Diana	184
32. Bi-wheel Prince Charles and Princess Diana	186
33. Sigmund Freud	208
34. Lucian Freud	209
35. Anita	214
36. Stella	216
37. Composite Anita and Stella	218
38. Bi-wheel Anita and Stella	220
39. Susan	222
40. Helen	224

41. Family tree of four generations	226
42. Maia	228
43. Leila	229
44. Helena	230
45 Benjamin	232
46. Judith	233
47. Nigel	236
48. Nick	238
49. Julie	242
50. Composite Julie and Anita	244
51. Bi-wheel Julie and Anita	246
52. Carl Jung	254
53. Composite Carl Jung and Sigmund Freud	256
54. Bi-wheel Carl Jung and Sigmund Freud	258
55. Emma	260
56. Emma's boss	262
57. Composite Emma and Emma's boss	264
58. Bi-wheel Emma and Emma's boss	265

Chapter 1
What We Are Talking About

Summary: A horoscope defines empirically the innate characteristics and the potential of any entity that comes into being in terms of the planets, signs, and houses that make up all horoscopes. Astrology transcends "good and evil" and it is a spiritual orientation to life that appreciates the combination of "fate" and "free-will" that determines our lives. Prophecy is about extrapolating present trends into the future. A game of cards is a useful metaphor for describing how we live our lives and interact with other people.

Basic Assumptions
The basic assumptions of astrology are that:

* every thing that comes into existence contains within it, for the whole of its existence, the qualities of the moment that it came into being.

* the qualities of any moment can be understood from the symbols of the horoscope for that moment, which is like an algebraic equation, the meanings of the "x's" and "y's" of which depend on the general nature of the entity under consideration (whether it be a human being, an animal, an inanimate entity such as an organization, an idea, or an event).

* a horoscope defines both the innate characteristics of what it describes and the unfoldment of the potential of

that entity, through passing geometrical patterns that are formed by " transits" (present planetary positions in relation to significant points in the original, "natal" horoscope) and "progressions" (symbolic ways of describing the unfoldment of the natal horoscope).

* all horoscopes are alike in containing all the "planets", "signs", and "houses" and uniquely different from each other in the juxtaposition of these components.

* the truths of astrology are empirical truths, developed by humankind in virtually every culture. We do not yet know how astrology works, but a likely theory (that will incorporate astrology into contemporary physics) is that the magnetic fields around all the planets resonate within our nervous systems in "tunes" which we individually recognize. In such a theory, each individual's "tuning" is determined by his or her genetic inheritance and we are born when, as it were, the current pattern of planetary positions "dials our number". Our horoscopes are thus descriptions of what we are, rather than - as is so often falsely presumed - the causes of what happens to us.

Good and Evil

For primitive man - and indeed for modern man up until about five hundred years ago - nothing was inanimate. The validity of astrology was never questioned since it was completely consistent with every human being's acceptance of himself and his life as participating in the life of nature as a whole, in which God was intrinsic. But the development of materialistic science challenged mankind's holistic view of the world and our relation to it as well as the existence of God; and by the beginning of the twentieth century the theories of science could confidently account for the most horrendous "acts of God" in materialistic terms. To very many more people than ever before, God was toppled and presumed dead.

But throughout the twentieth century and to the present day human consciousness has been bombarded with assaults on its new-found materialistic security. The implications of Heisenberg's uncertainty principle, Einstein's theory of relativity, and post-Einsteinian cosmologies, full of uncertainties and such nihilistic horrors as Black Holes and, most lately, Chaos Theory, have permeated the everyday existential consciousness of very large numbers of people. Without God to fall back on, we are left trembling at Nothing.

But we cannot change our minds and return to believing in God in the same way as we did before. We cannot effectively pretend not to know all that materialistic science has taught us. So an idea of God, to be convincing to contemporary humanity, needs to reconcile and synthesize the holism of the ancient world with the atomism of achieved scientific knowledge. And it may well be that, in due course, astrology will be that language that unites all religions in a new, non-anthropomorphic image of God while still retaining His superhuman awfulness, protection, and will.

We cannot manage without God because mankind's deepest need to believe in a meaning and purpose beyond our capacity fully to comprehend is timeless and universal in the face of pain and death. Astrologers are deeply religious people, steeped in awesome wonder at the order and meaning in the universe and the appreciation of even the smallest details of our lives as manifestations of the working of the Whole. Astrology is God-minus-his-long-white-beard, who, it is recorded in the first chapter of Genesis, has made available to us clues to His will through "lights for signs and seasons, for days and years".

"Good" and "evil" are mundane concepts that are fundamentally irrelevant to astrology. Astrology describes the ways things are and invites us, happily and serenely, to live in accordance with, or unhappily and agitatedly to stamp our feet in protest at, what is.

Thus astrology is, at core, a spiritual orientation to life that perceives everything, ultimately, to be the way it has to be, even if why things are the way they are is beyond our knowing. Nevertheless, in our mundane lives we cannot manage without the concepts of "good" and "evil", and it is worth considering why this is so.

As we are born, the first separated "facts" we apprehend are our bodily experiences of contentment versus pain. We like contentment; we don't like pain. In due course, this basic dichotomy gets refined by further differentiation, and we become able to calibrate and name our experiences as different degrees and kinds of contentment and pain. We continuously struggle to maintain contentment and eliminate pain from our lives but we never succeed for long. So the first truth we seek in our lives is that which makes sense of these two facts, contentment and pain. Contentment becomes "good" and pain becomes "bad".

Soon we come to realize that our attempts to eliminate pain from our lives are essentially and repeatedly doomed to failure, and this realization becomes another fact that needs to be made sense of in terms of theory. That is, we require a meta-theory that explains to us how the pain we continuously experience is necessary. Even when we are most contented, the pain of our knowledge of our mortality continues to haunt us. So the second essential theory we formulate invariably construes "good" and "evil" forces that permeate the universe. The unavoidable corollary to this truth is that, inasmuch as we ourselves are part and parcel of the universe, the good and evil forces of the universe must also be in us. Thus, irrespective of the variability of "truths" espoused by different individuals and different cultures, no individual and no culture can manage life without the concept of "good and evil" and the associated concepts of "blame and guilt" and "reward and punishment". These concepts are the necessary foundation for all our individual and collective meanings-of-life.

To the extent that we seek to evade the necessity to accept responsibility - for our badness and blameworthiness as well as our goodness and praiseworthiness - we invent "good luck" and "bad luck", by which we acknowledge the necessary existence of "good" and "bad" in the universe while at the same time dissociating them from goodness and badness in ourselves. In effect, we dissociate ourselves from the universe although, in truth, the only authentic use of the word "luck" is in reference to matters like just catching or just missing a bus; and in only a few of such events the good and the bad luck cancel out to zero.

There may, of course, be no meaning to life; the universe may be ultimately chaotic. Espousing this possibility as a "certainty" eliminates the need to make sense of pain. Pain becomes merely one of the contingent facts of life and no more explicable or inexplicable than any other. Everything is simply the way it is and neither good nor bad; so we are wasting our time asking why. Non-reflective playing out of our lives in keeping with the biological propellants of our constitution is all. This is the way of life for other species; and, paradoxically, this is also the position of the mystic, whose achieved attitude is of joyously interpreting everything we experience as "for no reason", just the way it has to be. The way of the mystic is called "transcendental"; but the same way, when we refer to other species is not. This is so because mystics have transcended their fear of death and other, derivative fears; animals don't have a conscious fear of death to transcend.

Our human life begins without any awareness of the separateness of ourselves from the universe. But from when we first say "I" we become more and more consciously differentiated from everybody else as we develop our individualities and our self-esteem. Our self-esteem, by rights, should grow and grow until, fully assured of our individual worth, we begin to transcend our pride in our separateness and, ideally, come full circle to oneness with the universe again, as achieved by the mystic.

The task of developing our self-esteem is essentially the task of struggling through our fears, and in the final analysis all our fears may be reduced to our fear of death. Knowledge of our mortality is the central pain of life and is universal, although each of us, in accordance with the individual differences between people, has specific fears and associated pains that we struggle to overcome. The struggle for a well-developed sense of our own individual importance in the world through our achievements is a manifestation of our doomed-to-fail quest for immortality.

Yet the universal quest for meaning in our lives bears witness to the fact that we never fully come to terms with the ultimate meaninglessness that death makes of all our mundane concerns. Some of us deny death by a belief in some form of eternal continuation of life; others seek a symbolic continuation of their lives after physical death by being remembered for their works or deeds; and most of us find some comfort in the knowledge of the survival of some of our genes in our children, grandchildren, and further descendants. One way or another, the happinesses that are available to us in our limited lives are contingent on us living life as if it has meaning, even if it doesn't.

Thus the courageous confrontation and growth of our individuality is the principal task of our lives, for as long as it takes. The mystical position of detachment, which may be the ideal goal for all of us, cannot be achieved pre-emptively. Nobody has yet transcended his or her individuality without first having an individuality to transcend. And whatever categories and concepts our minds may prompt us to impose on the universe, one formulation is absolutely necessary, irrespective of culture or individuality, and that something has to be "good and evil" with its derivative moral constructs which polarize blame and responsibility, righteousness and guilt.

Fate and Free-will

Thus armed with our basic dichotomous category of "good and evil", and with evil as the definitive "cause" of pain and death, we naturally seek to be "good" and thereby avoid pain and death. But we certainly can't avoid death, and although in multitudinous ways we do learn to attribute to our own "goodness" the avoidance of everyday pains, and it "serves us right" if we put our hands in fire and are burnt, we are forced to acknowledge that there is an incomprehensible gap in the perfect correspondence we would like to see between goodness and reward and evil and punishment. We do avoid the pain of being burnt by being "good" and not touching hot stoves; but a completely unpredicted gas explosion may set fire to our house and us. We avoid being arrested and sent to prison by being "good" and law-abiding; but Nazis can come and round us up and throw us into concentration camps. Love given is usually reciprocated; but sometimes love is responded to with a spit in the eye. Being "good" by eating a healthy diet and exercising does tend to keep us free from illness and pain and prolong our lives; but the young and "innocent" may be smitten with cruel and mortal illnesses while the "bad" live long and healthy lives.

We are left with the tantalizing ambiguity that pains - both physical and psychological - can demonstrably be shown to be at least delayed by our "goodness" - except when they are not! And this conundrum leads us inevitably to the second basic construct of the human mind, Fate versus Free-will. In the name of Fate we inevitably invent God, who becomes the Final Cause that determines both our inescapable mortality and the painful contingencies of our lives that we are unable to connect to our own causative "badness". However, for every instance of pain in our lives we are challenged to look first for the cause in our previous - however unconscious - freely-willed "badness"; and other people are often only too-willing to help find us "deserving" of our pains even when we ourselves are blind or deaf to the part we have played. Only death itself can safely be fully ascribed to Fate - that is, the totally unassailable will of God.

Thus at every moment in our lives "the problem of free-will" continues to daunt us. It cannot be solved, only dis-solved. The existence or non-existence of "meaning" and "fate" are concepts that refer to a "higher" state of consciousness than our own. An insect on the receiving end of the "free-will" of my foot in crushing it is experiencing its fate when the incident is interpreted simply in terms of my power over it. More complexly, wasn't the insect responsible for not seeing my foot and avoiding it? And even more complexly (from the insect's point of view) if I (whose power is infinitely greater than its) have chosen to crush it under my foot, why did I choose to do so? Maybe for the obvious (to it) sin it commited against me by stinging me. But maybe it didn't sting me and didn't even try, and in its dying moment it rages against me for my "injustice". (Think of all the insects who do sting people and get away with it!) Did I kill it punitively in accordance with a morality of my own outside its comprehension? From a "superior" position in order to demonstrate its "nothingness" to me? Because I am "evil"? It could never know. It - and we - can only solve the problem pragmatically by living at the highest level of free-will available to our consciousness, while accepting (from the evidence) that there are bound to be times in our lives when a higher consciousness than we are capable of mocks our lower level morality and conscious purposes. It is simply pragmatically the case that we live our lives most satisfactorily (to ourselves) when we behave as if our free-will is paramount.

The corollary to this pragmatic conclusion is that our free-will is contained in the responses we choose to make to our "fate".

Our responses are our choices, and these have consequences. We cannot avoid making choices. Passivity is the self-delusion of "no choice", but of course it is a choice and, like all others, has consequences. Psychotherapists are more aware than most other people that every moment of choice is the cause of the inexorable train of events that follows in its wake, to the natural conclusion of a "happening" in our lives. When a conclusion is painful we are loath to remember the moment of choice that determined it, although repression is never complete, and often the knowledge that we have chosen a path to pain is manifest as obsessive fear of that pain - too late - and a conscious struggle to avoid it. We actually do know (in our hearts) that we have made the choices we have which have led to their inevitable conclusions. In our most intense moments we are reduced to knowing, in all its simplicity, that in virtually - if not absolutely - everything that befalls us, we get exactly what we set out to get, and so what we deserve.

In the tiny number of occurrences in all our lives where even the inferential evidence of our unconscious motivations is not sufficient to account for what befalls us, we are reduced to impotent acquiescence to Fate - that is, God's will. All that is left for us to decide is whether we will deem God essentially benevolent or essentially malevolent - that is, whether on balance the universe is basically a friendly or an unfriendly place, whether "good" outweighs "evil", whether God Himself is benevolent or malevolent. Implicitly, the paranoic schizophrenic (and the paranoic component in us all) decides that, on balance the universe - that is, God - is an evil, malevolent force. The religious component in all of us decides that, on balance, God - as what is left over when "good" and "evil" have been balanced out - is good and benevolent. To the extent that we perceive good to be the pervasive dominating force in the universe we ourselves become "good"; to the extent that we perceive evil to be the pervasive dominating force in the universe we ourselves become "bad". Happiness is not guaranteed to those who perceive the universe to be, on balance, good; but unhappiness is inevitable for those who perceive the universe to be, on balance, evil.

So theologians seek to convince us that, no matter how we suffer, ultimately everything is for the best in this, the best of all possible universes. Indeed, they are even inclined to argue that pain and suffering are privileges implying future rewards not to be granted to those who do not suffer. All that we see is like the meaningless tangle of threads on the back of the tapestry, only God seeing the beautiful coherent picture on the front.

So it is, through a religious orientation to life, we are enabled to get rare glimpses of "the next level above us", at which level mundanely experienced incompatible opposites are contained in a higher unity. These privileged glimpses of a higher realm are contained in an experience of serene knowledge that everything is as it has to be, which experience is often the unexpected outcome of a long battle we have fought with an issue of "good and evil" in our mundane lives. Whether it be an event or a state of being, such moments in our lives fill us with wondrous awe, are very memorable to us, and have the power permanently to enhance our overall sense of well-being.

Free-will is maintained in the quality of our responses to our fate - basically whether, as the psychoanalyst Carl Jung put it, we "do gladly that which we must" or stamp at our fate with impotent rage. The religious orientation is to go willingly - however uncomprehendingly - with whatever fate metes out to us, the reward for which is eventually the beatitude of the mystic for whom even the fear of death is transcended. Religiously, destiny is fulfilment.

Prophecy

Amongst the people who angrily reject astrology on the pseudo-religious grounds that it is evil because it deploys prophecy, if we scratch just a little below the surface of their hostility we find terror. The terror is that astrology can forecast death and all the derivative mundane pains of life for an individual, which facts people do not want to know.

In truth, astrology cannot predict - and nor would any astrologer worthy of the name claim to be able to predict - with certainty, any particular manifestation in an individual's life or in the mundane world of events. Astrology is an algebra, the "x's" and "y's" of which we can use to enhance our ability to comprehend the past and the present and to choose the future in terms of the options available to us within the boundaries of the pre-determined general energies that will be operating in our lives. As in ordinary algebra, the same equation can be used to find the answers to a huge diversity of mundane "arithmetical" questions. And what a magnificent algebra astrology is! Nothing but astrology can see the equivalence of gas leaks, a sea voyage, film-making and mystical transcendence (Neptune); of underground explosions, surgery, demagoguery and psychological transformation (Pluto); of electricity, unexpected events, intuition and democracy (Uranus); of bones, concrete, fear, and self-discipline (Saturn); of obesity, good investments, lawyers and wisdom (Jupiter).

With or without astrology we are all making (short-term) predictions (Mercury) and (longer-term) prophecies (Jupiter) all the time, that is whenever we use the future tense. The accuracy of any prediction a person makes is a function of the depth and breadth of the knowledge he or she has concerning the subject-matter under consideration and the distance along the path into the future on which he or she is focusing. With the knowledge of myself that I have, my present prediction that I will light a cigarette in the next hour is a near-certainty; my prophecy that I will not end my days in the country in which I presently live is vague and subject to many intervening variables between now and then; my prediction that I will finish writing this book and find a publisher for it within the next year is likely. In broad terms we seem, on average, to be able to project ourselves accurately into own future up to about two years hence; thereafter, the image becomes rapidly more blurred due to our brain's incapacity to see, at a glance, the ever-increasing number of "moves" (as in a game of chess) that are possible between now and then. The famous astrologer Grant Lewi said, "Prophecy ... is merely the projection of the line of logic into the future. It is the extension of events along the line which they are already travelling, toward a goal which experience has led the prophet to expect..."

In life, as in chess, there are different degrees of skill in playing the game, which can be attributed to a combination of innate talent and devotion to the acquisition of techniques that can be learned. Grand Masters of life are the renowned prophets of history, rightly revered for their courage. Their courage consisted not so much of their willingness to be proven mistaken (for nothing is a certainty until it has actually happened) but for their willingness to know and announce the outcome of present trends while still being bound to the necessity of continuing along the path already chosen to its conclusion, however unpleasant they saw that conclusion to be. There are moments in all our lives when our knowledge and deep interest in some matter makes us minor prophets, epitomized most commonly perhaps in our knowledge of the "mistakenness" of some of our children's life decisions, while sadly and poignantly also knowing we must allow them to play out the consequences of their choices and learn their own lessons. It is our intense interest in and specialized knowledge of our children that enables us to make such actual predictions with our knowledge of the "mathematics of life" - which we call our experience.

Astrology is a precise formulation of the mathematics of human consciousness and experience. As algebra, astrology appeals to some people essentially for its intrinsic, abstract beauty; these people are the "pure mathematicians" of astrology. Most astrologers, though, want to use astrology in everyday life and, like applied mathematicians, their efficacy as prophets depends as much on their knowledge of relevant, other mundane subject-matters as on their knowledge of the tool of astrology. Thus, astrology can only be made to "work" well in medical matters when it is applied by doctors, in psychological matters by psychologists, in meteorology by weather forecasters, in money matters by economists, etc.

The language of astrology offers us a sublime vocabulary and grammar for disciplining and extending the understanding and prophetic wisdom towards which we are all striving in every aspect of living and throughout our lives.

However bound and constrained our lives may be by our natal horoscopes (and by transits and progressions to them) we are no more bound by them than we are by our more obvious genetically determined attributes, such as the colour of our eyes, our gender, our blood group, and the multitude of "programmes" manifest in such experiences as our acquisition of teeth, the onset of puberty, and the greying of our hair. A man four feet six inches tall would be simply foolish to deny that he will not be an Olympic high-jumper. How much energy he wastes and how much pain he causes himself hoping to be an Olympic high-jumper - energy he could use productively and pain he could avoid if only he aimed for what is actually possible for him! In exactly this way - and at deeper and subtler levels as well - astrology tells us just such truths about ourselves and so, by enabling us to avoid the pain of unrealistic hopes and expectations, is Good, not Evil.

No astrologer worthy of the title imposes unsolicited predictions and prophecies onto other people. To do so would be Evil to the extent that the astrologer would be falsely projecting onto another's consciousness thoughts which are not synchronous with the other's being. But once a question is voiced the astrologer has the ability to "complete" the question with an answer consonant with the question's meaning for the questioner. Questions and answers are two sides of the one coin of a given moment when the question becomes conscious to an individual, and seeing both sides of the coin creates psychological completion of that moment, enabling the individual to move on to another moment, unhampered by "unfinished business" from the past.

Life and Love as a Game of Cards

The two most fascinating considerations concerning people are the samenesses and the differences between them. We are all alike (in having all the same signs, houses, and planets in our horoscopes) and all uniquely different from everybody else (in the infinitely various configurations of the signs, houses, and planets in our individual horoscopes). Compatibility and incompatibility may be observed in samenesses between any two people; and compatibility and incompatibility may be observed in differences between any two people.

The first requirement for us to function effectively in any transaction with any other human being is a minimum knowledge of "human nature", through which we recognize the communality of all people everywhere in their general needs and frailties. People who interact with others with an implicit consciousness of the primary samenesses rather than the differences between all people exude a modest warmth that never fails to attract people to their presence. This is the necessary basis of all lovingness; but it is not sufficient for successful intimate relationships.

Without any knowledge of the differences between ourselves and any other, our essential self-love impels us to treat the other as if he or she were identical with ourselves; so whether or not we please him or her is bound to be a matter of chance. "Good manners" facilitate us in pleasing all people, at least within the bounds of the culture to which our particular "good manners" apply, at a minimal superficial level; but, to achieve any degree of intimacy with another, some acquired knowledge of our own and the other's idiosyncratic nature is needed.

The metaphor that I find provides the most precise image of the samenesses and the differences between us is that of a pack of cards, the games that can be played with it and the hands that can be dealt. God holds the pack which contains the totality of all that is possible; each of us is dealt a hand (our horoscope) which is one of a virtually limitless number of possible hands. Each hand may be likened to and contrasted with any other hand in a large number of ways, the ways chosen being determined by relevance to the game being played at any particular time.

We have no choice in the hands we are dealt; but we are free to choose which game or games we will play; and we are free to play our chosen games lightly or seriously, with desultoriness or enthusiasm, with attention or absent-mindedness, with good or bad grace, with clumsiness or artistry. No hand is intrinsically "better" or "worse" than any other; playing out a grand slam with a fistful of court cards and trumps can be as boring as playing an adroitly skilful game with no trumps or court cards can be joyful.

Shall we only play games where our own hand grants us a head-start towards winning? Or sometimes choose to play games where the below-average value of our hand grants us the pleasure of challenging us to stretch the boundaries of our innate limitations? Shall we learn to play one game supremely well? Or enjoy the variety of learning and playing a number of games with limited skill in each? Shall we play for high stakes or low? Shall we play games of high chance or high skill? In all these matters we are free to choose and are responsible for the consequences of our choices.

Seated across the table from our partners, what must we do to make the game as pleasurable as possible for both of us? We need explicitly to establish with our partners the conventions by which we will covertly communicate to each other the contents of our respective hands; sort our cards and categorize them in a way that makes most sense within the rules of the game; make sure we have all our cards in our hand and none is hidden behind another; ascertain the strengths and weaknesses of our hand and communicate them to our partner, within the rules of the game; attend carefully to our partner's communications to us, sorting out the components of his communication into responses to us and the information he is also giving us about his own strengths and weaknesses; arrive at a mutually agreed explicit contract; play the game cooperatively, attentively, and with finesse and pleasure; apologize for any errors we make, and happily forgive our partner for his or her errors, with the good sportsmanship derived from our knowledge that we are both "only human" and it is "only a game".

Exercises

1. Draw up a horoscope of 'Now' - that is, for the time, place, and date on which you are reading this, and make some comments on this horoscope for:

    (a) a baby girl
    (b) a baby boy
    (c) a cat

(d) a political party

(e) the beginning of your study of this course.

What mundane knowledge and assumptions of your own are you expressing in each of your comments?

2. Which of the planetary energies most closely expresses:
    (i) our struggles to overcome our fears and develop our self-esteem?
    (ii) love that transcends our concerns with ourself?
    (iii) unexpected events?
    (iv) the radical transformation of our lives?
    (v) logical thinking?
    (vi) ambition?
    (vii) maternal instincts?
    (viii) aggression?
    (ix) extravagance?
    (x) diplomacy?
    (xi) impulsiveness?
    (xii) changing conditions?
    (xiii) hard work?
    (xiv) optimism?
    (xv) pride?
    (xvi) dutifulness?
    (xvii) nervous energy?
    (xviii) original ideas?
    (xix) beauty?
    (xx) power?
    (xx1) laughter?
    (xxii) harmony?
    (xxiii) drug abuse?
    (xxiv) family influences?
    (xxv) computers and technology?
    (xxvi) talkativeness?
    (xxvii) brave action?
    (xxviii) obsessiveness?

(xxix) psychological depth?
(xxx) dreams?

Do think of human horoscopes as maps of the genetic endowment of people, whose lives can only be lived within the bounds of their innate potential, but whose fulfilment will come through working to the limits of their potential.

Don't think of any horoscope as "good" or "bad", but rather as an inevitable combination of talents and challenges to be used freely by the person to whom it is given.

Chapter 2
Elements, Modes, Planets and Nodes

Summary: Summary descriptions of each of the elements, modes, planets, and Moon's nodes are given.

I assume your knowledge of the general nature of the Elements (Triplicities) of Fire, Earth, Air, and Water; the Modes (Quadruplicities) of Cardinality, Fixity, and Mutability; and the significance of the North and South Nodes of the Moon. This chapter is a summary reminder of these concepts. Chapters 3 and 4 will consolidate your knowledge of the signs and houses and of planetary inter-aspects.

The Triplicities (Elements)
The Elements are Fire, Earth, Air, and Water. They act like adjectives, qualifying the basic energies of the planets that are in them.

Fire
Fire is inspired, enthusiastic, speculative, explorative idealistic. It represents the spiritual side of our natures and is forceful, ardent, and impulsive. Like fire itself, predominantly Fire sign people burn, crackle, consume, warm, and delight or annoy. They have a huge appetite for life, but tend to be impatient of more sensitive or gentler people. Fire feels that Water will extinguish it, that Earth will smother it, but that Air will fan its flames.

Astrological Symbols

Aries	♈	Sun	☉
Taurus	♉	Moon	☽
Gemini	♊	Mercury	☿
Cancer	♋	Venus	♀
Leo	♌	Mars	♂
Virgo	♍	Jupiter	♃
Libra	♎	Saturn	♄
Scorpio	♏	Uranus	♅
Sagittarius	♐	Neptune	♆
Capricorn	♑	Pluto	♇
Aquarius	♒	Moon's North Node	☊
Pisces	♓	Moon's South Node	☋
		Chiron	⚷
		Part of Fortune	⊗

Positively, Fire can be summarized as courageous, self-assertive, idealistic and visionary, stimulating of creative expression, active, ardent and strong.

Negatively, Fire is ruthless and self-imposing, fanatical, destroying the efforts of others, wasting energy through excess, self-indulgent and loud.

The Fire signs are Aries, Leo, and Sagittarius.

Earth
Earth is physical and has to do with material and practical affairs. It is possessive, work and achievement oriented, practical, cautious, and patient. It loves routine and attends to details. Predominantly Earth people are solid, dependable, capable, hard-working, sensible, and trustworthy. Earth feels that Air will dry it out, Fire will parch it, but that Water will refresh it.

Positively, Earth is a good provider, has a good sense of timing, deep understanding, and is utterly reliable.

Negatively, Earth is mean and hoarding, lacks emotional awareness, is ultra-conservative, and coarse.

The Earth signs are Taurus, Virgo, and Capricorn.

Air
Air is communicative, sociable, and detached. It represents the mental plane and plays a big part in interactions between people. It gathers knowledge and applies it through thought and objectivity. Predominantly Air people are inclined to reasoning and working in the realm of ideas. Air enjoys connecting people and ideas and is averse to extreme caution or emotional sensitivity in others.

Positively, Air is sociable, inventive, intelligent, alert, objective, and full of ideas.

Negatively, Air is superficial, garrulous, repetitious, hyperactive, nervous, aloof, and cold.

The Air signs are Gemini, Libra, and Aquarius.

Water
Water is emotional, needy, sensitive, and unstable. Like water itself, Water is calm when well-contained but can be turbulent and stormy and drag others down. Predominantly Water people are sensitive to art, music, poetry, and dance, but they tend to dislike other people who are boisterous or have strong personalities. Water feels that Fire will make it boil and Air will make it evaporate, but Earth will contain it.

Positively, Water is compassionate, understanding, artistic, romantic, and sensitively reserved.

Negatively, Water is paranoid and hysterical, lives in a fantasy world, manipulatively controls others, and exaggerates feelings histrionically.

The Water signs are Cancer, Scorpio, and Pisces.

The Quadruplicities (Modes)
The modes are Cardinality, Fixity, and Mutability. They act like adverbs, describing the ways in which the basic energies of the planets are expressed through them.

Cardinality
Cardinality is assertive, outgoing, active, dynamic, and go-getting. It is direct and to the point, but can also be overly-

impulsive, restless and impatient. It is initiating, ambitious, and entrepeneurial, likes creatively meeting challenges and then moving on to fresh ventures.

Positively, cardinality is enterprising, forceful and assertive, creative, and independent.

Negatively, cardinality is bossy, ruthlessly self-seeking, impatient and opportunistic.

The Cardinal signs are Aries, Cancer, Libra, and Captricorn.

Fixity
Fixity is manifest in patience and steadfast determination. It plans and organizes, is principled, disciplined, and resists change.

Positively, fixity is loyal, purposeful, reliable, and conservative of values and resources.

Negatively, fixity is opinionated, inflexible, stuffy, stubborn, and habit-bound.

The Fixed signs are Taurus, Leo, Scorpio, and Aquarius.

Mutability
Mutability is responsive, adaptable, easygoing, versatile, and enjoys interacting with others.

Positively, mutability is cooperative, compromising, flexible, and appreciative of all points of view.

Negatively, mutability is nervous, restless, lacking in conviction, and uncommitted.

The Mutable signs are Gemini, Virgo, Sagittarius, and Pisces.

The Planets

The planets are the core of all astrology. They are the nouns and the verbs of our being, representing all the ideas and energetic forces that the human mind is capable of construing.

The Sun

The Sun is the source of all life. Physiologically and anatomically it refers to our vitality, the heart, and the thymus gland. The Sun's primary function is the unfoldment of the self, self-sufficiency, and self-realization. It expresses ambition, creativity, organization, self-centredness and is associated with father, husband, boss, power, authority.

Positively, the Sun is bounteously energetic, courageous, and healthfully proud.

Negatively, the Sun is bossy, arrogant, ostentatious, and egocentric.

The Sun rules the sign of Leo and is associated with the 5th house of any horoscope.

The Moon

The Moon is the sustainer of life, rules body fluids, lymph glands, breasts, gall bladder, thyroid gland, female reproduction, and the sympathetic nervous system. Its primary function is nurturing and protection, expressing habitual responses and early childhood conditioning. The Moon is creative, adaptive, sympathetic, emotional, and os associated with wife, mother, and early childhood.

Positively, the Moon is protective, nurturing, kind and generous.

Negatively, the Moon is selfish, demanding, hyper-emotional, and possessive.

The Moon rules the sign of Cancer and is associated with the 4th house of any horoscope.

Mercury
Mercury is the communicator of life and rules the central nervous system and all the sense organs. Its primary function is communication and coordination. It is associated with youth.

Positively, Mercury is intelligent, reasoning, alert, and discriminating.

Negatively, Mercury is deceitful, nit-picking, nervous, and unsympathetic.

Mercury rules the signs of Gemini and Virgo and is associated with the 3rd and 6th houses in any horoscope.

Venus
Venus is the beauty of life. It rules the veins, parathyroid glands, and kidneys. Venus' primary function is the evaluation of feelings, and it expresses cooperation, sociability and the needs to appreciate and be appreciated.

Positively, Venus is artistic, kind, affectionate, cooperative, and gentle.

Negatively, Venus is greedy, self-indulgent, vain, lustful, and lazy.

Venus rules the signs of Taurus and Libra and is associated with the 2nd and 7th houses in any horoscope.

Mars
Mars is the action of life and rules the adrenal glands, the sympathetic nervous system, red blood cells, sexual desire muscles, fevers, accidents, and high blood pressure. Its primary function is energetic assertion.

Positively, Mars is enterprising, pioneeering, self-assertive, courageous.

Negatively, Mars is quarrelsome, selfish, aggressive, coarse, abusive.

Mars rules the sign of Aries and co-rules (with Pluto) the sign of Scorpio. It is associated with the 1st and 8th houses of any horoscope.

Jupiter
Jupiter is the wisdom of life. It rules the liver. Its chief function is growth of all kinds including the expansion of consciousness through knowledge, morality and orthodox religious beliefs, long-distance travel, and the law. It is philosophical, trustworthy, optimistic, jovial, and future oriented.

Positively, Jupiter is generous, expansive, open, humourous, and scrupulously honest.

Negatively, Jupiter is arrogant, snobbish, greedy, extravagant, bigoted, and opinionated.

Jupiter rules the sign of Sagittarius and co-rules (with Neptune) the sign of Pisces and is associated with the 9th and 12th houses of any horoscope.

Saturn
Saturn is (like Jupiter) the wisdom of life. It rules the skeletal system, skin, teeth, bones. Its primary function is formative processes and self-control. It preserves, is commonsensical, self-disciplined, self-reliant, practical, cautious, persistent, dutiful, conscientious. It is associated with delays, frustration, decay, death, suffering, fear, and responsibilities.

Positively, Saturn is helpfully limiting, patient, persevering.

Negatively, Saturn is bigoted, pessimistic, narrow-minded, defensive, cold, materialistic, and suspicious, mean, frightened and frightening.

Saturn rules Capricorn and co-rules (with Uranus) Aquarius and is associated with the 10th and 11th houses of any horoscope.

Uranus
Uranus is the liberator of life, rules the pineal and sex glands, ankles, and nervous disorders. Its function is to bring surprise and excitement into our lives. It rules electricity, technology, independence, originality, reforms, democracy, sudden events, intuition, eccentricity, and anarchy.

Positively, Uranus is original, inventive, intuitive, a social reformer, idealistic.

Negatively, Uranus is eccentric, erratic, rebellious, anarchistic.

Uranus is the co-ruler (with Saturn) of Aquarius and is associated with the 11th house of any horoscope.

Neptune
Neptune is the inspiration of life and rules the spinal cord, the thalamus, poisoning, and drowning. Its functions is to add refinement, sensitivity, imagination, dreams, and idealistic love to our lives. It rules inspiration, mysticism, trance, music, poetry, photography, hospitals, glamour, dreams, the sea.

Positively, Neptune is mystical , imaginative, sensitive, artistic, compassionate, fashionable.

Negatively, Neptune is deceptive, illusory, delusory, self-dramatizing, escapist, and addicted.
Neptune co-rules (with Jupiter) the sign of Pisces and is associated with the 12th house of any horoscope.

Pluto
Pluto is the transformer of life, rules regenerative processes, eliminative processes, and obsessions. Its function is irresistably to transform and to eliminate the outworn structures of life. It forces crises and brings about inevitable death and rebirth. It rules the underworld, terrorists, volcanoes, atomic energy, psychoanalysis, the sex act.

Positively, Pluto transforms, eliminates accumulated tensions, and is the agent of evolutionary forces.

Negatively, Pluto annihiltes, murders, obsessively controls.

Pluto co-rules (with Mars) the sign of Scorpio and is associated with the 8th house of any horoscope.

Chiron
Chiron is the wounded healer of life. It is a small heavenly body that orbits the solar system between Saturn and Uranus

and its nature is that of a very powerful hyphen linking the conservative, painful, fearful, disciplined qualities of Saturn with the sudden release into daring freedom and newness that Uranus brings. Chiron is where we are most wounded, where there is the greatest potential for the healing of our wounds, where we are capable of deeply wounding others and of healing others. Its function is to bring us new freedom and healing through forcing us to face issues we would rather ignore. In the charts of famous people Chiron often reflects what it is that these people are famous for.

Postively, Chiron is extremely sensitive to and tender towards our own ant others' deepest personal wounds.

Negatively, Chiron uses its sensitivity to reinforce and enlarge our own and others' deepest wounds.

The sign and house rulerships of Chiron are not yet established.

The Moon's Nodes

The Moon's Nodes, unlike the planets, are not energies or archetypal constructs of the human mind but are, nonetheless, extremely important parts of our horoscopes.

The Moon's Nodes indicate the point in space where the Moon crosses the ecliptic (the Earth's orbit around the Sun); In a given horoscope, the South Node by sign and house indicates some innate talent that the individual brings into this life, but which can become neurotic avoidance of personal growth. The North Node is what we are required to struggle towards in order to fulfil our most profound growth through healthy self-discipline in stretching our boundaries to fulfil our potential.

When an individual has worked sufficiently towards the fulfilment of his or her North Node potential, the South Node can then, through its easy talent, express what the North Node has learned.

For example, a man with his South Node in Gemini was born with a natural talent for verbal fluency and the ability easily to learn about lots of different subject-matters. By the time he was 25 he sensed that he was wastefully dissipating his mental abilities and he decided to go to university and study Law (North Node in Sagittarius). After he had studied Law for many years, he wrote, with great speed and fluency, an excellent legal textbook, (South Node in Gemini is rewarded.)

Exercises

1. Which element is
    a) practical?
    b) communicative?
    c) emotional?
    d) enthusiastic?

2. Which mode is
    a) persistent?
    b) flexibly responsive?
    c) go-getting and initiating?

3. Which planet most
    a) demands freedom of expresssion?
    b) communicates verbally?
    c) is compassionately idealistic?
    d) demands ruthless regeneration?
    e) expresses values?
    f) is hard-working and dutiful?
    g) reflects earliest childhood experiences?

h) expresses ambition?

i) is forcefully assertive?

j) expresses our deepest psychic wounds?

k) is optimistic, generous, and sometimes bigoted?

4. Which planet do you associate with
   a) bosses?
   b) red blood cells?
   c) jewellery?
   d) devastating war?
   e) film-making?
   f) lawyers?
   g) teeth and bones?
   h) computers?
   i) healing through confrontation?
   j) motherliness?
   k) telephones?

5. Which node represents
   a) our innate talents?
   b) the task we must struggle towards to fulfil our potential?

6. How do you experience Saturn in your horoscope? In what way does it handicap you and in what way do you use it to achieve your goals and overcome your fears?

7. How do you experience Chiron in your horoscope? How does it represent wounds that were inflicted on you in childhood?

What experiences has transiting Chiron brought you that have helped to heal your core wound?

8. To what extent are you struggling away from your South Node sign and house towards your North Node? How conscious are you of your North Node as a depiction of your deepest life-task?

Chapter 3
Signs and Houses

Summary: The general meanings of the Signs and Houses of the horoscope are summarized. Which House system? Angular, succedent, and cadent houses. The importance of the Ascendant-Descendant and IC-MC axes. Hemisphere emphases and chart shapes. The nature of the 12 Houses and their planetary rulers. A note on unknown times of birth.

Signs of the Zodiac
We will now summarize the positive (+) and negative (-) qualities of each of the signs of the zodiac - mentally, emotionally, and physically.

Aries (Cardinal Fire) is:

mentally	+ imaginative, alert, thriving on challenges - dogmatic, argumentative, sarcastic
emotionally	+ ardent, enthusiastic, honest - bad-tempered, self-centred, intolerant
physically	+ energetic, determined, courageous - foolhardy, heavy-handed, restless

Taurus (Fixed Earth) is

mentally	+ practical, deep-thinking, organized - stubborn, narrow-minded, blunt

emotionally	+ affectionate, loyal, wholesome - possessive, jealous, crude
physically	+ hard-working, persevering. strong - lazy, bull-in-a-china-shop, self-indulgent

Gemini (Mutable Air) is

mentally	+ alert, inquisitive, witty - sarcastic, superficial, impatient
emotionally	+ adaptable, responsive, versatile - unfeeling, fickle, uncommitted
physically	+ lithe, energetic, co-ordinated - restless, agitated, nervous

Cancer (Cardinal Water) is

mentally	+ intuitive, perceptive, has good memory - worrying, complaining, lost in dreams
emotionally	+ sympathetic, loyal, affectionate - hysterical, possessive, moody
physically	+ tenacious, relaxed, soft - fearful, devious, withdrawn

Leo (Fixed Fire) is

mentally	+ organized, confident, inspired - stubborn, arrogant, makes sweeping generalizations

emotionally	+ generous, charming, romantic - vain, proud, self-centred
physically	+ graceful, bold, impressive - ostentatious, overbearing, gaudy

Virgo (Mutable Earth) is

mentally	+ methodical, precise, analytical - critical, worrying, complaining
emotionally	+ independent, poised, helpful - distant, prissy, solitary
physically	+ hard-working, unobtrusive, modest - fussy, interfering, restless

Libra (Cardinal Air) is

mentally	+ fair-minded, intellectual, rational - indecisive, procrastinating, unbalanced
emotionally	+ charming, cooperative, poised - vain, moody, timid
physically	+ graceful, energetic, elegant - lazy, clumsy, self-indulgent

Scorpio (Fixed Water) is

mentally	+ perceptive, inquisitive, shrewd - critical, cynical, sarcastic

emotionally	+ magnetic, intense, deep - jealous, suspicious, secretive
physically	+ focused, assertive, courageous - obsessive, self-destructive, vengeful

Sagittarius (Mutable Fire) is

mentally	+ witty, inquisitive, broad-minded - blunt, prejudiced, opinionated
emotionally	+ zestful, enthusiastic, generous - bad-tempered, intolerant, grandiose
physically	+ active, bold, energetic - clumsy, bad-timing, crude

Capricorn (Cardinal Earth) is

mentally	+ deep, practical, methodical - narrow-minded, prejudiced, cynical
emotionally	+ responsible, conscientious, dutiful - resentful, bitter, inhibited
physically	+ hard-working, persevering, self-controlled - cowardly, withdrawn, resistant to change

Aquarius (Fixed Air) is

mentally	+ inquisitive, witty, original - argumentative, intolerant, absent-minded

emotionally   + independent, self-sufficient, whacky
              - bossy, contrary, distant

physically   + energetic, adventurous, coordinated
              - lacks team spirit, uncoordinated, timid

Pisces (Mutable Water) is

mentally   + intuitive, imaginative, witty
              - vague, confused, lacking discipline

emotionally   + gentle, sensitive, compassionate
              - cruel, moody, solitary

physically   + flexible, soft, gentle
              - fearful, aimless, nervous

Which House System?

The twelve house division of the horoscope defines the universal areas of living. All house systems are based upon the daily twenty-four hour rotation of the Earth on its axis, but there are many different systems of creating the twelve-house division, some based on space and some on time. In Western astrology, the two most often used house divisions are Equal House and Placidus, and the charts presented in this course will show Placidus divisions. The greater the latitude for which a horoscope is drawn up, the more differences will there be between the different house systems. It is suggested that, for the time being, you use Placidus and from time to time experiment with other divisions, and ultimately decide for yourself which system works best for you.

Angular, Succedent, and Cadent Houses

All house systems apart from the Equal House one have the 1st, 4th, 7th and 10th houses as angular houses beginning respectively at the Ascendant, IC, Descendant, and MC, which are very important and sensitive points of the horoscope. These four houses - the 1st, 4th, 7th, and 10th houses - are called angular houses. The beginning points of these houses are called the angles of the horoscope and any planets close to these points will be very powerfully expressed. The Ascendant-Descendant axis refers to our basic ways of expressing ourselves as individuals and in intimate encounters (personal or business) with other people. The IC-MC axis refers to our basic sense of our own power and our ways of expressing our power in the pursuit of our worldly ambitions and status.

Succedent houses have a quality of fixity. The 2nd, 5th, 8th, and 11th houses of the horoscope are the succedent houses and generally refer to our resources, the 2nd to do with our own money and our non-material values, the 5th with our family resources in the form of our children and our creativity in general, the 8th with the monetary resources and values that partners bring to us, and the 11th with the connections we make in the wider world through the creative ideals we share with others.

Cadent houses have a quality of mutability. The 3rd, 6th, 9th, and 12th houses of the horoscope are the cadent houses and refer to our various transitory ways of relating to ourselves and to other people, the 3rd to do with short-distance travel, the 6th to our everyday work and care of our health, the 9th to long-distance travel and education, and the 12th to the influences of hidden enemies and our own neurotic behaviour.

Chart Shapes

It is always useful, before beginning a detailed analysis of a horoscope, to notice any marked overall pattern in the placement of the planets, which will give a general sense of the way the life will be lived. There are seven general patterns.

A splash pattern is one in which the planets are distributed quite evenly round the whole 360 degrees of the horoscope. Such a horoscope implies universal interests and a possible difficulty in choosing the focus for ambitions.

A bundle pattern is one where all the planets are contained within a 120 degree segment of the horoscope. The course of life is likely to be within quite narrow bounds of opportunism.

A locomotive pattern is one where all the planets are contained within 240 degrees and implies an orientation of self-driving individuality, led by the energy of the planet leading the other planets in a clockwise direction.

A bowl pattern is one where all the planets are clustered in one half of the horoscope. All the planets above the horizon implies a concentration on objectivity and events in the outer world; below the horizon, the concentration will be on the subjective life and the inner world. When all the planets are on the rising (Ascendant) side of the chart, the life will tend to be initiating and determining of one's own destiny; when all are on the setting side of the chart, the life is likely to be lived receptively, fulfilling one's destiny in response to the stimulation of other people and events.

A bucket pattern (a bowl with a single planet providing a "handle") will give a very particular and uncompromising direction to the life effort, with the planet forming the "handle" dominating over all other considerations.

A see-saw pattern (two roughly opposed groups of planets) implies a constant consideration of and sensitivity to opposed views and contrasting possibilities.

A splay pattern (sharp, irregular aggregations of planets) suggests special, individualistic responses to life and a person whom it is difficult to pigeon-hole.

The Twelve Houses and Their Rulers

The First House is ruled by Mars and is associated with Aries. It is the most prominent of the houses because it involves the overall manner in which the personality and the attitudes and outlook on life are expressed. Because this house describes the overall temperament, it also refers to health, because general health and specific types of illnesses have association with different temperaments.

The Second House is ruled by Venus and is associated with Taurus. It has to do with inner resources and values as well as financial resources, and the sign on the cusp may give some indication of the way the individual earns his or her living.

The Third House is ruled by Mercury and is associated with Gemini. It refers to the written and spoken word and all forms of everyday communication with other people, including short-distance travelling in the pursuit of daily affairs. It is also associated with neighbours and with near relativies, especially brothers and sisters.

The Fourth House is ruled by the Moon and is associated with Cancer. It refers to our deepest desire to put down roots and create a home and also to the kind of family into which an individual was born. It rules the parent who was the greater nurturing influence during childhood, usually but not always the mother.

The Fifth House is ruled by the Sun and is associated with Leo. It is the house of creativity, play, children, romance, and all that is primarily pleasure-seeking. It can also indicate the kind of relationship the individual is likely to have to his or her children.

The Sixth House is ruled by Mercury and is associated with Virgo. It is the house of work and health, and the sign on the cusp will describe the manner in which the individual approaches his or her daily work and their way of being of service to other people.

The Seventh House is ruled by Venus and is associated with Libra. It rules all one-to-one personal relationships and partnerships of a contractual kind, both marriage and business. It indicates the general manner in which the individual deals with other people.

The Eighth House is ruled by Mars and Pluto and is associated with Scorpio. It concerns matters of life and death, sexuality, and the monetary and other resources brought to the individual through partnership relationships, including inheritances. Planets in this house are intensely felt but may find difficulty in outward expression.

The Ninth House is ruled by Jupiter and is associated with Sagittarius. It rules the intellect and is associated with higher education, philosophy and morality, religious observance, and long-distance travel.

The Tenth House is ruled by Saturn and is associated with Capricorn. It rules career, ambition, and achievement and shows the kind of respect the individual will earn in the world. It describes the parent who was most influential in encouraging the child's worldly ambitions, usually but not always the father. In a woman's chart it may also describe her husband because, even in our time, when women have careers of their own, their status is still, to some extent, a reflection of their husband's standing in the world.

The Eleventh House is ruled by Saturn and Uranus and is associated with Aquarius. It describes the individual's friends and associations in the wider world of career and humanitarian ideals. It describes hopes and wishes for a better world.

The Twelfth House is ruled by Jupiter and Neptune and is associated with Pisces. It rules places of solitude and places of incarceration, including prisons and hospitals. It is often referred to as "the house of self-undoing" because the energies in this house have great difficulty finding outward expression and are often turned inward in self-destructive ways. Serving the needs of suffering others and/or finding creative forms of expression for our 12th house energies are the ways to avoid neurotic suffering and self-destructive behaviour.

A Note on Unknown Times of Birth

When a birth time is not known, it is appropriate to draw up the horoscope for dawn for the place at which the birth occurred. In such cases we need to be cautious is analyzing the houses of the horoscope, bearing in mind the unknown time of birth, although dawn horoscopes do seem to have a validity of their own, even including the houses. Indeed, dawn horoscopes are the basis of all the astrological columns that are written for newspapers and magazines. For example, if your Sun sign is Virgo and you look up the predictions for Virgo in a newspaper column, the predictions are based on assuming 0 degrees of Virgo on the Ascendant and an equal house division of the zodiac from that point. And such horoscope readings (when written by competent astrologers) definitely seem to work. So when you are required to analyze a horoscope of an unknown time of birth it is recommended that you include an interpretation of the house positions of the planets, taking the position of the Sun at dawn as the natural Ascendant.

However, in the interpretation of relationships where one or both times of birth are unknown it is probably wise not to refer to the houses in the inter-relationship between the two people. There are, anyway, plenty of other precisely known factors between the horoscopes of two people to delineate the essence of their relationship with confidence.

Exercises

1. Which combinations of planets and signs could be described as:

    a) ardent, loyal love?

    b) talkative, flirtatious love?

    c) imaginative, responsive compassion?

    d) sociable, assertive communication?

    e) sensitive, controlled feelings?

    f) practical, critical assertiveness?

    g) enthusiastic, go-getting ambition?

    h) unstable, moody dutifulness?

    i) enthusiastic, moral dutifulness?

    j) conservative, inflexible beliefs?

    k) warm, creative healing?

    l) conservative but flexible beliefs?

2. Which house refers to:

    a) our general outlook on life?

    b) the way we earn our money?

c) our career?

   d) our everyday work?

   e) our business partnerships?

   f) our neurotic tendencies?

   g) our friendships?

3. The following statements describe a sign on a house cusp together with the sign's ruler in a particular house. Work out which sign is on which particular house cusp and how that area of life finds expression through the planet which rules the sign but is placed in a different house.

   a) She has a very serious, ambitious attitude to her career as a marriage guidance counsellor.

   b) He earns his living by many and varied communications, which involves him in a lot of long-distance travel.

   c) Her personality is very sensitively compassionate, which she expresses particularly in her care of her crippled husband.

4. Write brief meanings of the following:

   a) Moon in Virgo in the 4th house

   b) Mars in Sagittarius in the 8th house

   c) Jupiter in Capricorn in the 7th house

   d) Venus in Leo in the 5th house

   e) Mercury in Libra in the 11th house

   f) Saturn in Aries in the 12th house

   g) Chiron in Taurus in the 1st house

   h) North Node in Cancer in the 2nd house

(Example: Mars in Gemini in the 5th could be, "She asserts her-self in a communicative way in her romantic affairs and in her relationships with her children".)

5. Using equal or Placidus houses, write down the house position of the ruler of each house in your horoscope. For example, if the sign on your Ascendant is Capricorn, look at the house position of Saturn and assess how you use Saturn in this house to express your basic personality (First House). If your 6th house cusp is Virgo, look at the house position of Mercury in your horoscope and assess how you use Mecury in this house in your everyday work and how it affects your health. Repeat this procedure for each of the 12 houses of your horoscope.

6. Compare your own timed birth horoscope to a dawn horoscope for the date and place of your birth. How true to your experience if yourself are the houses and planetary placements in them of each of these two horoscopes?

Do notice interesting chart shapes and the significance of clusters of planets in particular houses and signs. Don't get swamped by detail. Houses and signs are only qualifiers of the planetary energies whose aspects with each other are the core dynamic meaning of the horoscope.

Don't over-interpret individual items in a horoscope. The whole is bigger than the sum of its parts.

Chapter 4
Planetary Aspects

Summary: The major aspects between planets are defined. Brief interpretations are given of the positive and negative manifestations of each pair of planets in combination and of each planet in combination with the Ascendant, Midheaven, and Moon's North Node.

Aspects
Every planet is, strictly speaking, in aspect to every other planet in the horoscope. However, certain specific degree aspects are known to be particularly potent in a clearly manifest way, and we will consider these aspects in this chapter. The closer to exactitude the more powerfully will an aspect manifest.

How large an orb to use as the limit of significance of any given aspect is an empirical matter, but for each kind of aspect most astrologers are in general agreement, and these orbs will be given as guidelines.

Orbs allowed for planetary inter-aspects in a natal horoscope are also appropriate when analyzing a relationship between two people in terms of the planetary inter-aspects between their horoscopes.

A conjunction (0 degree aspect) is the most powerful of all aspects and is fundamentally neutral in nature. A conjunction represents a blending of energies, and the ease of its expression will depend on the natural harmony or tension between the two energies involved. The strength and meaning of the conjunction will generally be influenced by the nature of the planet that is strongest in its own nature. Allow a maximum orb of about 8 degrees.

A sextile (60 degree aspect) represents an opportunity for easy creativity in the harmonious expression of the planetary energies involved. Many opportunities will come to people having many sextiles in their horoscopes and may be associated with great creative productivity. Allow a maximum orb of about 6 degrees.

A square (90 degree aspect) is a tense aspect. The two planets involved have difficulty working together but struggle hard to do so. The person expressing a square is expressing a dynamic, thrusting tension that provides energy for constructive achievement and productivity. Allow a maximum orb of about 8 degrees.

A trine (120 degree aspect) is an extremely easy-flowing, harmonious energy between two planets. It is an aspect of talent that requires no energy to activate it, but may be taken for granted by the person possessing it, who may therefore fail to fulfil its potential. Motivation needs to come from more dynamic aspects in the horoscope for a trine to be expressed productively. Allow a maximum orb of about 8 degrees.

An opposition (180 degree aspect) is a powerful aspect of conflict and/or compromise. The person usually identifies with one of the planetary energies and experiences the other, opposed planetary energy as a frustrating circumstance or person in their environment. Unconsciously, the person attracts others who provide a rationalization for the conflict that is actually inside him- or herself. Allow a maximum orb of about 8 degrees.

An inconjunct (150 degree aspect) is an aspect that is halfway between a trine and an opposition. The two planets involved are neither harmonious nor disharmonious, but have very different orientations. Each needs to make adjustments to accommodate the needs of the other. In intimate relationships, inconjunct aspects between the planets in one person's horoscope and the other person's horoscope are often experienced by the people involved as elusive, erotic tension between them. Both in the individual horoscope and in relationships the inconjunct calls for the person to give appropriate value and expression to each of the energies in turn. Allow a maximum orb of about 5 degrees.

"Hard" aspects (the square, opposition, inconjunct and some conjunctions) alone are often frustrating; "soft" aspects (the sextile, trine, and some conjunctions) alone are often lazily apathetic. A combination of hard and soft aspects in a horoscope is often a blessing of motivation that finds fulfilment.

Planetary Inter-aspects

Sun/Moon
Positive expression: A harmonious personality, inner balance, self-assertion and emotions work well together.

Negative expression: Inner discontent, an unbalanced personality, self-assertion and emotional life in conflict.

Sun/Mercury
Positive expression: A clear mind, consciousness of objectives, organizing ability, prudence.

Negative expression: Lack of clarity, absent-mindedness, aimlessness.

Sun/Venus

Positive expression: The feeling of love, attractiveness, artistic leanings, sense of beauty, sociability.

Negative expression: Self-indulgence, hedonism, superficial attachment to appearances.

Sun/Mars

Positive expresssion: Energy, leadership, virility, determination.

Negative expression: Aggression, obstinacy, hastiness, quarrelsomeness.

Sun/Jupiter

Positive expression: Good health, good morality, the will to expand consciousness.

Negative expression: Materialism, extravagance, wastefulness, ostentation.

Sun/Saturn

Positive expression: Firmness, perseverance, ability to be absorbed in a subject, modesty.

Negative expression: Inhibitions in mental or physical development, pessimism, depression.

Sun/Uranus

Positive expression: Originality, individuality, a far-seeing mind, a reformer.

Negative expression: Rebelliousness, self-will, impatience, trouble-making.

Sun/Neptune
Positive expression: Active imagination, mysticism, the cultivation of inner-life experiences.

Negative expression: Gullibility, weakness, addictions.

Sun/Pluto
Positive expression: Creative power, leadership, intense commitment to ambitions.

Negative expression: Power struggles, obsessive-compulsive disorders.

Sun/Chiron
Positive expression: Healing of own and others' wounds through creative self-expression.

Negative expression: Inhibition of self-expression through fear of rejection and pain, arrogant insensitivity to others' vulnerabilities.

Sun/North Node
Positive expression: Preference for associations and teamwork, the search for intellectual contacts.

Negative expression: A disharmonious attitude towards living or working with others.

Sun/Ascendant
Positive expression: Desire to gain esteem and importance within one's personal environment, self-confidence.

Negative expression: Disharmonious relationships, excessive or misplaced self-confidence.

Sun/Midheaven
Positive expression: Consciousness of goals and ambitions, a positive attitude to life.

Negative expression: Lack of clarity concerning goals and ambitions, a wrong or misguided outlook on life.

Moon/Mercury
Positive expression: Adaptability, sympathetic kindness, good judgement.

Negative expression: Liking for gossip, changeable thinking, propensity for lying.

Moon/Venus
Positive expression: Expression of tenderness, an affectionate nature, good judgement concerning the value of all things, cheerful disposition, gracefulness.

Negative expression: Moodiness, shyness, easily led, poor powers of judgement.

Moon/Mars
Positive expression: A forceful and purposeful nature, openness and frankness, honesty, sincerity.

Negative expression: A harsh judge of self and others, quarrelsomeness, rashness, irritability.

Moon/Jupiter
Positive expression: Kindness, benevolence, an obliging and helpful nature.

Negative expression: Negligence, inner conflicts with regard to one's outlook on life, rebellion.

Moon/Saturn
Positive expression: Self-control, thoughtfulness, dutifulness, conscientiousness.

Negative expression: Uncommunicativeness, feelings of inferiority, depression, anxiety, humourlessness.

Moon/Uranus
Positive expression: Emotional excitability, attentiveness, confidence in own convictions.

Negative expression: Excessive self-will, fanaticism, tendency exaggeration, restlessness.

Moon/Neptune
Positive expression: Sensitivity, sympathetic nature, inner vision, imaginative perception.

Negative expression: Illusions or delusions, self-deception, tendency to tell lies.

Moon/Pluto
Positive expression: Very intense, focused feelings, excitability in emotional expression.

Negative expression: Emotional outbursts of negative feelings, such as jealousy, vulnerable to feeling insulted by others.

Moon/Chiron
Positive expression: The ability to sense moods, feelings and emotions in others and to understand them deeply.

Negative expression: Powerful insecurity and need to feel superior to other people.

Moon/North Node
Positive expresssion: Dominance of feeling in personal relationships and in relationship to the world.

Negative expression: Lack of adaptability, tendency to have unhappy, disruptive relationships.

Moon/Ascendant
Positive expression: Harmonious behaviour in the presence of others. Adaptability and obligingness.

Negative expression: A disharmonious attitude towards other people, hyper-sensitivity, easily annoyed.

Moon/Midheaven
Positive expression: Appreciation of spiritual values, desire to care for others, appreciation of home and family.

Negative expression: Volatile disposition and rapidly changing moods, unreliability.

Mercury/Venus
Positive expression: A sense of form and design, intellect strongly influenced by feeling, a light-hearted, cheerful nature.

Negative expression: Vanity or conceit, self-indulgence, hypersensitivity.

Mercury/Mars
Positive expression: Love of discussion and argument, quickness of response in speaking, wit.

Negative expression: Grumbling, fault-finding, quarrelsome, irritability, exploitation of other people's ideas for own benefit.

Mercury/Jupiter
Positive expression: Wealth of ideas, sound commonsense, oratorical talent, optimism, love of learning, interest in literature.

Negative expression: Frivolity, absent-mindedness, unreliability, grandiose speech, tactlessness, arrogance or conceit.

Mercury/Saturn
Positive expression: Logical thinking, thoroughness, concentration, love of tidiness, organizing ability, hard-working, methodical, philosophical thinking.

Negative expression: Mistrust, shyness, narrow-mindedness, uncommunicative and reserved disposition, obstinacy.

Mercury/Uranus
Positive expression: A revolutionary spirit and mind, shrewdness, a talent for speaking, intuitive, interest in science, intellectual flexibility.

Negative expression: Tendency to scattered thinking, nervous haste, tactlessness, contradictoriness for its own sake.

Mercury/Neptune
Positive expression: The power of imagination, a sympathetic and compassionate understanding of people, intuitive thinking, idealism.

Negative expression: Wrong thinking, gullibility, confused ideas, nervous sensitivity, fantasy, untruthfulness or the tendency to tell lies.

Mercury/Pluto
Positive expression: Good powers of observation, a quick grasp of every situation, intellectual depth.

Negative expression: Hasty thinking, speaking or acting, opposition for its own sake, irritability, grandiosity.

Mercury/Chiron
Positive expression: Great intuitive sensitivity to other people's thoughts.

Negative expression: Communicates with others in hurtful ways and is vulnerable to being hurt by others' innocent remarks.

Mercury/North Node
Positive expression: Sociableness, desire to exchange ideas and thoughts with other people, intellectual interests.

Negative expression: An unsociable disposition, propensity to gossip.

Mercury/Ascendant
Positive expression: Defining self in relation to others, enjoying the exchange of ideas and thoughts with others.

Negative expression: Tendency to gossip and to criticize and belittle others.

Mercury/Midheaven
Positive expression: Thinks a great deal, forms own opinions, self-knowledge, clear aims and ambitions.

Negative expresssion: Over-estimation of self, lack of self-criticism, aimlessness.

Venus/Mars
Positive expression: Passionate love, desire, a warm heart, artistic creativity, a lively expression of feelings.

Negtive expression: Disharmonious emotional and sexual life, irritability, dissatisfaction, tactlessness, sudden outbursts of extreme passion or sensuality followed by coldness.

Venus/Jupiter
Positive expression: A warm heart, grace, tact, attractive personality, harmonious relationships.

Negative expression: Inclination to laziness, falsity in love relationships, wastefulness, excessive expression of feeling.

Venus/Saturn
Positive expression: A sense of reality, sobriety, reserve, loyalty and faithfulness, self-control.

Negative expression: Emotionally inhibited, hard-heartedness, being dissatisfied, unhealthy expression of sexuality.

Venus/Uranus
Positive expression: Strong excitability in love expression, impulsive expression of sensations and feelings, artistic talent.

Negative expression: Self-will in love, fickleness, moodiness caused by repressed emotional desires, urge for independence in love, strange love relationships.

Venus/Neptune
Positive expression: Sensitivity in love, great appreciation of beauty, art, and music, good taste, dreaminess, high ideals.

Negative expression: Illusion or delusion in love, lack of good taste, indecisiveness, sexual aberrations.

Venus/Pluto
Positive expression: Ability to see through false values and role-playing, appreciation of lasting values.

Negative expression: Hostility towards women (especially by men who are unconsciously uncomfortable with the feminine side of their own nature), impressed by superficial fashions and values.

Venus/North Node
Positive expression: Adaptability, obligingness, a pleasant and engaging personality.

Negative expression: Lack of adaptability, unwillingness to oblige people, a disagreeable nature.

Venus/Ascendant
Positive expression: A harmonious attitude towards other people, sociableness, an appreciation of beauty and artistry in personal environment.

Negative expression: A disharmonious relationship to personal environment, lack of good taste, wastefulness.

Venus/Midheaven
Positive expression: An affectionate disposition, kindness and benevolence, a harmonious nature, a sense of beauty and art.

Negative expression: Vanity and conceit, jealousy.

Mars/Jupiter
Positive expression: A love of enterprise, the joy of living, a sense of honour, the urge for freedom, creative power.

Negative expression: Rebelliousness against rules and regulations and against authority, inclination to exaggerate, hasty or premature action.

Mars/Saturn
Positive expression: Endurance, indefatigibleness, the power of resistance.

Negative expression: Self-destructiveness or violence towards others, harshness, bitterness, obstinacy, selfishness.

Mars/Uranus

Positive expression: Sudden expression of extraordinary amount of energy, urge for freedom and independence, quick determination, courage

Negative expression: An argumentative disposition, inclination to contradict others, self-willed obstinacy, a fighting spirit, violence.

Mars/Neptune

Positive expression: The control of feelings and passions through a spiritual outlook, abstemiousness, talent for percussion instruments and conducting.

Negative expression: Will without the ability to act, self-destructive use of drugs, irritability, feelings of inferiority.

Mars/Pluto

Positive expression: Ability to demonstrate extraordinary force and vigor, great self-confidence and ambition.

Negative expression: Ruthlessness, brutality, cruelty, violence.

Mars/Chiron

Positive expression: Potential for overcoming great obstacles, ability to heal self and others.

Negative expression: Tendency to harm self and others, inclination to violence and bad temper.

Mars/North Node
Positive expression: Desire to cooperate with others, team spirit, desire for children.

Negative expression: Disharmonious collaboration with others, quarrelsomeness, lack of good feeling for others.

Mars/Ascendant
Positive expression: Ability to lead others resolutely, active team-work.

Negative expression: Fighting and aggression in relationships, inclination to violence.

Mars/Midheaven
Positive expression: Readiness for action, decisiveness, clear consciousness of aims and ambitions, the power to succeed in chosen career, resoluteness.

Negative expression: Over-excitability, acting under emotional stress, premature action, impulsiveness.

Jupiter/Saturn
Positive expression: Patience, perseverance, consciousness of objective, straightforwardness and honesty, philosophical thinking.

Negative expression: Emotional tensions and inhibitions, lack of self-confidence, pessimistic and self-destructive thoughts.

Jupiter/Uranus
Positive expression: The desire for knowledge, good intuition, organizing ability, quick grasp of situations, farsightedness, philosophical interests.

Negative expression: Desire for freedom, obstinate opposition to other people for the sake of being difficult, exaggeration, inconstancy, tactlessness.

Jupiter/Neptune
Positive expression: Richness of emotional expression, an active and intense imagination, idealism, enjoyment of art and music, interest in metaphysical and religious problems, great love of humanity.

Negative expression: Impressionability, easily seduced, dreaminess, inclination to escapism, being misunderstood by others, inclination to speculation and wastefulness.

Jupiter/Chiron
Positive expression: Full of original ideas, unusual abilities as a teacher, great self-assurance, strong convictions.

Negative expression: Self-righteousness, intolerance, unwillingness to be taught.

Jupiter/North Node
Positive expression: A harmonious relationship to other people, adaptability, compromise, tact.

Negative expression: Lack of good fellowship, exploitation of other people for own ends.

Jupiter/Ascendant
Positive expression: A pleasant disposition, a harmonious personality and a positive attitude to other people, generosity, a liking for abundance and comfort in physical surroundings.

Negative expression: Excessive desire to be important, disharmonious attitudes to other people, wastefulness.

Jupiter/Midheaven
Positive expression: A happy and harmonious person, striving for success, consciousness of aims and ambitions, optimism, generosity, contentment.

Negative expression: Self-importance, ruthless pursuit of ambition.

Saturn/Uranus
Positive expression: The ability to cope with every situation, power of endurance, indefatigability, willpower, determination.

Negative expression: Great emotional tensions and strains, irritability, emotional conflicts, rebellion, provocative behaviour, violence, frustrated urge for freedom.

Saturn/Neptune
Positive expression: Willingness to make sacrifices for others, taking care of others, self-restraint, cautiousness, foresight.

Negative expression: A struggle between materialism and spirituality, frequent mood changes, insecurity, depression.

Saturn/Pluto
Positive expression: Tenacity and toughness, endurance, ability to do very difficult work with extreme self-discipline.

Negative expression: Hardness, cold-heartedness, severity, tendency to violence, fanaticism.

Saturn/Chiron
Positive expression: Determination to heal the wounds of childhood by courageous transformation of self.

Negative expression: Great inhibition and self-deprecation.

Saturn/North Node
Positive expression: Attracted to people older than self, contacts with mature and experienced people.

Negative expression: Great difficulties in cooperating with others, inhibitions in the presence of other people.

Saturn/Ascendant
Positive expression: Maturity of outlook, gain of experience through everyday life.

Negative expression: Tendency to feel hindered and depressed, a negative outlook, suffering from poor circumstances in life.

Saturn/Midheaven
Positive expression: Patient work for the achievement of aims in life.

Negative expression: Emotional inhibitions, lack of courage, feelings of inferiority.

Uranus/Neptune
Positive expression: Inner vision, enlightenment, inspiration, idealism, an interest in spiritual subjects, mysticism, artistry.

Negative expression: Confusion, emotional imbalance, nervous sensitivity, wrong ideas.

Uranus/Pluto
Positive expression: Creative energy and power, fighting for innovations and reforms, untiring effort, endurance.

Negative expression: Impatience, tendency to scatter energies, fanaticism, violence and destruction.

Uranus/Chiron
Positive expression: Conscious expression of individuality, integrity in the face of opposition to own unconventional ideas.

Negative expression: Eccentricity for its own sake, insensitivity to what is sacred.

Uranus/North Node
Positive expression: A lively and active manner in the company of other people, desire to share new experiences in life with others, the search for change and variety.

Negative expression: A restless disposition, nervousness, irritability in the presence of others.

Uranus/Ascendant
Positive expression: An original, quickly responding personality, love of change and variety, inventive ability.

Negative expression: An unstable personality, inconstancy, irritability, a tendency to disturb other people.

Uranus/Midheaven
Positive expression: Pursuit of aims and ambitions with great energy, power to be successful in life, readiness for action, prudence and vision, originality.

Negative expression: Emotional instability, frequently changing aims, premature action, unreliability, bad temper.

Neptune/Pluto
Positive expression: Great sensitivity, a highly active imagination, clairvoyant visions, love of mysticism.

Negative expression: Confusion, delusion, falsehood, deception.

Neptune/Chiron
Positive expression: Great sensitivity and imagination, a spiritual teacher.

Negative expression: A self-important or deceptive teacher or guru.

Neptune/North Node
Positive expression: A communal, spiritual lifestyle.

Negative expression: A lack of social feeling, inclination to deceive and cheat other people.

Neptune/Ascendant
Positive expression: Impressionability, sensitivity, compassionate understanding of other people, artistry.

Negative expression; Lack of stamina, inclination to be negatively influenced by other people, moodiness.

Neptune/Midheaven
Positive expression: Interest in the unconscious mind and spiritual understanding, artistic career.

Negative expression: Confusion about aims in life, insecurity, lack of self-confidence, vulnerability to deceptive influences.

Pluto/Chiron
Positive expression: Ability to transform situations for the betterment of self and others.

Negative expression: Seeks control over others to exploit them for own selfish aims.

Pluto/North Node
Positive expression: Urge to associate with many people, desire to become a public figure and exert influence.

Negative expression: Feeling of being burdened by association with others, suffering from others.

Pluto/Ascendant
Positive expression: Willpower, ambition, the striving for power, lifelong personal growth and transformation, charisma.

Negative expression: Dictatorial control of other people, repulsive behaviour.

Pluto/Midheaven
Positive expression: Growth and development of strength, power to be successful, vision, authority.

Negative expression: Foolhardiness, promiscuity, abuse of power, tendency to invoke resistance of others and enmity towards self.

Chiron/North Node
Positive expression: Self-healing through associations in the larger world, potential for healing others.

Negative expression: Self-destructiveness in badly-chosen relationships, the infliction of suffering on other people.

Chiron/Ascendant
Positive expression: An excellent counsellor, teacher, or healer.

Negative expression: Makes own suffering the basis of all relationships to others, self-pitying.

Chiron/Midheaven
Positive expression: An excellent teacher, charismatic healer of the masses.

Negative expression: Exploitation of others' suffering for personal gain, a charlatan.

North Node/Ascendant
Positive expression: Harmonious relationships in family, social, and working environments.

Negative expression: Disharmonious relationships, an anti-social outlook.

North Node/Midheaven
Positive expression: Desire to seek out people with same ideas as self, enthusiasm for shared ideals.

Negative expression: Inconstancy in the pursuit of joint objectives, putting own interests above shared group interests.

Exercises

1. Which aspect expresses

    a) the complete blending of energies?
    b) having to compromise between our own impulses and the demands of other people or the world?
    c) opportunity?
    d) two impulses in ourselves that we cannot express simultaneously?

e) easy, harmonious blending of energies?

f) a tense, dynamic struggle to blend energies within ourselves?

2. What aspects between planets could be described in the following ways? (The answers given on p.293 are not the only possible correct ones. Think of equally possible other aspects for yourself.)

a) She finds it difficult to be simultaneously a mother and a loving wife.

b) He expresses his love for another aggessively.

c) There is a natural blending of rationality and imagination in him, which sometimes deludes him and sometimes enables him to communicate very eloquently.

d) She experiences life and other people as making great demands of her and she works very hard to fulfil her ambitions.

e) She struggles to reconcile her dreams with her responsibilities.

f) She has great talent as a musician and poet.

g) She is always gossiping and talking about her feelings.

h) He is a natural salesman.

i) She expresses her feelings very suddenly.

j) He expresses his feelings with charming originality.

k) She expresses her feelings in sudden outbursts that imply a mistrust of other people.

l) He expresses himself and his ambitions very assertively.

m) He expresses himself and his ambitions with abundant optimism.

n) He expresses himself and his ambitions in a frowningly serious way.

Do think of the interaction of the archetypal energies of any two planets as primary, irrespective of the aspect connecting them.

Do think of hard aspects as dynamically motivating; and soft aspects as gifts that can only be rewarding when used effortfully, especially in combination with hard aspects.

Don't think of hard aspects as "bad" and soft aspects as "good".

Chapter 5
The Science, Art, and Profession of Astrology

Summary: Three examples of horoscope interpretation are given: one systematic and analytical, the others intuitive and holistic.

The professional principles pertaining to being an astrologer are outlined.

Introduction
When, with their horoscope in front of us, we come face to face with a client in readiness to interpret their horoscope for them, we already know a great deal, without even looking at the horoscope. First, we know that the horoscope we are about to interpret is that of a human being. We also know their gender, their age (from the data needed to draw up the horoscope) and, if they share our own race and nationality, a multitude of quite confident, though largely sub-conscious assumptions about their general orientation to life which we take for granted are the same as our own. Thus the possible particular meanings of the "x's" and "y's" that make up the "algebraic equation" of the horoscope are hugely diminished. So even before we begin to speak to our client we are in a generally good position to make some "educated best guesses" about how the symbols of this person's horoscope are likely to manifest in this person's life.

Sometimes our "educated best guesses" will be mistaken; more often, the combination of our general understanding of human nature, our understanding of the vocabulary and grammar of astrology, and our accumulated experience both of life and the reading of horoscopes, will tend to make our "educated best guesses" very accurate and precise. Never be fearful or ashamed of making mistakes in interpretation. So long as the interpretations you offer are astrologically plausible you have not actually made a mistake but just offered a likely expression of the symbols that happens not to be true at the mundane level of the person's experience of themselves; and the more you are willing sometimes to be mistaken the more skilled you will become.

However, for the practical purpose of giving the most valid and useful interpretation of the horoscope of a particular person, the more you know about the actual life of the person the better. Are they married? Do they have children? What is their educational level? What is their career? Do they have any hobbies? Are they religious? etc., the answers to which will all help you narrow your focus and give them interpretations that are relevant to the ways in which they themselves have already freely chosen to crystallize the general meaning of their horoscopes as well as pointing out to them the areas of potential in themselves that they have not so far made use of. Remember, our horoscopes describe both what we are and the potential that the cosmos is asking us to fulfil in the whole course of our lives.

Systematic Interpretation

1) General nature. Analyze any obvious pattern to the planetary aspects and any imbalance of the elements and modes. Analyze the Ascending sign and its ruler, and the Sun and Moon and their house positions.

2) Mentality. Look to the 3rd and 9th houses for mental outlook and to the 5th house for creativity. Look to the 8th and 12th houses for intuitional ability and to Mercury and its aspects for special abilities.

3) Career. Analyze the 10th house and its tendencies, the 6th house for everyday work. Look at the comparative strengths of Jupiter and Saturn for easy success and obstacles to be overcome. Refer to the 7th house for partners and business associates and the 2nd and 8th houses for money matters.

4) Hobbies and spare time activities. The 1st house refers to the general orientation to life, the 5th house to pleasures. The Sun and Moon will also be associated with the activities that most appeal to the person.

5) Personal contacts. Look to the 11th house for friends, the 5th house for romantic relationships, the 7th house for marriage, the 8th house for sexual love. Venus and its aspects describe the general capacity for intimate relationships, and Mars and its aspects for the expression of sexuality. The sign and aspects to the Sun in a woman's chart are associated with the kind of men she is attracted to; and the sign and aspects to the Moon in a man's chart are associated with the kind of women he is attracted to.

6) Family The 4th and 10th houses refer to the parents (the 4th to the parent who was most tenderly nurturing, generally but not always the mother, the 10th to the parent who gave the most explicit advice concerning how to succeed in life, generally but not always the father). Saturn and its aspects describe the kind of discipline imposed on the child by the parents. The 3rd house pertains to brothers and sisters; and the 5th house to one's own children.

7) Health. The 1st house describes the general physical and constitutional type of the person. The 6th house describes health and particular kinds of health vulnerabilities. The Sun describes general vitality and the heart; the Moon functional disorders; Mars burns, cuts, fevers, and accidents; Jupiter liver trouble; Saturn chills, falls, rheumatic conditions, tooth decay; Uranus circulation problems, breaks

and sprains; Neptune psychosomatic illnesses; Pluto psychological problems, especially obsessions and compulsions; and Chiron where we feel most wounded and will seek to heal ourselves and/or others.

8) Travel. Look to the 3rd and 9th houses and to Mercury and Jupiter.

9) The importance of the Ascendant. Whatever else the chart shows, it can only act through the medium of the Ascendant. For instance, a strong Mars in the 1st house may be shown, but it will act very differently through a dominant sign like Aries compared with the same Mars in a gentle sign like Pisces.

10) Intercepted signs. When one sign is at the beginning (on the cusp) of a house and the next sign is wholly contained within that house, the house is understood to be ruled jointly by both signs, so the affairs of that house and the expression of the planets within that house will have the "flavour" of both signs.

11) Aspects. In the print-out of all the horoscopes in this course some "minor" aspects between planets are included, which you need not pay attention to at this stage in your learning. The major aspects of conjunction, sextile, square, trine, opposition, and inconjunct are quite sufficient to give a very comprehensive reading of any horoscope.

12) Repetition. It will often be found that personality characteristics are repeated several times from a number of different configurations in the horoscope. This is a sure sign that the characteristic described is a very important part of the nature. Indeed, most important characteristics of a person will almost always be discernable several times from quite separate components of the horoscope.

A Systematic Analysis of a Horoscope - Daniel (Chart 1)

Biographical information. Daniel was born in Calcutta, India, of European parents. He left home at age 16 and spent nine years moving around a number of countries and doing various jobs. He is highly intelligent although he was a rebel in his early years and failed to complete his secondary schooling. He has never married although he has had many love affairs. He came to England in 1978 and, together with his sister, started a business which has been very successful.

The following interpretation is written for Daniel. The justifications for my interpretations, in brackets in the text, are for the sake of the student reading it and would not normally be included for the client.

Dear Daniel, It is important in reading the following astro-analysis to understand the principles behind it.

Contrary to widespread misunderstanding, astrology is not a fatalistic interpretation of people's characters and the events that occur in their lives. It is rather an interpretation of the unique pattern of energies that existed in the cosmos at the moment of an individual's birth, which pattern is understood to correspond to the individual's innate and lasting predispositions. With reference to the pattern of the birth moment, a tentative prognosis can be made as to the most likely ways that the particular individual will experience himself and his relationships to other people and to the world at large.

Your birth chart may be thought of as a map of your genetic inheritance. Modern psychology testifies to the profound importance of the experiences of the first few years of our lives as well as to our genetic inheritance in determining our final characters, personalities, and destinies, so biographical data

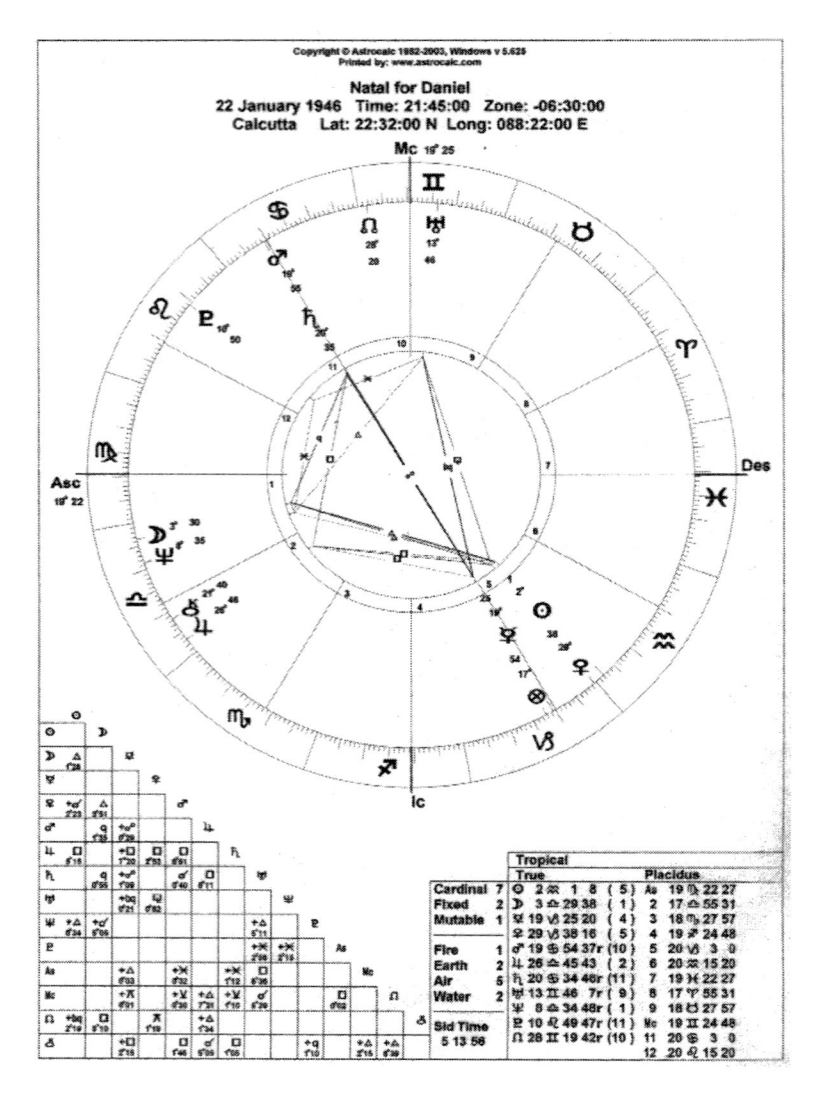

Chart 1

must always be taken into account as tending to support or modify the potentials contained in the birth chart.

The planetary energies, in combination with the "signs" and "houses" in which they are found find expression in an enormous variety of ways in everyday life. "Difficult" aspects are as capable of granting great productivity and satisfaction in life as of tension and frustration; and "easy" aspects are as capable of expression as lethargy and boredom as of contentment and creativity. Our free-will is our attitude to and use of the unique set of energies we are given.

All the signs of the zodiac are present in the birth horoscopes of everybody, as are all the planets and the sun and the moon, although each of these significators will vary in its importance for different people. Popular sun-sign astrology emphasizes the importance for an individual of the sign containing his or her Sun at the time of his or her birth. While to the serious astrologer the Sun-sign is considered to be of very great significance to the whole chart, a multitude of other factors contribute to the overall character and personality of every individual. In particular, the sign ascending over the eastern horizon at the moment of birth is understood to be of equal if not greater significance than the sign containing the sun.

Your horoscope shows that:

the sign ascending is Virgo

the sign containing the Sun is Aquarius.

You would therefore be described astrologically as "Sun in Aquarius with Virgo Ascendant". These significators, together with all the many other factors in your horoscope, define your unique individuality.

Your general nature. You are an extremely dynamic, self-motivating man, with a determination to do things your own, original way (7 cardinal planets, T-square involving Mercury opposition a Mars-Saturn conjunction, all square Jupiter, locomotive shape led by Uranus). You have a great need to be of service to other people (Ascendant Virgo) in a gentle and compassionate way (Moon conjunction Neptune in the 1st house) and you are most likely to fulfil this aim by your communicative creativity (Mercury ruler of Ascendant in the 5th house).

Mentality. You are full of ideas (5 planets in Air signs) and have a well-disciplined, creative mind (Mercury in Capricorn on the cusp of the 5th house). Expressing your mental creativity is central to your whole life (Mercury ruler of Ascendant) which you do with great assertive energy (Mercury opposition Mars), grandiose aims (Mercury square Jupiter), although probably with some resistance from the world (Mercury opposition Saturn) and some uncertainty about whether your communications serve your overall ambitions well (Mercury inconjunct Midheaven).

Career. Your worldly ambitions blend easily with your deepest life goals (Midheaven Gemini, Moon's North Node in Gemini in the 10th house), and you express your creative communicativeness with self-discipline and originality in the pursuit of your ambitions (Mercury ruler of the Midheaven on the 5th house cusp in Capricorn, supported by Sun and Venus in the 5th house in Aquarius). You have the ability to be a successful businessman and to heal your own deepest psychological wounds through earning a lot of money (Jupiter conjunction Chiron in the 2nd house).

You will succeed best in business through being in partnership (Libra on the 2nd house cusp) although, within any partnership you have in the wider world, you will be very self-assertive in a self-disciplined way (Aries co-ruler of the 7th and 8th houses and Mars, ruler of Aries, conjunction Saturn in the 10th-11th house). You will have a very sympathetic and caring attitude towards your business partner(s) out of your great desire to look after them in a selfless way (Pisces on the cusp of the 7th house and Neptune, the ruler of Pisces, conjunction Moon in the 1st house in the (partnership) sign of Libra). Your energy and ambition, compared to most people, are boundless (Jupiter square Sun square Mercury, square Mars) although you work very hard for the achievement of your ambitions (Saturn in the 10th-11th houses) and with very prudent, and perhaps anxious, calculation of the proper balance between caution and risk-taking (Jupiter square Saturn).

Hobbies and spare-time activities. You are likely to be attracted to hobbies that enable you to develop your mental or practical skills as well as expressing yourself creatively through these skills (Virgo Ascendant, Mercury ruler of the Ascendant in the 5th house).

You always want to express yourself with original flair (Sun in Aquarius) and you are likely to enjoy creating beautiful things (Sun conjunction Venus in the 5th house) and with much feeling and imagination (Sun trine Moon conjunction Neptune in the 1st house).

Personal contacts. You tend to prefer romance to marriage (Sun and Venus in the 5th house and 7th house untenanted) but if you do marry you want your marriage to have a very spiritual quality, and you may choose a partner who has some special neediness in order to be able to look after her in a selfless way (Pisces on the cusp of the 7th house opposition Moon conjunction Neptune in the 1st house). Sexually, you express yourself with uncomplicated masculine assertiveness (Aries on the 8th house cusp) and wholesome sensuality (Taurus co-ruler of the 8th house). You are attracted to women who have a harmonious, gentle, and imaginative nature (Moon *conjunction Neptune in Libra) and whom you probably first get to know as friends (Moon ruler of Cancer on the 11th house cusp). Much of your personal growth comes through your friendships, in which you express yourself warmly and with great intensity (Leo co-ruler of the 11th house, Pluto in Leo in the 11th house).*

Family. You probably experienced your parents as very intelligent and even intellectual (Sagittarius-Gemini IC-MC). One of your parents (probably your father) may have been unstable in some way or too preoccupied with his own interests to have been fully available for you (Uranus conjunction MC). You may also have experienced your father as being sternly repressive of your natural masculine assertiveness (Mars conjunction Saturn) and may have felt your mother failed to defend you appropriately because of her weakness or passivity (Moon conjunction Neptune). You are likely to have had intense relationships with any brothers or sisters (Scorpio on the cusp of the 3rd house) but likely also to think of them as very good friends (Mars and Pluto, co-rulers of Scorpio both in the 11th house). Any children of your own that you have are likely to bring you much joy and they may well be beautiful (Sun conjunction Venus in the 5th house).

Health. You have a tendency to be a hypochondriac (Virgo Ascendant) and may be vulnerable to chills, rheumatism or tooth-decay (Mercury, ruler of Ascendant, in Capricorn) or circulatory problems or vague psychosomatic disorders (Aquarius and Pisces co-rulers of the 6th house). You may suffer burns or other injuries from carelessly over-reaching yourself (Mars square Jupiter) although you are generally careful to express yourself physically in a well-controlled way (Mars conjunction Saturn).

Travel. You are likely to do quite a lot of travelling in the course of earning your living (Jupiter in the 2nd house) and your overall career (Mercury ruler of Midheaven). You probably experience travelling as mind-expanding and exciting but also quite stressful (Uranus in Gemini in the 9th house and Mercury square Jupiter opposition Saturn).

Yours sincerely, Mavis Klein.

An Intuitive Analysis of a Horoscope - Michael (Chart 2)

Biographical information. Michael was born in London, England, of middle-class parents. He is the third of his parents' four children, all the others being girls. He was interested in art and photography from an early age and trained as a graphic designer and photographer, from which occupations he has always earned his living. He lost his virginity to the woman who became his wife - by whom he says he was raped - in 1972, when he was 24. In order to marry his Israeli wife he converted to Judaism in 1974 (his own father having a Jewish mother) and emigrated to Israel. They have a daughter born in 1976 and a son born in 1978. They were divorced in 1985. In 2004, finding it difficult to make a living as a commercial artist in Israel, he returned to England, where he now lives. He continues to struggle to earn an adequate livelihood. His father died in 1992 and his mother in 1999.

The Moon forming a trine to his Mercury-Neptune conjunction bears witness to his artistic talent and his ability to use his imagination (Neptune) to express his feelings (Moon) in communicative ways (Mercury, graphic design) and photography (Neptune). But the Moon also being in close opposition to Pluto suggests difficult relationships to women, probably starting with his relationship to his mother. And Pluto being in the second house (money and possessions) denotes both the determination and struggle he has had earning an adequate living through his creativity (2nd house Leo), which is exacerbated by Saturn (difficulties and restrictions) also being in Leo in the 2nd house).

81

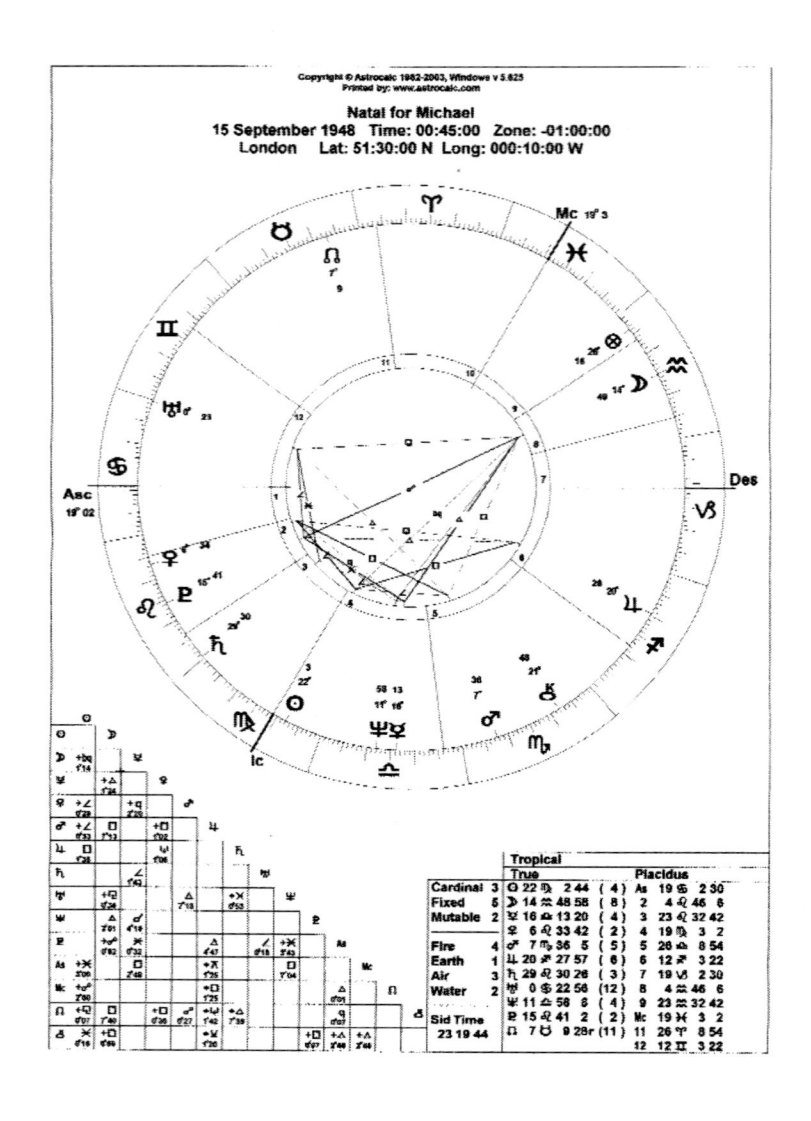

Chart 2

All of these configurations relating to the Moon are inevitably very important in his life, since his Ascendant (Cancer) ruler is the Moon, and the Moon being in the 8th house signifies a great need for emotional security through sex in marriage. But the Moon being in Aquarius suggests he might find it difficult to relate in a fully emotional way, and Uranus (the ruler of the Moon's sign) is in the sign that rules the Moon (Cancer) in the 12th house (deep-seated psychological problems). The close square between Venus and Mars also suggests difficulty in combining tenderness with passion in intimate relationships.

The Sun in Virgo bears witness to the meticulousness involved in his chosen career, and the Sun's square to Jupiter (in its own sign in the 5th house) testifies to his struggle to fulfil his creative ambitions, which struggle has beset him throughout his life (5 planets in fixed signs).

The time of his marriage was associated with Neptune (romantic love, illusion) transiting his Venus (relationships) by trine aspect; and Saturn (structure) transiting conjunct his Ascendant (the beginning of a new era in life), conjunct his Uranus (restiction of freedom) and square his Neptune (reality and dreams do battle with each other).

His children's births coincided with many major transiting aspects including, in 1974, Saturn opposition Moon, conjunction Venus, square Mars, sextile Neptune, conjunction Pluto; Uranus square Venus, conjunction Mars, opposition North Node; Neptune sextile Moon, sextile Neptune; and Pluto trine Moon, conjunction Neptune. And, in 1976, he experienced his first Saturn return (Saturn transiting conjunction Saturn, becoming truly grown-up); Uranus square Moon, square Pluto; Neptune square Midheaven; and Pluto trine Moon, square Ascendant - all rare and powerful symbols of radical changes in the life.

Michael's father's death was associated with Saturn (sorrow) transiting conjunct his Moon (deepest roots of emotional being) and opposition Pluto (profound transformation); while Pluto formed a sextile aspect to his Sun (father, animus). His mother's death was associated with Saturn (sorrow) transiting in square aspect to his Moon (mother); and Uranus (sudden transforming events) transiting conjunct his Moon (mother).

Doctor S. - A Gentle Murderer (Chart 3)

At the time of writing, the newspapers in England are full of the trial and conviction of Dr. S., a middle-aged doctor who has been found guilty of murdering at least twenty-five and possibly as many as two hundred of his middle-aged and elderly patients, the vast majority of whom were women. He killed them by injecting them with huge doses of morphine. None of the women was mortally ill, and most of them were quite healthy. All of Dr. S's patients died sitting up, fully clothed, in their chairs, some of them with a cup of tea at their sides, looking as if they had just fallen asleep.

The information we have about this man is that he was brought up in relative poverty and was extremely ambitious to achieve status in life. When he was seventeen he witnessed his mother dying a very painful death from lung cancer. He worked extremely hard in his studies to become a doctor, and for the past thirty years he has been much respected and very affectionately regarded by his patients for his gentle and compassionate nature. He married and has three adult children. At his trial he insistently denied his guilt, arguing that all he had ever done was ease his patients' passing from life to death. In this perception he was either lying or declaring himself criminally insane. Psychologically, it seems obvious that he was profoundly traumatized by his mother's death and particularly the pain she suffered, from which he

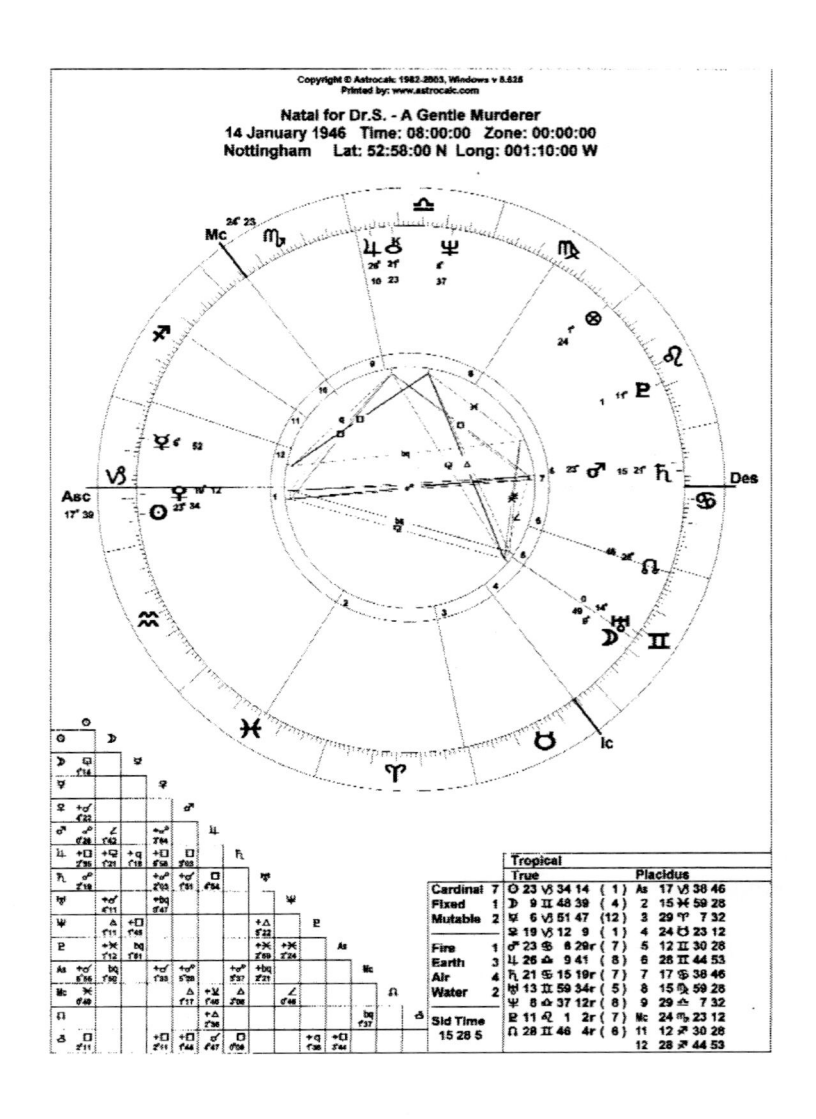

Chart 3

has never recovered. I hypothesise that every time he murdered one of his women patients with morphine he was seeking to re-write his personal history - impossible of course - by making his mother die a painless death. (Perhaps the relatively few male patients he murdered were stand-ins for himself in a subsidiary bid to end his own suffering.) Each murder was a failed bid by him to change his unbearable memory.

What can we see in his horoscope? (His time of birth is unknown, so the chart is drawn for dawn.)

The Sun (his core spirit, ambition, masculinity) is in conjunction with Venus (love and relating to others) in the sign of Capricorn, which gives his loving spirit a deep, sober, conscientious, emotionally reserved, ambitious quality. The ruler of Capricorn, Saturn (burdens, sorrows) is in close conjunction with Mars (aggressive action), both being in the sign of Cancer (mother). This conjunction is in close opposition to the Sun-Venus conjunction (love versus sorrowful anger). With 7 planets in cardinal signs, this man has to act out his impulses.

While we cannot be sure of the exact position of the Moon (because of the unknown time of birth) we can fairly confidently assume that it is conjunction Uranus (the sudden acting out of emotional impulses) and, for Dr. S., an original bid to "free" (Uranus) his mother (Moon), out of his compassion for her (Neptune trine Moon).

Accepting the validity of the dawn chart in its own right (irrespective of the actual time of birth), the Sun conjunction Venus opposition Mars conjunction Saturn lies right across the Ascendant-Descendant axis (self in intimate relationship to others). Chiron (the wounded healer) is conjunction Jupiter (benevolent largesse, grandiosity) in Libra, the sign of intimate relationships and, together with Neptune, in the 8th house of death.

Neptune (illusion, delusion, dreams, fantasies, compassionate idealism) reaches out, on the one hand to Mercury (rational thought) in a square aspect and on the other hand in a trine to the Moon, convincingly suggesting the total contamination of fantasy and rationality and compassionate caring that constitutes the core of this man's psyche.

I think we can safely infer that he was not lying in court. Within the construction of this man's agonized consciousness he was indeed expressing nothing but tender love to those he murdered.

But, of course, Dr. S's horoscope did not make him have his consciousness and its horrific expression. Thousands of other people born on the same day have not become mass murderers. There are, in principle, limitless ways in which any horoscope, in all its part and its wholeness, can manifest, but once it has manifested, the horoscope is a wondrous witness to that manifestation.

Professional Practice

Being a professional of any kind means confidently and reassuringly looking after people in some way that they need to be looked after in return for money paid. No human being is capable of being completely self-sufficient, and in modern civilized life nearly everybody is fundamentally dependent on many other people's professionalism for their survival as well as for the fulfilment of their non-survival needs and desires. And in seeking out the plumber to unblock our sink, the accountant to sort out our money problems, the dentist to fix our teeth, the taxi driver to get us to the airport in a hurry, the hairdresser to make us beautiful ... what we are looking for, above all else, is that person's assurance that what we hope for can be done and that he or she is capable and willing to do it for us promptly. If we have the choice between any two professionals equally competent in their skills we always choose - and choose again - the one who makes us feel secure in his or her confident care of us in the fulfilment of our needs.

And nowhere is the need for the caringness of professionalism more pronounced than in those areas of our lives that concern our physical or psychological health and well-being; and being an astrologer is such a profession. People consult astrologers as they do their doctors and dentists, with some, however unfounded, anxiety or even apprehension, and it behoves us immediately on meeting them (or even before, if a telephone appointment is made) to reduce and, if possible, eliminate their anxiety by the reassuringness of our smiles, the tone of our voice, and the words we choose.

While this book is not about predictive work in astrology, it is important for you to bear in mind that most clients, however well-educated, have a certain degree of apprehension that an astrologer can see "bad things" about to happen to them in a fatalistic way, and they need to be disavowed of this misapprehension immediately and in a very firm way. Ultimately, people's deepest fear is of death and, thankfully, there is no way that death can be read in the horoscope. Nor can "bad times" of any kind be predicted; Saturn in or transiting the 7th house of our horoscope can as easily stand for the new structure in our lives created by getting married as it may stand for painful issues needing to be faced in an existing marriage; Jupiter transiting the 7th house can as easly stand for the liberation and/or the litigation experienced in association with getting divorced as it may stand for the happiness associated with newly-married bliss. And, irrespective of the external factual realities in our lives, as Shakespeare so wisely said, "There's nothing good or bad but thinking makes it so".

Nevertheless, there is information in the horoscope that can be a very valuable guide to people, especially when the client's present pre-occupations are known. For example, if somebody has decided to leave their job and become a freelance consultant but is worried about the consequences, it is appropriate to interpret Saturn about to transit their 2nd house as an indication that money is likely to be short for a couple of years, until that transit has passed; or to predict for somebody who has been unsuccessfully trying to sell their home for several months that they are likely to succeed in three months time when Jupiter will transit conjunction their Moon and trine their Saturn.

Exercises

1. Look at charts 4, 5, 6, 7, 8, 9, and 10. They are the horoscopes of the following:

Mahatma Gandhi

Uri Geller

Muhammed Ali

Shinichi Suzuki

Bill Gates

The moment when Louis and August Lumi re-recorded the first ever moving film

Princess Diana

Which chart does each of the above belong to? (You may, of course, use the dates of birth of the different horoscopes to help you sort them.)

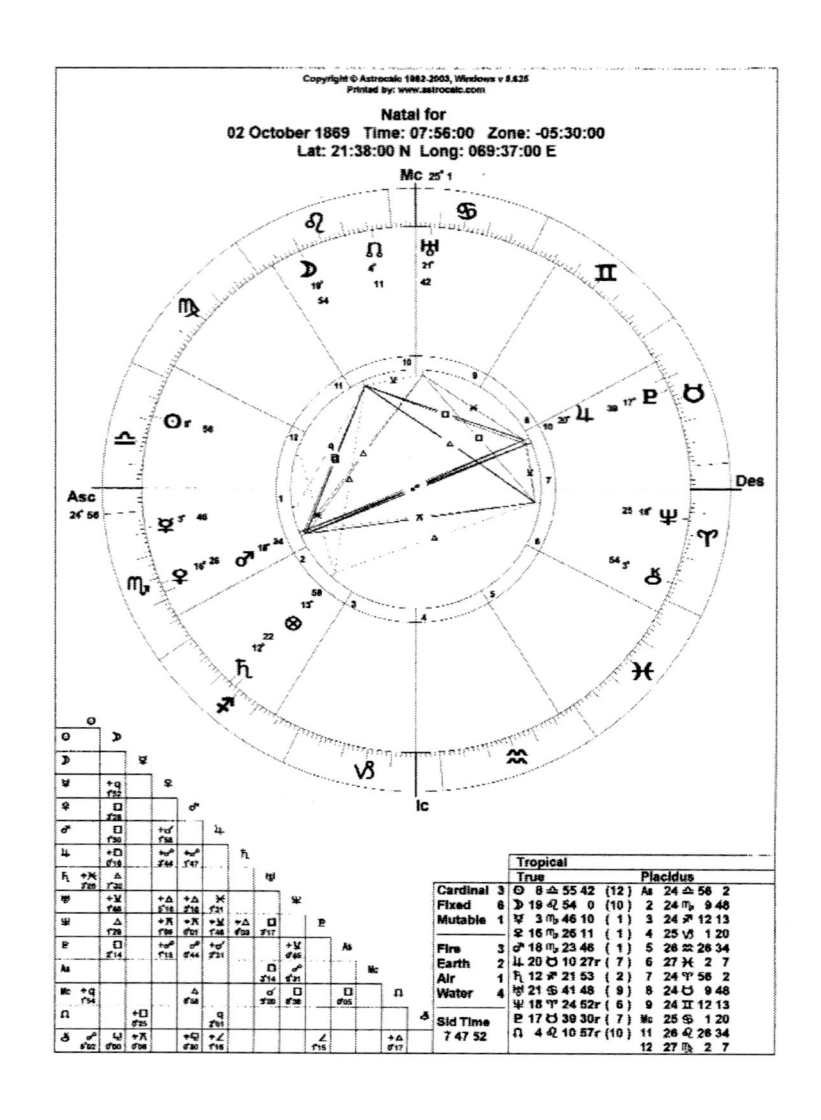

Chart 4

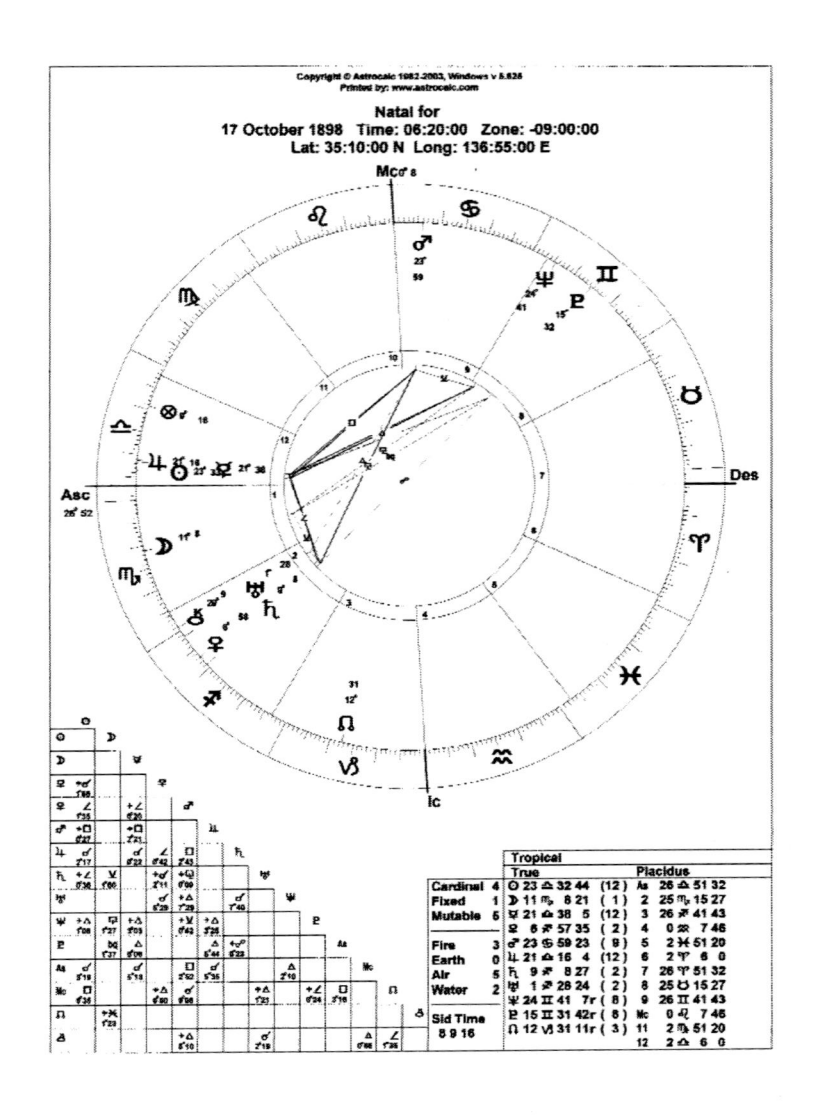

Chart 5

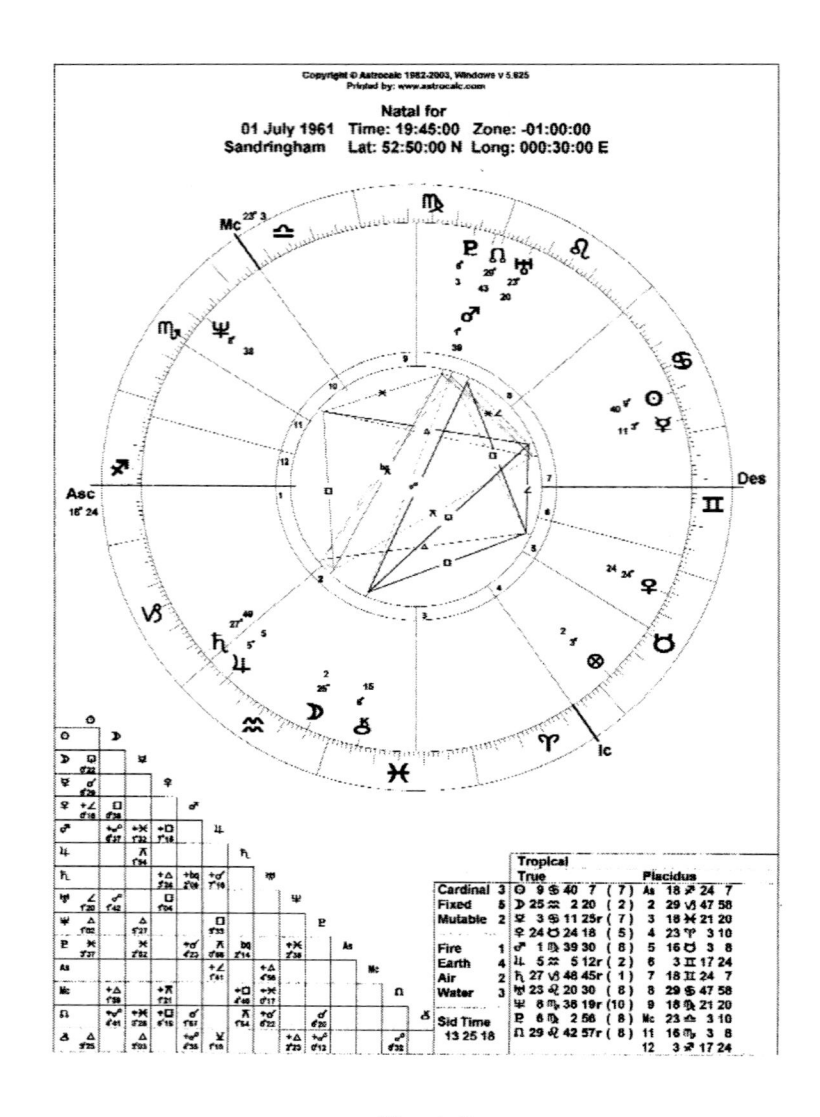

Chart 6

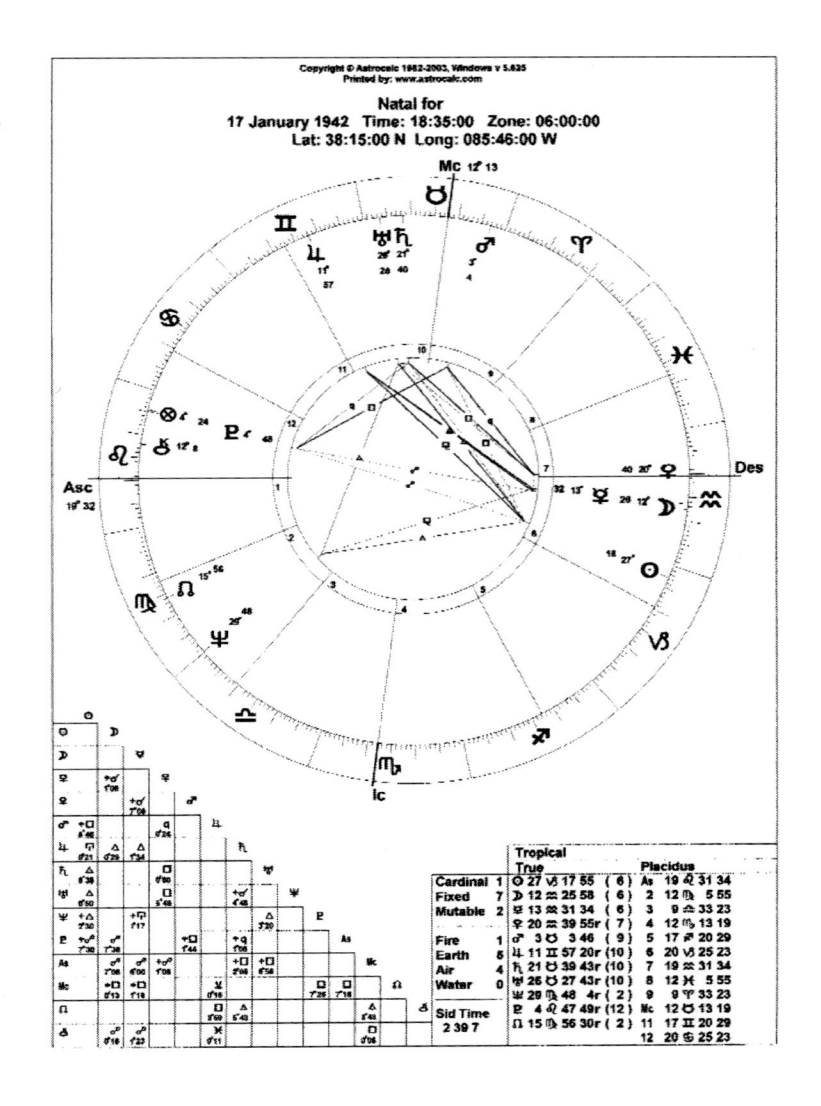

Chart 7

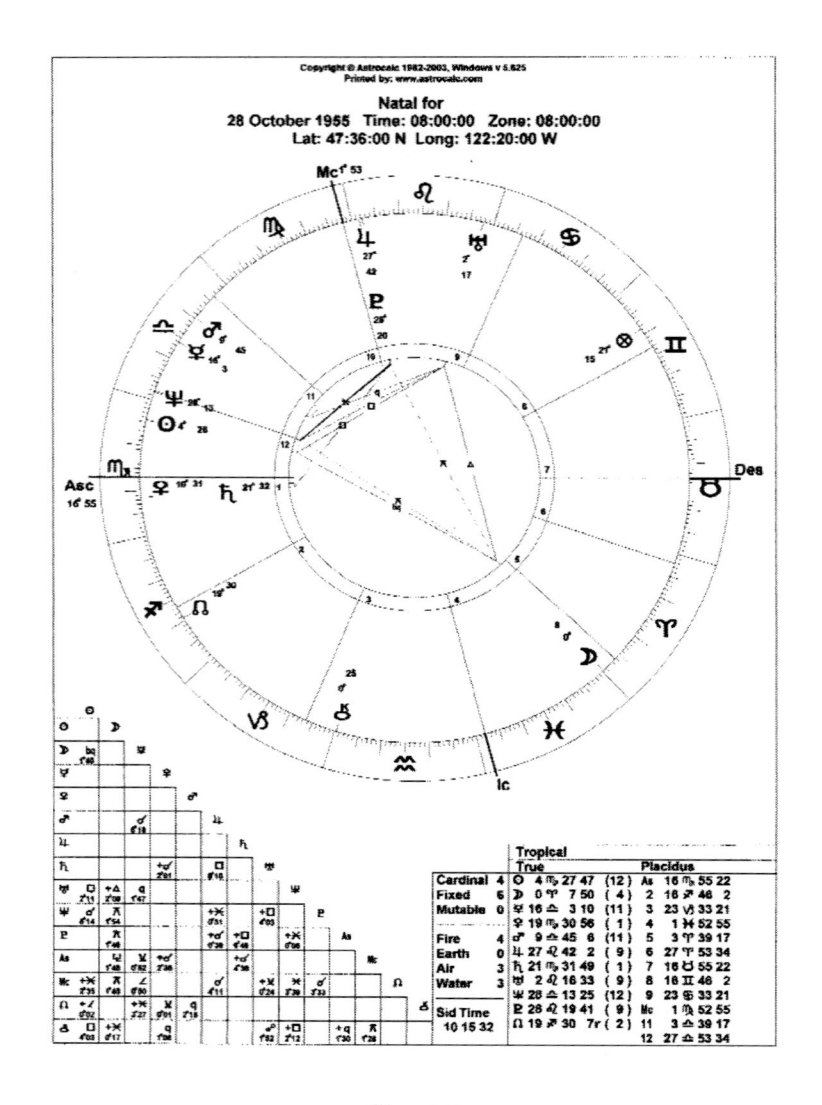

Chart 8

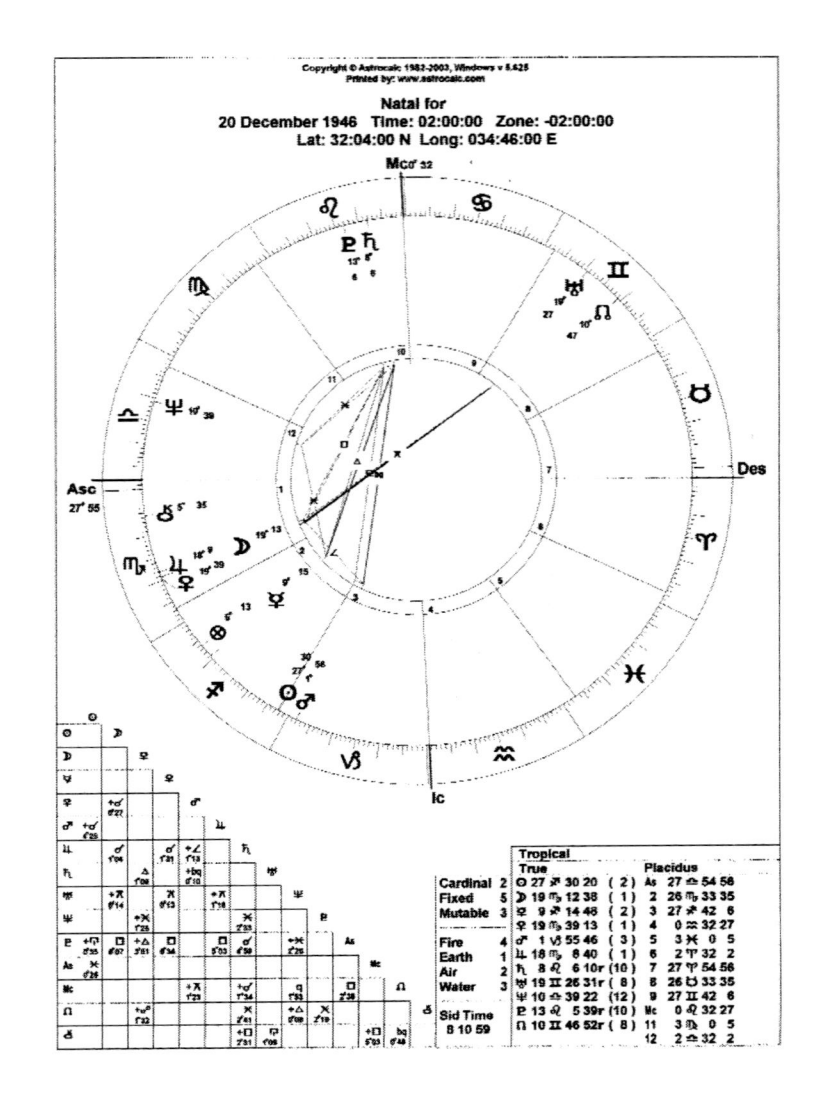

Chart 9

95

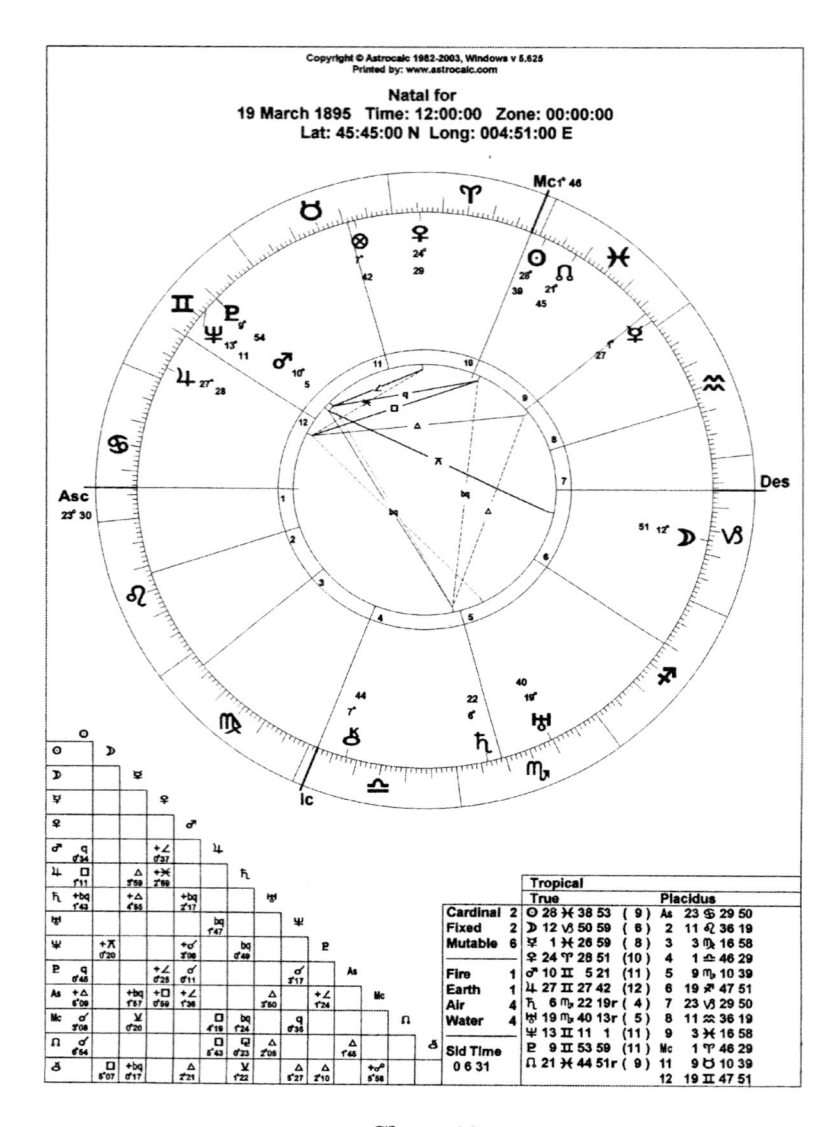

Chart 10

Here are some clues.

Chart 4. The Grand Trine in Water (emotional idealism) involving Venus, Mars, Uranus, and Neptune describes this person's life and work very well. Notice also the Libra Ascendant (peace-maker) and the self-assertive cluster of energies in the 1st house.

Chart 5. Notice the many aspects to Neptune (imaginative artistry) on the border of the 8th house (transformation) and 9th house (teaching). Notice Mars in Cancer (purposeful nurturing) in the 9th house, close to the Midheaven.

Chart 6. The T-square involving the Moon, Venus, Mars, Uranus, Pluto and the Node says a lot about this person's life.

Chart 7. Mars, Jupiter, Saturn, and Uranus all clustering around the Midheaven of this chart describe well the person's career. The Leo Ascendant (very high opinion of self) together with the Sun (ruler of the Ascendant) in the 6th house and Jupiter in Gemini in the 10th house describe well the person's way of presenting him/herself and career.

Chart 8. Jupiter conjunction Pluto in the 10th house in Leo (hugely successful transformation in a self-dramatizing public image) provides a vivid description of this person's career.

Chart 9. Saturn conjunction Pluto in the 10th house in Leo (intensely controlled power to transform through a self-dramatizing public image) is a core description of this person's career.

Note the similarities and differences between charts 8 and 9. Jupiter conjuction Pluto in Leo in the 10th and Saturn conjuction Pluto in Leo in the 10th aptly describes both a similarity and difference between these two people.

97

Chart 10. Note the Grand Trine involving Mercury, Jupiter, and Saturn (structured expansion of communication) in water (fantasy) and the equal abundance of planets in Air signs (communication) and the Mars, Neptune, Pluto conjunction and Jupiter in the 12th house (imagination) which are all apposite to this horoscope.

2. In interpreting a horoscope, which house refers to

   a) parents?
   b) children?
   c) marriage?
   d) friends?
   e) open enemies?
   f) hidden enemies?
   g) hobbies?
   h) travel?
   i) neighbours?
   j) brothers and sisters?
   k) inheritances?
   l) sexuality?
   m) religious outlook?

3. What is your first responsibility to anybody who consults you as a professional astrologer?

4) Is it possible to be a professional without accepting payment for your services?

5) Which horoscope configuration expresses special talent?

6) Which horoscope configuration expresses dynamic motivation?

7) Re-read the sections on "Fate and Free-will" and "Prophecy" in Chapter 1. Learn by heart, "There's nothing good or bad but thinking makes it so". (Shakespeare)

Do enjoy yourself interpreting horoscopes and be willing to make thoughtful guesses.

Do be warm and cheerful towards your clients, and allay their anxieties by emphasising that there are no "bad things" indicated in horoscopes, only challenges that they can freely and happily choose to meet.

Don't try to say everything that can be said in interpreting a horoscope - only God can do that.

Interpreting Relationships

Chapter 6
Pain and Joy in Intimate Relationships

Summary: All relationships contain both pain and joy. While we all believe we only seek joy, we also deeply need and seek to be challenged by pain in order to grow and fulfil our potential. While we want to understand our own sexual and other deeply intimate relationships very fully, summary and brief analyses of many relationships are sufficient for many purposes. A number of techniques for rapid analysis are outlined and a marriage and a love affair are analyzed by these means.

What is Intimacy?

Intimacy is the expression of free, spontaneous, truthful, non-damaging closeness between people. It is the ideal form of interaction between all people because it gives us our times of greatest happiness. But being intimate with others also makes us excruciatingly vulnerable to the deep pain that may be inflicted on us by others if they choose so to use the knowledge of us we have given them. So intimacy involves risk, and many people, sadly, deeply presume that if others know them intimately they are bound to be hurt and rejected by them. As a result, many people are frightened of intimacy and never allow others to get really close to them. Thus people's overall willingness to be intimate with others depends on the general level of trust they have that those others are essentially benevolent towards them.

The wonderful (and terrible) thing about other people is that, in their presence, our horoscopes become unavoidably entangled in theirs by virtue of the interaction between the planets and houses of their horoscope and the planets and houses of our own. People often talk metaphorically of the "chemistry" between two people but, astrologically, this is literally the case. The planets in one horoscope form aspects to the planets in the other in exactly the same way as they do in an individual horoscope, and the planets in one horoscope "light up" the houses in which they are placed in the other horoscope.

While, in principle, "there's nothing good or bad but thinking makes it so", being human, we do make judgements of other people or at least acknowledge our spontaneous like or dislike of them according to whether it is their Jupiter or Saturn that is sitting on our Moon.

Commonsense might suggest that choosing to form intimate relationships with others with whom we have the greatest possible number of harmonious aspects is the path to happiness. The actual (though anti-commonsensical) truth is that we are complexly driven to seek pain as well as joy in our intimate relationships. The complexity derives from two needs that are intrinsic to human nature: our needs to make sense of our experiences and to feel righteous.

Our first need is to experience life as being as orderly and predictable as possible, by virtue of which we decide, in our earliest months and years of life, that this is the way I am, this is the way the world is, and this is the way other people are and the way they will be to me. These decisions, construed from our objective experiences interpreted by our individual natures as delineated in our horoscopes, become the essentially immutable existential decisions in which, and through which, we live out our interactions with other people and the physical world. The value of the certainties we thus provide ourselves with overrides all other values. Our avowed conscious quest for joy over pain is true to the extent that the interaction between our earliest environmentally imposed experiences and our horoscopes leads us to joyful interpretations of ourselves, the world, and other people. But when our environmentally imposed experiences combine with our horoscopes to lead us to painful interpretations of ourselves, the world, and other people our primary need for predictable certainty overrides our quest for joy. We all have some painful as well as joyful decisions at the core of our being, and throughout our lives we get satisfaction (however masochistic) by compulsively seeking experiences that confirm our earliest decisions. For all of us, the world is found constantly to be full of what we have idiosyncratically decided to be the case.

But seeking pain does not make sense to our conscious minds, and we are wired to delude ourselves that our pains are thrust upon us by other people or circumstances outside our control. Because we are human we are glad to accept responsibility for the joy and beauty and good in our lives, but prefer to perceive the pain and ugliness and bad in our lives as fortuitously "happening" to us or imposed on us by other people. Denial and projection are the chief devices by which we preserve the inherent narcissism of our fragile egos, which I observed in unadorned simplicity in one of my granddaughters. Then aged two, she dropped and broke a cup and simply said, "I didn't". A few months later, sitting opposite me at the kitchen table, she accidentally knocked some food off her plate onto the floor and, without any consciousness of the transparency of her ego's now more sophisticated ability to defend itself, she stared straight at me and said, "I think you did that". As grown-ups our quest for righteousness hides from itself in webs of camouflage that we sophisticatedly spin, but our primary aim in every instance of pain, ugliness or evil in which we participate is to maintain the perception of our own righteousness. A "you did it" projection implies a developed concept of "self" and equivalent "selves" in others, which is the usual baseline on which we build the edifices of our self-esteem.

So we are attracted to others who, by the interactions of their horoscopes with our own, provide us with plausible justification for projecting onto them blame for our core pains, thus reffirming our own righteousness. This is probably an important factor in the statistical popularity of intimate relationships between near-contemporaries whose outer planets are closely posited to ours, for it is difficult aspects between our own inner and outer planets that describe our most painful decisions. If, in my horoscope, Pluto is square my Moon in a 3 degree orb and your Pluto is exactly square my Moon, what more could I ask to fulfil my need to blame someone (other than myself) for that pain in my being!

However, we are saved from being forever stuck in get-nowhere righteousness by the reality that we are given the opportunity for working through and beyond our pains (as manifest in our horoscopes) both by natural transits to our horoscopes and by the dynamic influence of the aspects formed to our horoscopes by the planets in another person's horoscope. The ultimate justice of the cosmos is declared in the fact that the strength of another's Saturn, especially in its hard aspects (conjunction, square, opposition, and inconjunct), not only allows us to find masochistic gratification in reaffirming the "truth" of our painful decisions and a suitable other person to blame, but also offers us the serenity and wisdom, over time, of appreciating that we each create the world with our own thoughts. Relationships between people who have few or no Saturn inter-aspects between their horoscopes do not last!

We know - however unconsciously - within minutes if not seconds of meeting another all the pain and joy that is potential between us. In a potential sexual relationship we all immediately instinctively thrust our best Venus and Mars feet forward, then our (deeper) Sun and Moon energies, and then, reluctantly, display our Saturns.

Venus and Mars aspects (hard or soft) declare our sexual relatedness. Sun and Moon aspects (hard or soft) declare our deepest connectedness of spirit and sould. Soft aspects from our own Saturn to another's horoscope declare the other's compassionate tolerance of our ego's defences. Hard aspects from our own Saturn to another's horoscope declare our courage in meeting the opportunity and challenge to outgrow our righteous fears and inhibitions in favour of extending the boundaries of our being, and growing in wisdom and serenity. And all aspects between any of the outer planets (Chiron, Uranus, Neptune, and Pluto) in one horoscope to the inner planets of another will manifest as passionately challenging dynamic interactions between the couple which, over time, can lead to the deepest and most healing growth for each of them.

There are no "wrong" or "bad" relationships. All relationships that are formed are, by definition, serving the deepest purposeful existential needs of both parties for as long as the relationship lasts. Relationships formed between people who are irrelevant to each other's purposeful existential needs soon dissolve because they contain no real joy and no real pain. Mild, short-lived disappointment in oneself for one's misperceived hope is the usual price paid, but even such abortive relationships may be seen as having the purpose of teaching the individuals the necessity for deeper discrimination in the choice of an intimate other.

God (or the powers-that-be) in their wisdom almost always send us a mixed bag of pain and joy in the relationships between our own and another's horoscope. To the extent that we want to use our free-will consciously to choose to enter into an intimate relationship for maximum benefit and growth and joy, we need to weigh up the balance of harmony and tension between our own and another's horoscope, even though Neptune (the romantic) in all of us seeks "perfect peace and harmony" (which would actually be very boring!)

When, for one or both of the partners in an intimate relationship, pain has outstripped joy, and the purpose of the pain is known to have been served, whether or not the relationship still has life-enhancing meaning depends on what is left between the couple once the sado-masochistic gratifications are removed. When one or both partners no longer needs to play out with the other the patterns of greatest pain in their relationship, and decisively desists from initiating or reacting to invitations to mutual pain, what remains is seen with clarity. Sometimes there is a lot left that happily justifies the continuance of the relationship. New dimensions can then be added to the relationship to replace the old, new purposes consciously articulated between the couple that serve the continued unfoldment of the life potential of each of them; and they may become more deeply united in appreciation of the growth that each of them has achieved by living through and transcending the now redundant painful structures of the past.

But when the pain between a couple has served its purpose and one or both desist from initiating or reacting to further invitations to pain, and there is little or no compatible joy observable in their relationship, the only authentic thing to do is to part, with as little mutual blame and the greatest mutual appreciation they can muster for the past value of the relationship to each of them.

Quick and Easy Techniques for Understanding Relationships

1) Sun-Sign Comparison

The quickest and easiest way to get a broad sense of the quality of a relationship between two people is to assess the interaction of their two Sun signs. This, of course, means dividing the whole world into only twelve categories, which people sometimes thoughtlessly infer means that Sun-sign astrology is rubbish, which is not the case.

Categorizing is the primary function of the brain in making sense of anything and everything. Human vanity is offended by this fact because it reduces the significance of the exceptional characteristics of ourselves in which most people take such pride. But, outside our essential narcissistic frame of reference, the two most interesting observations that can be made about people are always their differences and their samenesses. Male or female is the first categorization of any person that we all immediately make. "It's a girl" or "It's a boy" is the first ever observation made about any human being, and a very large number of other dichotomous characterizations by which we describe people, concepts, and the inanimate world can readily be seen to be closely derived from the basic category of gender.

Which categories we apply and how far we go in refining any of our categorizations by sub-categories depends on the context in which the person, idea, or thing is being described. "Men" is sufficient in the context of public lavatories, "female, 162 cm., 95-62-90" is sufficient for a beauty contest, and "intelligent, moderate socialist" may be sufficient for selecting a candidate for a local council election. So it goes on, to the limiting case of a beloved other whom we wish to describe and know down to the tiniest freckle of his or her physical and psychological being.

In the context of astrology, a very good case can be made for the primacy of Sun signs in categorizing people (analogous to the primacy of gender in ordinary categorizing of people).

The sun is the lone star around which all the matter of the planets in our solar system revolve, as it is, analogously, in our personal horoscopes, the core dynamic spirit of our being.

Of course the Sun-sign columns in newspapers, when they are written by a non-astrologer, are rubbish. But when they are written by a competent astrologer they are valid and useful, even though they say little more than the equivalent of a weather forecast that might say, "Tomorrow will be hot and sunny. Light-skinned people should stay indoors, dark-skinned people will be in their element".

So it is always worth comparing the Sun signs of any two people in an existing or potential relationship for a broad but useful idea of the likely components of ease and stress between them.

Here is a brief description of how each of the possible pairs of Sun signs get on with each other, positively and negatively. These descriptions are not intended to be definitive, but to suggest quite likely attributes of the relationships. Add your own ideas to the ones listed below.

Aries-Aries. + Enjoy each other's go-getting, active attitude to life. - Accuse each other of selfishness.

Aries-Taurus. + Aries appreciates Taurus's stability, and Taurus enjoys Aries' liveliness. - An irresistable force (Aries) meets an immovable object (Taurus).

Aries-Gemini. + Aries loves Gemini's mind, Gemini enjoys Aries" easy extraversion and friendliness. - Aries is made insecure by Gemini's elusiveness, Gemini resents Aries' dominating bossiness.

Aries-Cancer. + Aries enjoys being looked after by Cancer, and Cancer enjoys Aries' dependency. - Aries feels suffocated by Cancer's emotionality, Cancer feels assaulted by Aries' loudness.

Aries-Leo. + Aries enjoys Leo's loyalty, Leo enjoys Aries' lively child-likeness. - They compete with each other to be the centre of attention.

Aries-Virgo. + Aries enjoys the servicing of his or her needs by Virgo, Virgo feels enlivened by Aries. - Aries thinks Virgo stuffily boring, Virgo is offended by Aries' bossy loudness.

Aries-Libra. + Great sexual attraction (if of opposite sexes) and enjoy each other's go-gettingness. - Tend to dislike each other (if of same sex) and there is conflict over who is boss.

Aries-Scorpio. + Enjoy each other's intensity. - Aries finds Scorpio sulky and secretive, Scorpio finds Aries shallow.

Aries-Sagittarius. + Love being "on the go" and travelling together. - Aries objects to Sagittarius' moralizing attitudes, Sagittarius accuses Aries of irresponsibility.

Aries-Capricorn. + Aries enjoys the security of Capricon's sober and responsible attitude to life, Capricorn feels enlivened by Aries. - Aries accuses Capricorn of being unfeeling, Capricorn accuses Aries of being hysterical.

Aries-Aquarius. + Aries appreciates Aquarius' independence, Aquarius enjoys Aries' impetuousness. - Aries is made angry by Aquarius' refusal to be bossed, Aquarius objects to Aries' aggression.

Aries-Pisces. + Aries enjoys Pisces' willingness to be led, Pisces feels enlivened by Aries. - Aries is driven crazy by Pisces' passivity, Pisces feels abused by Aries' aggression.

Taurus-Taurus. + Appreciate each other's wholesome, stable, sensual attitude to life. - Accuse each other of stubbornness.

Taurus-Gemini. + Taurus feels enlivened by Gemini, Gemini feels safe with Taurus. - Taurus is made insecure by Gemini's flightiness, Gemini feels stifled by Taurus' possessiveness.

Taurus-Cancer. + They share the aims of enjoying the good things of life and feeling materially and emotionally secure. - Taurus finds Cancer neurotically unstable, Cancer finds Taurus stolid and emotionally insensitive.

Taurus-Leo. + Taurus enjoys Leo's romantic nature and generosity, Leo appreciates Taurus's steadfastness and loyalty. - Mutual accusations of stubborn inflexibility.

Taurus-Virgo. + Respect each other's shyness, and enjoy each other's quiet sensuality. - Taurus objects to Virgo's fussiness, Virgo objects to Taurus's unchangingness.

Taurus-Libra. + Share a love of beauty and order in their surroundings. - Taurus dislikes Libra's bossiness, Libra dislikes Taurus's stolidness.

Taurus-Scorpio. + Great sexual attraction (if of opposite sexes), enjoy each other's quiet depth. - Tend to dislike each other (if of same sex), Taurus dislikes Scorpio's secretiveness, Scorpio dislikes Taurus's bluntness.

Taurus-Sagittarius. + Taurus feels enlivened by Sagittarius, Sagittarius enjoys Taurus's stability. - Taurus dislikes Sagittarius's restlessness, Sagittarius feels stifled by Taurus's practicality.

Taurus-Capricorn. + Taurus values Capricorn's ambition and seriousness, Capricorn enjoys Taurus's conservative values. - Taurus finds Capricorn mean, Capricorn finds Taurus extravagant.

Taurus-Aquarius. + Taurus admires Aquarius's independence, Aquarius appreciates Taurus's quiet stability. - Taurus accuses Aquarius of being cold, Aquarius feels his or her mind intruded by Taurus.

Taurus-Pisces. + Taurus is appreciative of Pisces softness and emotional sensitivity, Pisces enjoys Taurus's warm sensuality. - Taurus dislikes Pisces' elusiveness, Pisces dislikes Taurus's nagging.

Gemini-Gemini. + Enjoy each others' intelligences and talking to each other. - Mutual accusations of uncaring irresponsibility.

Gemini-Cancer. + Gemini enjoys being looked after by Cancer, Cancer enjoys Gemini's child-like dependence. - Gemini feels smothered by Cancer, Cancer feels abused by Gemini's emotional insensitivity.

Gemini-Leo. + Gemini appreciates Leos's warmth and generosity, Leo enjoys Gemini's lively extraversion. - Gemini feels Leo is too demanding, Leo feels Gemini is too restless and flighty.

Gemini-Virgo. + Appreciate each other's minds. - Gemini objects to Virgo's nit-pickingness, Virgo accuses Gemini of being facile and shallow.

Gemini-Libra. + Both enjoy exchanging ideas and talking and laughing together. - Gemini dislikes Libra's bossiness, Libra dislikes Gemini's lack of commitment.

Gemini-Scorpio. + Gemini appreciates Scorpio's stable reliability, Scorpio appreciates Gemini's liveliness. - Gemini feels threatened by Scorpio's reserve, Scorpio feels misunderstood by Gemini's insistence on talking about everything.

Gemini-Sagittarius. + Great sexual attraction (if of opposite sexes), enjoy exchanging ideas and travelling together. - Tend to dislike each other (if of same sex), Gemini finds Sagittarius self-righteous, Sagittarius finds Gemini irresponsible.

Gemini-Capricorn. + Gemini feels safe and secure with Capricorn, Capricorn feels enlivened by Gemini. - Gemini objects to Capricorn's criticism and stuffiness, Capricorn objects to Gemini's childishness.

Gemini-Aquarius. + Gemini admires Aquarius's independence, Aquarius enjoys Gemini's intellectual liveliness. - Gemini feels criticized by Aquarius, Aquarius objects to Gemini's childishness.

Gemini-Pisces. + Appreciate each other's tolerance of the other's need for privacy. - Gemini feels smothered by Pisces emotionality, Pisces feels abused by Gemini's emotional detachment.

Cancer-Cancer. + Feel very looked after by each other. - Conflict about who needs looking after most, and each accuses the other of being too demanding.

Cancer-Leo. + Cancer basks in Leo's warmth and generosity, Leo feels valued by Cancer's neediness. - Cancer feels insecure in response to Leo's gregariousness, Leo finds Cancer too clinging.

Cancer-Virgo. + Cancer enjoys being looked after by Virgo, Virgo enjoys Cancer's neediness. - Cancer feels criticized by Virgo, Virgo feels unappreciated by Cancer.

Cancer-Libra. + Cancer admires Libra's independence, Libra appreciates Cancer's sensitivity. - Cancer feels abused by Libra's forthrightness, Libra feels smothered by Cancer's clingingness.

Cancer-Scorpio. + Identify with each other's intense emotionality. - Cancer feels insecure in response to Scorpio's self-sufficiency, Scorpio feels overwhelmed by Cancer's demandingness.

Cancer-Sagittarius. + Cancer admires and enjoys Sagittarius's easy sociability, Sagittarius admires Cancer's caringness. - Cancer is hurt by Sagittarius's bluntness, Sagittarius is upset by Cancer's extreme sensitivity.

Cancer-Capricorn. + Great sexual attraction (if of opposite sexes), identify with each other's needs for emotional and material security. - Tend to dislike each other (if of same sex), Cancer accuses Capricorn of being coldly controlling, Capricorn accuses Cancer of being infantilely demanding.

Cancer-Aquarius. + Cancer admires Aquarius's emotional independence, Aquarius respects Cancer's sensitivity. - Cancer feels inferior to Aquarius, Aquarius feels stifled by Cancer's neediness.

Cancer-Pisces. + Cancer feels safe with Pisces, Pisces is gratified by Cancer's neediness of him or her. - Cancer feels unresponded to by Pisces, Pisces feels nagged and criticized by Cancer.

Leo-Leo. + Appreciate each other's warmth and loyalty and enjoy spending money together on the good things of life. - Accuse each other of being too vain and proud.

Leo-Virgo. + Leo appreciates Virgo's modesty, Virgo enjoys Leo's largesse. - Leo finds Virgo prissy and lacking in exuberance, Virgo finds Leo vain and extravagant.

Leo-Libra. + Leo admires Libra's charm and love of beauty, Libra basks in Leo's admiration, and loves him or her wholeheartedly in return. - Leo objects to Libra's bossiness, Libra objects to Leo's stubbornness.

Leo-Scropio. + Leo enjoys Scorpio's passionate sexual responsiveness, Scorpio appreciates Leo's loving faithfulness. - Leo objects to Scorpio's secretiveness and jealousy, Scorpio objects to Leo's loud extraversion.

Leo-Sagittarius. + Appreciate each other's easy-going gregariousness and warmth. - Leo dislikes Sagittarius's restlessness, Sagittarius dislikes Leo's easily hurt vanity and pride.

Leo-Capricorn. + Leo admires Capricorn's ambition, Capricorn appreciates Leo's liking for the finer things of life. - Leo finds Capricorn mean, Capricorn finds Leo extravagant.

Leo-Aquarius. + Great sexual attraction (if of opposite sexes), Leo admires Aquarius's detachment, Aquarius enjoys Leo's warmth. - Tend to dislike each other (if of the same sex), Leo finds Aquarius cold, Aquarius finds Leo boastful and vain.

Leo-Pisces. + Leo admires Pisces' gentleness, Pisces admires Leo's easy extraversion. - Leo finds Pisces unappreciative of love and gifts given, Pisces finds Leo arrogant and self-centred.

Virgo-Virgo. + Appreciate each other's quiet self-effacingness. - Accuse each other of being too critical and perfectionistic.

Virgo-Libra. + Virgo admires Libra's elegance and charm, Libra admires Virgo's modesty. - Virgo finds Libra bossy and vain, Libra finds Virgo an irritating fuss-pot.

Virgo-Scorpio. + Appreciate each other's quiet presence. - Virgo accuses Scorpio of stubbornness, Scorpio accuses Virgo of being too critical.

Virgo-Sagittarius. + Virgo enjoys looking after Sagittarius, Sagittarius enjoys having his or her physical needs reliably taken care of. - Virgo finds Sagittarius selfishly demanding, Sagittarius accuses Virgo of being a confining nag.

Virgo-Capricorn. + Mutual appreciation of each other's quiet sensuality. - Virgo feels unappreciated by Capricorn, Capricorn feels nagged by Virgo.

Virgo-Aquarius. + Enjoy rational discussions with each other. - Virgo feels Aquarius is too emotionally detached, Aquarius feels Virgo is too concerned with petty details.

Virgo-Pisces. + Great sexual attraction (if of opposite sexes), mutual appreciation of each other's quiet sensitivity and unselfishness. - Tend to dislike each other (if of the same sex), Virgo finds Pisces impossibly impractical, Pisces finds Virgo unimaginative.

Libra-Libra. + Share a love of beauty and harmony and enjoyment of luxury. - Compete for dominance.

Libra-Scorpio. + Libra enjoys Scorpio's passionate sexiness, Scorpio enjoys Libra's erotic artfulness. - Libra feels unloved by Scorpio's silences, Scorpio feels intruded upon by Libra's insistent talking.

Libra-Sagittarius. + Enjoy each other's minds and easy-going sociability and optimism. - Libra finds Sagittarius crude and offensively blunt, Sagittarius finds Libra vain and bossy.

Libra-Capricorn. + Enjoy each other's sense of humour. - Libra finds Capricorn a miserable pessimist, Capricorn finds Libra wasteful and vain.

Libra-Aquarius. + Enjoy each other's friendship and detached interest in the world. - Libra finds Aquarius coldly arrogant, Aquarius finds Libra self-centred and vain.

Libra-Pisces. + Appreciate each other's gentleness and liking for peace. - Libra finds Pisces too passive, Pisces finds Libra too bossy.

Scorpio-Scorpio. + Mutual emotional depth and intensity. - Accuse each other of possessive jealousy.

Scorpio-Sagittarius. + Scorpio admires Sagittarius's honesty, Sagittarius is intrigued by Scorpio's self-control. - Scorpio dislikes Sagittarius's crudeness and social clumsiness, Sagittarius is intimidated by Scorpio's piercing insight.

Scorpio-Capricorn. + Admire and appreciate each other's serious attitudes to life. - Scorpio finds Capricorn overly materialistic, Capricorn is suspicious of Scorpio's secretiveness.

Scorpio-Aquarius. + Enjoy intellectual analysis with each other. - Mutually accuse each other of obstinacy, Scorpio finds Aquarius too detached, Aquarius finds Scorpio too intense.

Scorpio-Pisces. + Are at ease with each other's silent presence. - Scorpio finds Pisces too tolerant, Pisces finds Scorpio too rigid.

Sagittarius-Sagittarius. + Enjoy each other's boisterous good-nature. - Accuse each other of selfish inattentiveness to the practicalities of life.

Sagittarius-Capricorn. + Sagittarius admires Capricorn's self-discipline, Capricorn admires Sagittarius's easy extraversion. - Sagittarius dislikes Capricorn's dour pessimism, Capricorn feels invaded by Sagittarius's boisterousness.

Sagittarius-Aquarius. + Enjoy sharing and discussing intellectual ideas with each other. - Sagittarius finds Aquarius cold, Aquarius dislikes Sagittarius's intrusive bluntness.

Sagittarius-Pisces. + Sagittarius enjoys and respects Pisces' spirituality, Pisces appreciates Sagittarius's wide-ranging ideas. - Sagittarius finds Pisces too vague, Pisces finds Sagittarius too blunt.

Capricorn-Capricorn. + Appreciate each other's serious, self-disciplined approach to life and desire for achievement. - Feel personally neglected by each other's concentration on worldly ambitions.

Capricorn-Aquarius. + Appreciate each other's seriousness and detachment. - Capricorn finds Aquarius too idealistic, Aquarius finds Capricorn too materialistic.

Capricorn-Pisces. + Capricorn admires Pisces' spirituality, Pisces admires Capricorn's self-motivation. - Capricorn dislikes Pisces' passivity, Pisces dislikes Capricorn's materialism.

Aquarius-Aquarius. + Enjoy each other's intelligent, detached observations. - Accuse each other of obstinate inflexibility.

Aquarius-Pisces. + Aquarius admires Pisces' spirituality, Pisces admires Aquarius's intellectuality. - Aquarius finds Pisces too emotional and passive, Pisces feels rejected by Aquarius's independence.

Pisces-Pisces. + Share a compassionate sensitivity to each other's and the world's suffering. - Accuse each other of being confused and unrealistic.

2) Composite Charts

While it is, of course, true that people's relationship needs are revealed in their individual horoscopes, it is quite valid to analyze a relationship between two people without reference to their individual horoscopes. However unconsciously, people are only ever attracted to another because - at least at that time - they know the other can serve a purpose in the fulfilment of their individualistic potential. Thus, we can take for granted that if two people have got together then some purposes will exist in the relationship, and our task is primarily to read what that purpose is all about, and this can be done very reliably without reference to their separate horoscopes. Indeed, premature reference to the individual horoscopes can induce mental "overload" in the astrologer, so I recommend that, in the first place, you analyze the relationship in its own right and only later refer to individual horoscopes to confirm or challenge the fulfilment of the individuals' needs through the relationship.

One quick and reliable way to assess the meaning of a relationship between any two people is through a "composite chart", which describes not one person or the other, nor the experiences each have of the other as individuals, but the relationship itself, which is, as it were, an entity in its own right. In every relationship between two people there are three entities - the two people and the relationship their two individualities create.

If you have an astrology software program, it probably contains the means for calculating a composite chart out of two individual charts, at the touch of a button. In case you do not have this facility, here is how to calculate a composite chart.

A composite chart consists of the mid-points of the pairs of planetes in the two charts: the midpoint of the two Suns creates the composite Sun, the midpoint of the two Moons creates the composite Moon ...etc. The mid-point of the two Midheavens also creates the composite Midheaven, but the composite Ascendant and house divisions are calculated from the composite Midheaven, using tables of houses for where the two people live or where the relationship is taking place.

Calculate the planetary and Midheaven positions of the composite chart by converting the planetary and Midheaven positions of the natal charts into absolute longitude (starting at 0 degrees Aries), add them together, divide by two, and reconvert the result into the degree of the sign. It will help you to use the table below.

0 degrees Aries = 0
0 degrees Leo = 120
0 degrees Sagittarius = 240

0 degrees Taurus = 30
0 degrees Virgo = 150
0 degrees Capricorn = 270

0 degrees Gemini = 60
0 degrees Libra = 180
0 degrees Aquarius = 300

0 degrees Cancer = 90
0 degrees Scorpio = 210
0 degrees Pisces = 330

Examples: If the Sun in one horoscope is at 18 degrees Gemini and the Sun in the other horoscope is at 1 degree Libra, the Suns convert to 78 degrees and 181 degrees in absolute longitude. They add up to 259 degrees. Divide this by 2, which gives 129.5 degrees of absolute longitude. Reconvert this and we have the Composite Sun at (approximately) 9 degrees of Leo.

If the Midheaven of one horoscope is at 4 degrees Pisces and the Midheaven of the other horoscope is at 13 degrees Capricorn, they respectively convert to 334 degrees and 283 degrees of absolute longitude. These add up to 617 degrees of absolute longitude. Divide this by 2, which gives 308.5 degrees of absolute longitude, which re-converts to a composite Midheaven at (approximately) 8 degrees of Aquarius. (If the added longitudes of any pair of planets exceeds 720 degrees, subtract 360 degrees before re-converting.)

Important note: There are actually two mid-points between any two planets, which will be 180 degrees apart (exactly opposite each other). Always choose the one that is the mid-point of the shorter distance between the planets in the two horoscopes. The two examples above fulfil this condition, but consider another example.

Moon is one horoscope is at 29 degrees Taurus, in the other 18 degrees Capricorn. They convert to 59 degrees and 288 degrees absolute longitude. These add up to 347 degrees and divided by 2 gives 173.5 degrees, which converts to (approximately) 23 degrees Virgo. But this is not the shortest distance between the two Moons, so the composite Moon is at 23 degrees Pisces, not Virgo.

Once you have set up the composite chart, intepret it in the same way as you would a natal chart, but bear in mind that this is the chart of a relationship, not an individual. So, for example, the Ascendant of the composite chart refers to the overt personality of the relationship, not either of the individuals who have created it. And one difference between natal and composite charts seems to apply; the experience of many astrologers in interpreting composite charts is that, relative to natal horoscopes, the houses seem to be more important than the signs in composite charts.

In interpreting a composite chart, take particular note of:

* any strong house emphasis (four or more planets in a house)

* the houses of the Sun and Moon

* aspects to the Sun and to the Moon

* house positions and aspects to Venus and Mars

* planets in aspect to the angles of the chart

* house position and aspects to Saturn.

For love relationships, the 1st, 5th, 7th, and 11th houses will be particularly relevant.

For business relationships, the 2nd, 6th, 7th, and 10th houses will be particularly relevant.

For friendships, the 5th and 11th houses will be particularly relevant.

3) How to Analyze a Relationship Quickly and Efficiently

Step 1. Write down, for each person, the number of planets in cardinal, fixed, mutable and in Fire, Earth, Air, and Water signs. Compare them for obvious complimentarities (sex and love) and samenesses (friendship).

Step 2. Look at each person's Sun, Moon, Mercury, Venus, Mars and Ascendant and write down the aspects between them by sign only. E.g. Mars at 28 degrees Gemini is trine Mars at 1 degree Libra (even though square by degree). This kind of delineation shows whether the archetypal energies of the couple are on harmonious or inharmonious wavelengths.

121

Step 3. Using the same orbs as you would for natal aspects, and using only the aspects of conjunction, sextile, square, trine, and opposition (i.e. excluding the inconjunct aspect), count how many aspects there are to each person's Sun, Moon and Saturn from the other person's chart. By your own intuition, decide whether there are enough aspects to each person's Sun and Moon for there to be an assurance of deep significance in the relationship for each of the people involved. Decide if there are enough aspects to each other's Saturns for the relationship to be binding for both people. Take particular note of any marked disparities in the number of aspects to the respective Suns, Moons, and Saturns, which will describe one person as being more involved in the relationship than the other.

Step 4. Make a list of the "double-whammies" between the charts. For example, the Moon in Chart A in aspect to the Moon in Chart B; Mercury in Chart A in aspect to Jupiter in Chart B and Mercury in Chart B in aspect to Jupiter in Chart A. Note whether the inter-aspects in the double-whammies are harmonious or inharmonious. Whether harmonious or inharmonious, the archetypal energies of the double-whammies between people will be very conscious and significant foci of their relationship.

Step 5. Note aspects between the outer planets (Chiron, Uranus, Neptune, and Pluto) of one chart to the inner planets (Sun, Moon, Mercury, Venus, and Mars) and Ascendant and Midheaven of the other chart. (Discount these where the same outer planets of the two charts are close to conjunction, i.e. when the two people are near-contemporaries). Aspects between the outer planets of one chart to the inner planets of the other chart refer to powerful, dynamic (but often painful) transformative potential for each of the two people through the relationship.

Chiron to inner planet aspects suggests healing or wounding of deep pain in either or both of the parties.

Uranus to inner planet aspects suggest excitement and instability in the relationships.

Neptune to inner planet aspects suggest romance, illusion, and disappointment in the relationship.

Pluto to inner planet aspects bring intensity, transformation, and power struggles to a relationship.

In all the relationships you will be looking at and analyzing from now on, you will be presented with the two natal charts, the composite chart, and "bi-wheel". A bi-wheel consists of one horoscope at the centre of the chart with the planets and house cusps of the second chart surrounding the first chart, on its rim. This is a valuable visual aid to seeing clearly the most significant inter-aspects between the two horoscopes.

Brief Analysis of a Marriage
Michael (Chart 2) was married to Ruth (Chart 11)

1) We look at their two Sun-signs. Michael's is Virgo (mutable Earth) and Ruth's is Aquarius (fixed Air). These signs form an inconjunct in the zodiac and so, although not antagonistic, require much thoughtful adjustment on the part of each to understand the other's very different nature. They are likely to enjoy rational discussions with each other, but Michael is likely to complain that Ruth is too emotionally detached, and Ruth is likely to complain that Michael is too concerned with petty details.

2) Michael has 3 cardinal, 5 fixed and 2 mutable planets, while Ruth has 4 cardinal, 5 fixed and 1 mutable planet. So Ruth is likely to be the leader in the relationship (she has

123

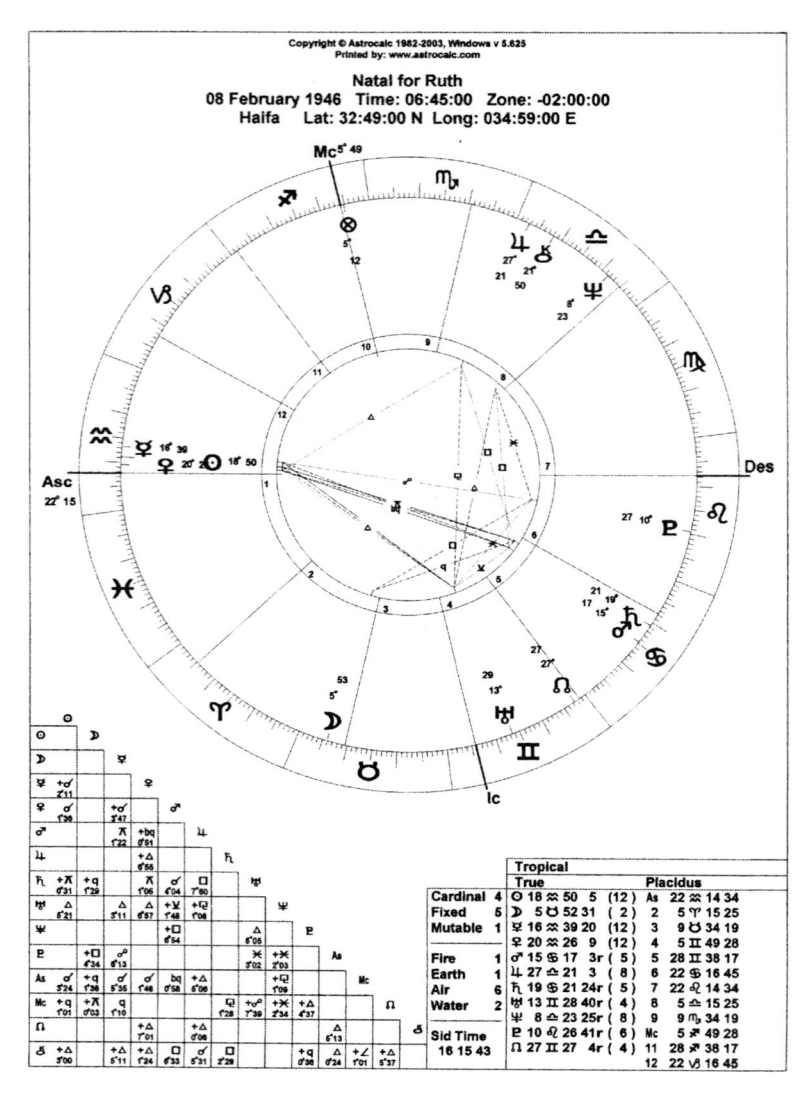

Chart 11

124

more cardinality), although the overwhelming theme between them is huge fixity (5 fixed planets each) imlying great stubbornness in each of them, with virtually no flexible responsiveness to the other (shortage of mutability). Michael has 4 Fire, 1 Earth, 3 Air and 2 Water planets, while Ruth has 1 Fire, 1 Earth, 6 Air and 2 Water planets. The combination of his Fire and her Air could make for a lot of inspired ideas - but also a lot of hot air! especially because of the very little Earth (practicality) between them.

3) Their Suns are inconjunct by sign.
   Their Moons are square by sign.
   Their Mercurys are trine by sign
   Their Venuses are in opposition by sign.
   Their Marses are trine by sign.

(We do not have Ruth's time of birth, so her horoscope has been set for dawn, but her actual Ascendant is not known.)

The Venus and Mars aspects (by sign) suggest the relationship began through sexual excitement (opposition) and compatibility (Mars), but the square Moons imply great tension due to incompatible family/emotional backgrounds.

4) Between their horoscopes there are 0 aspects to Michael's Sun, 2 aspects to Michael's Moon, and no aspects to Michael's Saturn; 2 aspects to Ruth's Sun, 2 aspects to Ruth's Moon, and 2 aspects to Ruth's Saturn. From these we can infer that Ruth has no direct bearing on Michael's career (no aspects to his Sun), she is significantly relevant to his deepest emotions (2 aspects to his Moon), but he does not feel bound to her (no aspects to his Saturn). But her status in the world is significantly related to Michael (2 aspects to her Sun); he is relevant to her deepest emotions (2 aspects to her Moon); and she feels significantly bound to him (2 aspects to her Saturn).

5) In the synastry between their horoscopes there are some very difficult planetary aspects. His Mercury square her Mars and Saturn suggest he experiences her as aggressive (Mars) and squelching (Saturn) in response to whatever he says (Mercury); and, indeed, he claims she criticized him constantly. Conversely, his Mars opposing her Moon would make her experience him as aggressively discounting of her feelings. Yet she probably understood his feelings (her Mercury conjunct his Moon) and he was probably stimulated by her ideas (his Mercury trine her Uranus).

The only double-whammie between their horoscopes is Mercury trine Mercury, implying that talking to each other was a central feature of their relationship and, given that it is a trine aspect, it was probably being able to talk to each other that helped draw them together at the beginning of their relationship.

6) Finally, looking for outer planet (Chiron, Uranus, Neptune, Pluto) aspects from either horoscope to the inner planets (Sun, Moon, Mercury, Venus, Mars) of the other, or from Ruth's horoscope to Michael's (known) Ascendant or Midheaven, we find Michael's Chiron squaring Ruth's Sun, Mercury and Venus and trining her Mars and Saturn; and her Chiron sextiles his Jupiter and squares his Ascendant, all of which implies they were each seeking - largely unsuccessfully - to heal their deepest wounds (Chiron) through their relationship. His Pluto opposing her Sun and Mercury and her Pluto squaring his Mars add a risk of violence between them as well as chronic power struggles.

Having completed our analysis of the relationship, we may now look to the individual horoscopes to see how the relationship fulfils the needs and compulsions of the two people in it.

Referring back to our analysis of Michael's horoscope (pp. 82-84), we can see how he would almost inevitably be drawn to a difficult marriage in order to rationalize and justify the difficulties in his own nature. In particular, Ruth's Aquarius Sun enables him to project his own difficulty in being fully emotionally involved (his Moon in Aquarius) onto her.

On her part, Ruth has some very difficult aspects to her Sun (the men in her life), including inconjuncts to her Mars-Saturn conjunction (angry frustration in adjusting to the men in her life) and an opposition to her Pluto (power struggles with the men in her life). Her Sun, Mercury and Venus form trine aspects to Uranus, suggesting her attraction to excitingly "different" realtionships to men. Thus, in an overall way, they were each initially attracted to the exciting unfamiliarity of the other, which became, in combination with all the other aspects between them, a nervous and fraught battle of incompatibility. (After Michael and Ruth were divorced, he discovered she had been having a clandestine affair for most of their marriage - another manifestation of her Sun conjunction Venus trine Uranus)

A Painful Love Affair - Bill Clinton and Monica Lewinsky Charts (Charts 12, 13, 14 and 15)

Her Sun is in Leo, his Sun is in Leo. They appreciate each other's warmth and loyalty and enjoy spending money together on the good things of life. They may be inclined to accuse each other of being too vain and proud.

Their composite chart has Libra, the sign of intimate relating, on the Ascendant and its ruler, Venus, in the 12th house, the house of neurotic self-destructiveness. Neptune in the 1st house in Scorpio, suggests romantic and sexual confusion and delusion as the basic nature of the relationship, and Neptune is the ruler of Pisces, which rules the 6th house of work,

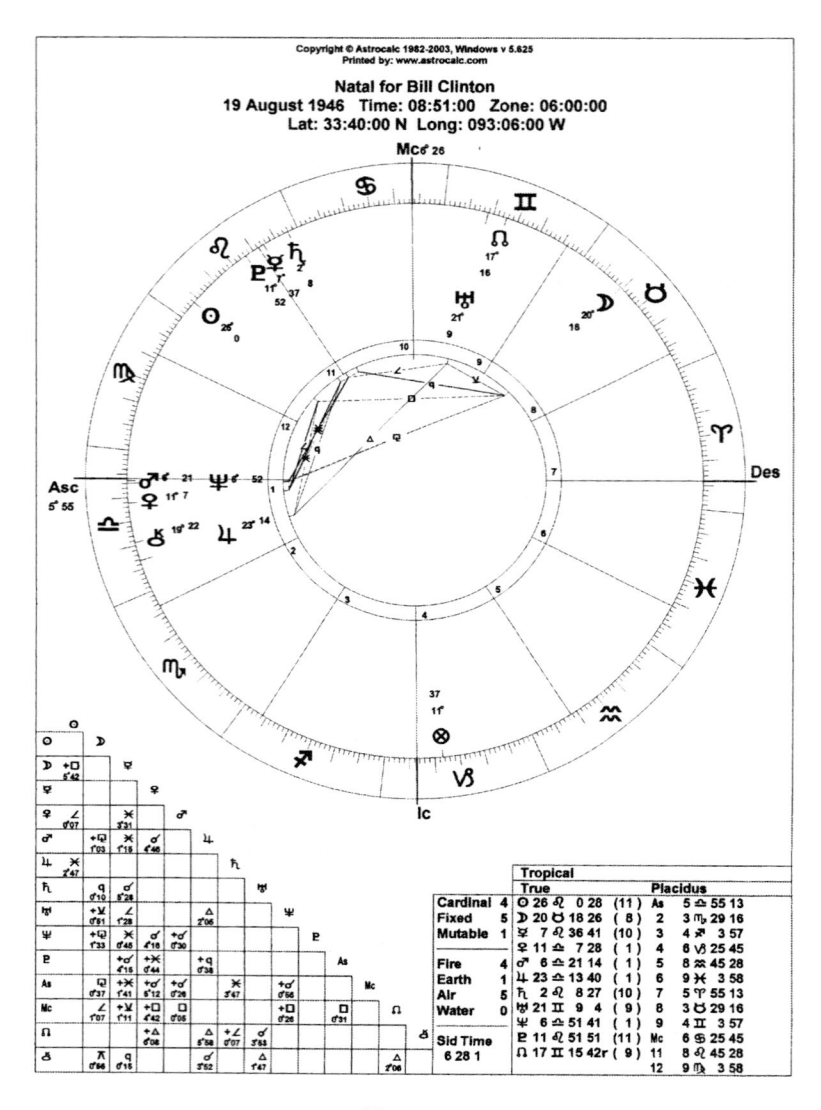

Chart 12

which house contains the Moon's North Node, defining the essential purpose of the relationship as working together, but this being deflected, confusedly, into the illusory and delusory intimacy (1st house Neptune) which led to the scandal (Neptune).

The stellium of planets in the 10th house (Sun, Mercury, Mars, Saturn, and Chiron) reinforce the Moon's North Node in the 6th house, emphasizing that their relationship was principally a relationship of careers. But the Moon (feelings) dominates the rest of the relationship, being the "handle of the bucket" of the rest of the chart and in Taurus in the 8th house (down-to-earth sexuality) and ruling Cancer (feelings), the sign on the Midheaven of the chart. The Moon is in a close square to the Sun, describing the tense conflict between the career purpose of the relationship and the feelings between this couple. Mars on the Midheaven (assertive expression of career goals) is in a close square to the Ascendant, and Mars is the ruler of the Descendant, again describing the conflict between this couple's legitimate career relationship and their personal relationship.

The exact sextile between Chiron and Venus enabled them to heal each other's relationship wounds, but Chiron being conjunction Saturn in the 10th house made this also the signature of the public shame (Saturn) that befell the relationship.

Uranus and Pluto in the 11th house describes the sudden and powerfully transforming effect their relationship had on the world-at-large.

He has 4 cardinal, 5 fixed, and 1 mutable planets, she has 4 cardinal, 4 fixed, and 2 mutable planets, making them equally go-getting. They are both stubborn, he slightly more so than she (he "won" in the end). He has 4 Fire, 1 Earth, 5 Air, and 1 Water planets, she has 4 Fire, 1 Earth, 4 Air, and 1 Water

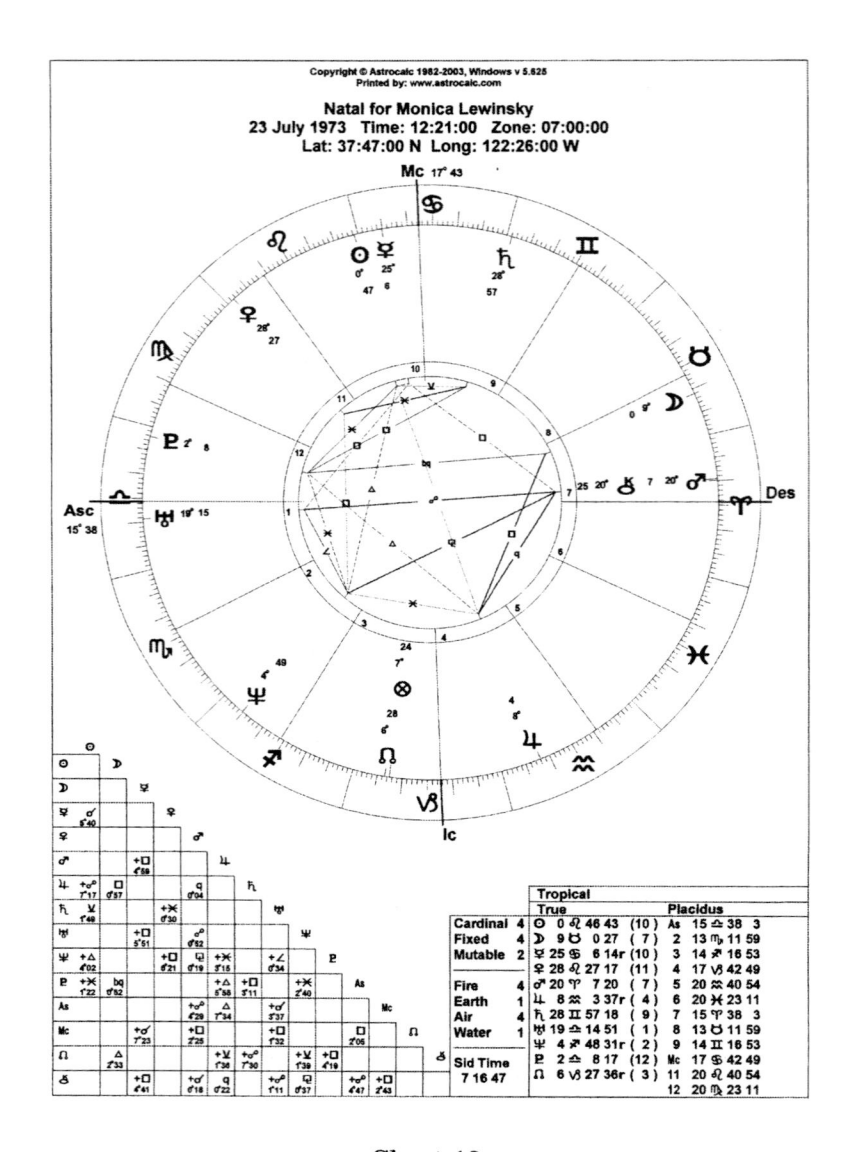

Chart 13

planets, underlining the similarities rather than complementarity that was the essence of their relationship, which was overwhelmingly impetuous and lacking in practicality.

Their Suns are conjunction by sign.
Their Moons are conjunction by sign.
Their Mercurys are in semi-sextile by sign.
Their Venuses are sextile by sign.
Their Marses are opposition by sign.
Their Ascendants are conjunction by sign.

Thus their overwhelming similarities to each other are confirmed, although it was probably the Mars opposition that precipitated Monica in blowing the whole relationship sky high.

Between their charts, there are:

1 aspect to Bill Clinton's Sun, 0 aspects to his Moon, and 3 aspects to his Saturn; 1 aspect to Monica Lewinsky's Sun, 2 aspects to her Moon, and 0 aspects to her Saturn.

From these we can infer that she was significantly emotionally involved in their relationship (2 aspects to her Moon), but he was not (0 aspects to his Moon). However, he found it very difficult to free himself from the relationship (3 aspects to his Saturn) whereas she did not (0 aspects to her Saturn).

From their bi-wheel chart, we can extract the following major inter-aspects between them.

His Sun is conjunction her Venus - a clear love connection, he being attracted to her way of being a woman, she attracted to

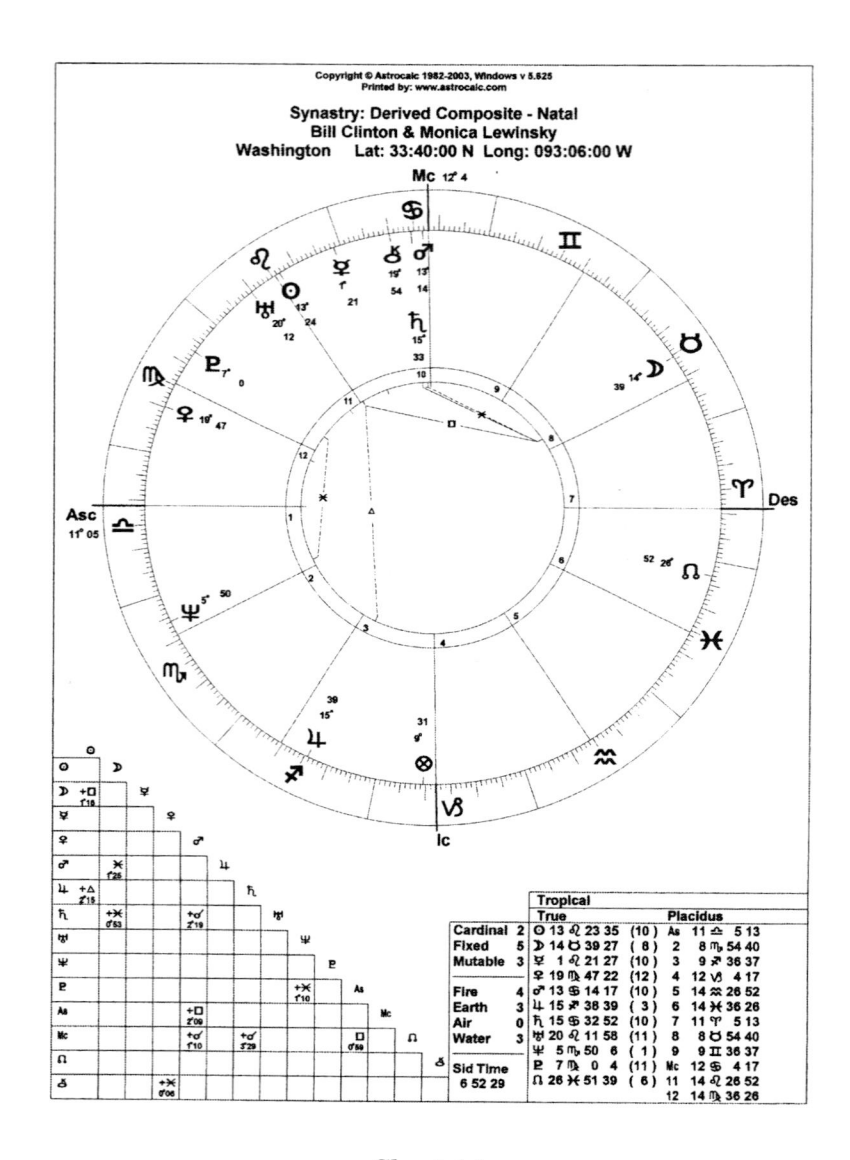

Copyright © Astrocalc 1982-2003, Windows v 5.625
Printed by: www.astrocalc.com

Synastry: Derived Composite - Natal
Bill Clinton & Monica Lewinsky
Washington   Lat: 33:40:00 N   Long: 093:06:00 W

Tropical				
True			Placidus	
Cardinal 2	☉ 13 ♌ 23 35	(10)	As	11 ♎ 5 13
Fixed 5	☽ 14 ♉ 39 27	(8)	2	8 ♏ 54 40
Mutable 3	☿ 1 ♌ 21 27	(10)	3	9 ♐ 36 37
	♀ 19 ♍ 47 22	(12)	4	12 ♑ 4 17
Fire 4	♂ 13 ♋ 14 17	(10)	5	14 ♒ 26 52
Earth 3	♃ 15 ♐ 38 39	(3)	6	14 ♓ 36 26
Air 0	♄ 15 ♋ 32 52	(10)	7	11 ♈ 5 13
Water 3	♅ 20 ♌ 11 58	(11)	8	8 ♉ 54 40
	♆ 5 ♏ 50 6	(1)	9	9 ♊ 36 37
Sid Time	♇ 7 ♍ 0 4	(11)	Mc	12 ♋ 4 17
6 52 29	☊ 26 ♓ 51 39	(6)	11	14 ♌ 26 52
			12	14 ♍ 36 26

Chart 14

his power. His Mercury square her Moon opposition her Jupiter and trine her Neptune - the things he said (Mercury) seduced her (Neptune) and led her to expect more than he would deliver (Jupiter), and ultimately described the conflict between his communications and her feelings (Moon). His Venus trine her Jupiter - a naturally loving aspect. His Mars trine her Jupiter sextile her Neptune square her Moon's North Node - she flattered his masculine self-esteem (Mars-Jupiter), she was seduced by him (Mars-Neptune), but his sexuality was ultimately in conflict with her life-goals (Mars-North Node).

His Jupiter square her Mercury opposition her Mars basically describes her being led to expect more from him than he was actually willing to give.

His Saturn conjunction her Sun trine her Neptune sextile her Pluto: he suppressed her natural exuberance in the relationship (for the obvious reasons of his responsibilities and his fear of being found out - Saturn-Sun), but she happily submitted to this out of her romantic projection onto his discipline (Saturn-Neptune), through which she may well have experienced him as the "good" father that she experienced her own father as not being), and she experienced the relationship as offering her the opportunity to transform her life (Saturn-Pluto).

His Uranus sextile her Mars trine her Uranus - very exciting sexuality.

His Neptune trine her Jupiter square her Moon's North Node - he, too, was seduced by her (Neptune-Jupiter), although his fantasies about the relationship were at odds with her life-goals (Neptune-Moon's North Node).

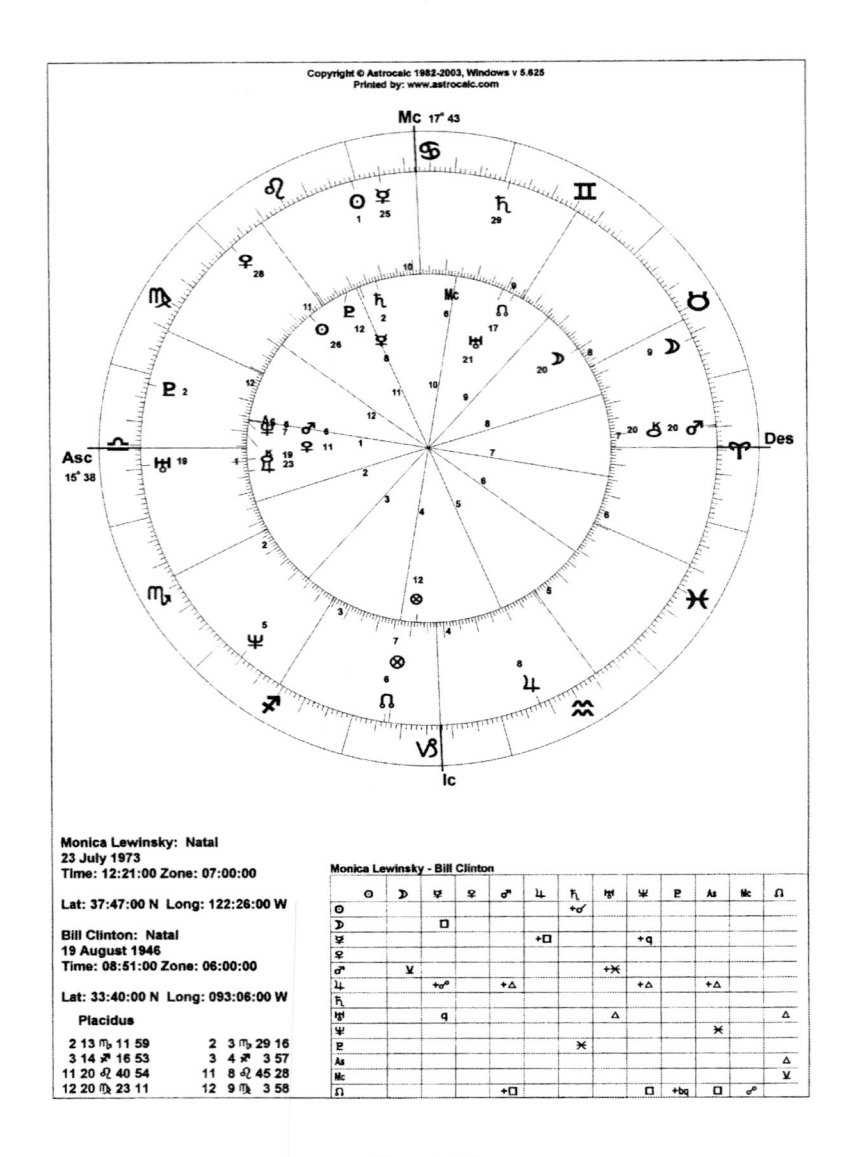

Chart 15

His Pluto square her Moon: there was great tension between them out of the conflict arising from his bid to control her free emotional expressivenss.

His Ascendant trine her Jupiter sextile her Ascendant, square her Moon's North Node: he felt himself expand (Jupiter) in her presence, they identify with each other (Ascendants) but - again - his essential nature (Ascendant) is in conflict with her life goals (Moon's North Node).

The double-whammies between their horoscopes are:

Mercury-Jupiter (opposition, square) and Uranus-Uranus (trine), which describe the grandiose misunderstandings and irresistible excitement which were at the forefront of their awareness in the relationship.

Looking for the deep transformation implied in outer to inner planet aspects, her Neptune trines his Mercury, sextiles his Mars, trines his Saturn, and sextiles his Ascendant, implying her ability to teach him how to express himself - verbally and sexually - in a romantic way and to overcome his inhibitions through her leading him into fantasy in their relationship. All these aspects to her Neptune also describe her being seduced into the relationship, which was, inevitably, deeply disappointing and disillusioning for her.

His Pluto square her Moon means he exerted great power over her emotionally, but which caused her much pain (square), although probably also permanently transformed her emotional expression.

Finally, let us look to each of their individual horoscopes to check how well they each fulfilled their relationship needs. Monica Lewinsky has Uranus in Libra on the Ascendant opposition Mars conjunction Chiron in her 7th house. Thus, notwithstanding any protestations she might make to the contrary, she is actually drawn to relationships which do not involve commitment (Uranus) but which bring her a lot of aggravation (Mars) and painful lessons (Chiron). Her Moon in the 7th house also suggests that in her intimate relationships she will seek fluctuating emotional security (Moon). She is attracted to men who are powerful in their careers (Sun in the 10th house) and who seduce her into romance, which ends in disillusionment (Sun square Neptune). Her emotional expectations are grandiose (Moon square Jupiter). Her love relationships tend to be formed out of friendships or associations she makes through her career (Venus in the 11th house), and she is attracted to men who have powerful intellects from whom she can learn (Venus sextile Saturn in Gemini in the 9th house). Pisces is on the cusp of her 5th house, which is ruled by Neptune, and the many aspects to her Neptune from Bill Clinton's horoscope fulfil her romantic expectations. Thus the relationship with him was a very meaningful one for her.

Bill Clinton's well-publicized compulsive and deceitful sexual relationships are described by his Venus, Mars, and Neptune all conjunction his Ascendant in Libra. All being in Libra, he is inclined to rationalize his sexual escapades as important intimate relationships, until he is confronted with his own excesses (Chiron conjunction Jupiter in the 1st house). His Moon in the 8th house describes him as a man who is ultimately much more looking for emotional security than sex for its own sake (as is known from his very unsatisfactory relationship to his mother). With Aquarius on the cusp of his 5th house, whose ruler, Uranus, is conjunction his Moon's North Node, we have a man who is inclined to form romantic relationships suddenly and excitingly, and these are an important aspect of his life destiny.

Thus, in this relationship, notwithstanding its pain for both parties, each actually got what they deeply sought in love relationships. Loath as we are to admit it, we all compulsively seek to reiterate the pains in our lives as well as the joys. Ultimately, we all get what we want under the disguise of what we deserve.

Exercises

1) What is the negative feeling that all people seek through their relationships?

2) What makes us compulsively repeat our painful (as well as our joyful) experiences?

3) Name the two most common defences of our egos.

4) Which inter-aspects between our own and another's horoscope most help us to grow our consciousness?

5) Which planet is needed to maintain stability in a relationship?

6) Which planets in ourselves do we first show towards somebody we are sexually attracted to?

7) Which planet expresses where we are most sensitive to being wounded?

8) Which planet expresses where we are most able to be healed of our wounds?

9) Which of the following relationships tend to be tense and which easily harmonious?

   a) Sun Aries with Sun Cancer
   b) Sun Taurus with Sun Virgo
   c) Sun Libra with Sun Gemini
   d) Sun Libra with Sun Capricorn

10) What is the name we give to the horoscope of a relationship?

11) Which houses are particularly relevant to a love relationship?

12) Which houses are particularly relevant to a business relationship?

13) What do we call an inter-aspect between two people's horoscopes that goes both ways, e.g. His Sun trine her Mars and her Sun square his Mars?

14) Which planet in a relationship expresses excitement and instability?

15) Which planet in a relationship expresses power struggles and transformation?

16) Which planet in a relationship expresses romance and illusion?

17) What is the name of a chart in which the horoscope of one person is surrounded by the horoscope of another person?

18) Which of the following relationships are most likely to have a strong basis of sexual attraction?

   a) His Sun in Gemini, her Sun in Leo

   b) His Sun in Gemini, her Sun in Sagittarius

   c) His Sun in Cancer, her Sun in Capricorn

   d) His Sun in Virgo, her Sun in Cancer

19) Which two planets do you think are most important in assessing domestic harmony between two people?

20) Which two planets are most important in assessing the sexual relationship between two people?

21) Which two planets are most important in assessing the deepest level compatibility between two people?

22) In the same ways as Graham and Carol's relationship and Bill Clinton and Monica Lewinsky's relationships have been analyzed in this chapter, analyze the relationshipof Yoko Ono and John Lennon (Charts 18, 19, 20 and 21).

Do realistically assess the pains and joys intrinsic to any relationship for each of the partners.

Don't judge any relationship as "good" or "bad". People need the difficult relationships they are in for as long as they choose to remain in them.

Chapter 7
Synastry

Summary: As well as by the methods described in Chapter 6, a relationship between two people can be understood through a detailed analysis of the planetary inter-aspects between them; through analyses of the interactions of one person's planets with the houses of the other person's horoscope; and by the inter-aspects between each persons's horoscope and the composite chart of the relationship. The relationship between Elizabeth Taylor and Richard Burton is analyzed in detail.

Synastry means literally "between the stars" and, more broadly, is taken to be any understanding of two people's relationship through an analysis of the inter-aspects between their individual horoscopes. The wholeness of each of us as individuals and the wholeness of any relationship are made up of the separate and combined fragments of planetary inter-aspects, modified by signs and houses. Planetary inter-aspects between two people can be interpreted as they would be in an individual horoscope, as set out in Chapter 4, supplemented by the mutual experiences of one person's planets in the houses of another person's horoscope, and the wholeness of their relationship further refined by the synastries between their composite chart and the individual horoscopes of each of them.

Planetary inter-aspects
The dynamic core of any relationship between two people's horoscopes (as of any individual horoscope) is represented by the planetary inter-aspects. Planetary inter-aspects give very vivid and accurate pictures of people's experiences of each

other, even without reference to house placements. The aspects that somebody else's planets form to the planets in your horoscope will be experienced by you very similarly to the ways you experience transits to your horoscope. And if the other person's outer planets form close aspects to your inner planets, that person is going to exert a very powerful influence on you. When you experience outer planet transits to your horoscope, they are often once-in-a-lifetime occurrences (and may be less than once-in-a-lifetime); but if another person's outer planets aspect your inner planets, they will stimulate you to great growth whenever you are in their presence. No wonder intimate relationships are such challenges to us, as they are the greatest source of our personal growth and the fulfilment of our potential.

The relative importance of particular inter-aspects between two people will vary according to the type of relationship they have, and these differences will be highlighted in the chapters following this one. Nevertheless, do remember, as already discussed in Chapter 6, that in all relationships planetary inter-aspects that occur both ways (e.g. his Mercury aspects her Moon and her Mercury aspects his Moon), which we call "double whammies", will be experienced by the two people as a very conscious and central components of their relationship.

Apart from the double-whammies in the synastry between two people's horoscopes, some aspects will be more dominant in the consciousness of both people than others. This is partly because some aspects are closer to exactitude than others and are therefore felt more powerfully. But it is also the case that out of the huge complexity of all the inter-aspects between two people they may actually choose to "use" some aspects often and to generally ignore others, even though all the inter-aspects between them are potentially manifest in their experiences of each other. It may help you to appreciate this if you think of your commonsense, non-astrological understanding of human relationships. You probably have a number of friends each of whom you enjoy for different reasons. That is, certain parts of you regularly interact with one friend and different parts of you interact with another friend. And sometimes, after knowing somebody for some time, we discover new parts of them - for better or worse - that we haven't noticed before and may now widen our relationship to them. The astrological analysis of a relationship reflects this. Long-term intimate relationships between people (whether viewed astrologically or commonsensically) are so rich because they give us enough time to get to know the multitudinous possibilities of our relationship that a brief or superficial relationship cannot give.

When interpreting the planetary inter-aspects between two charts, use the same orbs as you would in interpreting planetary inter-aspects in an individual horoscope. (See Chapter 4). In relationships between men and women there are often subtle but important differences between the meaning of a given planetary inter-aspect, depending on which planet is in the horoscope of the man and which in the horoscope of the woman. E.g. his Sun trine her Moon, is likely to manifest in quite different ways from her Sun trine his Moon. Use your intuition to be sensitive to these differences.

Planets in Houses in Synastry

Your experiences of somebody else are represented by the placement of his or her planets and the Ascendant and Midheaven on your chart (as represented in a bi-wheel). For example, his or her Sun in your 10th house "lights up" and energizes your career goals; his or her Moon in your 1st house implies that you are immediately sensitive to his or her feelings.

Conversely, if you want to know how another person experiences you, place all your planets and Ascendant and Midheaven on his or her chart. For example, if your Venus falls in his or her 5th house, he or she will feel romantically loved by you; if your Saturn falls in his or her 2nd house, he or she will experience you as controlling his or her spending (which he or she may value or resent!)

Synastry Between an Individual and a Composite Chart

When considering a relationship in the finest possible detail - and you are only likely to want to do this quite rarely - you can look at the synastry between each individual's planets and the planets and angles of the composite chart. Whereas the planetary inter-aspects between the two individual horoscopes describe how each person experiences he other, the planetary inter-aspects between an individual's planets and the composite chart of his or her relationship to another person describe how that individual experiences the relationship.

The Tempestuous Relationship of Elizabeth Taylor and Richard Burton (Charts 20, 21, 22, and 23)

Elizabeth Taylor has been a famous film-star since she was a child. She is renowned for her beauty and her many marriages and divorces. Richard Burton was a renowned Shakespearian actor, risen from lowly origins. He was an alcoholic. Elizabeth Taylor and Richard Burton were twice married and divorced from each other.

Her Sun is in Pisces, his is in Scorpio, so their core natures blend harmoniously, she being more changeable (mutable) and he more controlled (fixed).

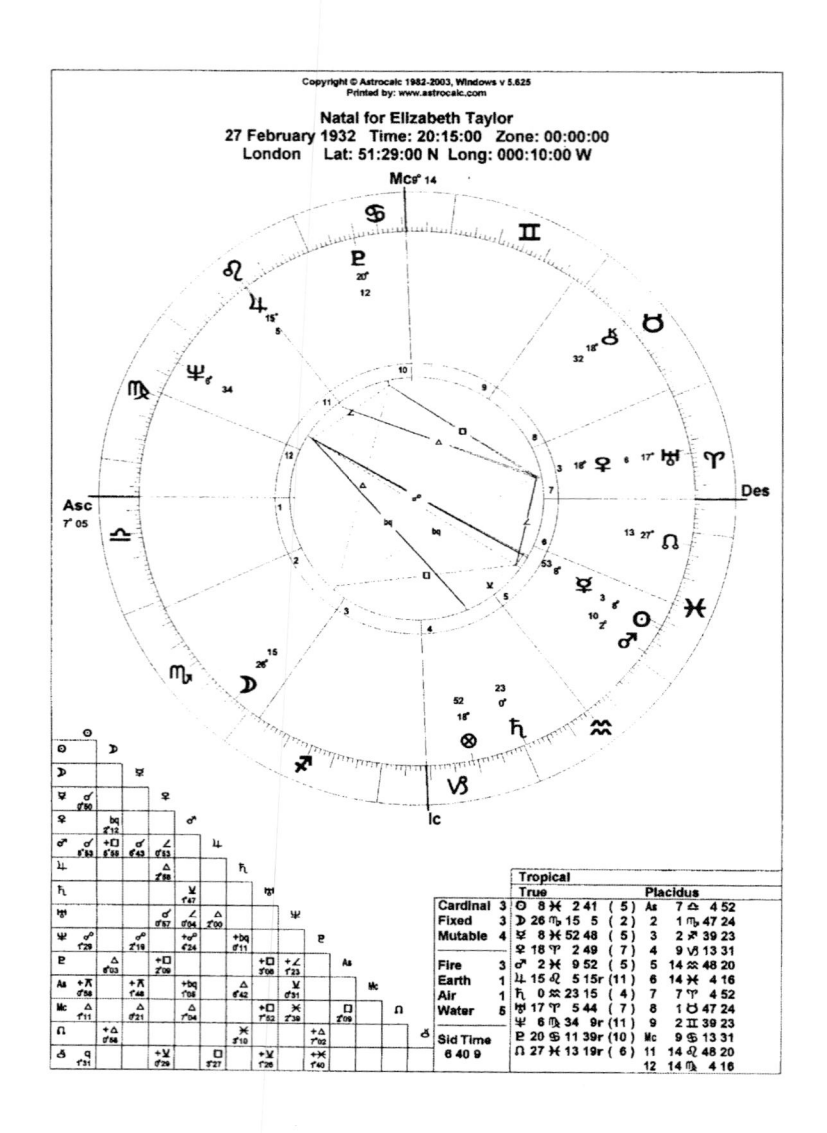

Chart 20

In their composite chart, the volatile nature of their relationship is immediately evident from Uranus on the cusp between the 7th and 8th houses of (intimacy, marriage, sex, and transformation). Neptune trine Sun describes the high romance of their relationship (but even a trine aspect from Neptune makes whatever it touches vulnerable to delusion and disappointment!) and Neptune in the 12th house of self-destructiveness is the ruler of the 7th house of marriage, (which, in a composite chart, also refers to the way the relationship is seen by the public). The Moon squaring both Mercury and Pluto is the very painful emotional power struggles between them.

How each of them experienced the relationship (as distinct from how they experienced each other as individuals) is shown in the aspects the composite chart makes to each of their individual horoscope.

Composite to Elizabeth Taylor

Sun Square Venus
Sun inconjunct Jupiter
Sun square Uranus
Moon opposition Venus
Moon sextile Jupiter
Moon opposition Uranus
Moon square Pluto
Mercury sextile Moon
Mercury opposition Pluto
Mercury sextile North Node
Venus square Moon
Mars sextile Mars
Mars trine Neptune

Composite to Richard Burton

Sun sextile Sun
Sun conjunction Jupiter
Sun sextile Saturn
Sun opposition Pluto
Moon square Jupiter
Moon inconjunct Uranus
Moon sextile Neptune
Moon square Pluto
Mercury sextile Sun
Mercury square Mars
Mercury conjunction Jupiter
Mercury sextile Uranus
Mercury inconjunct Neptune

145

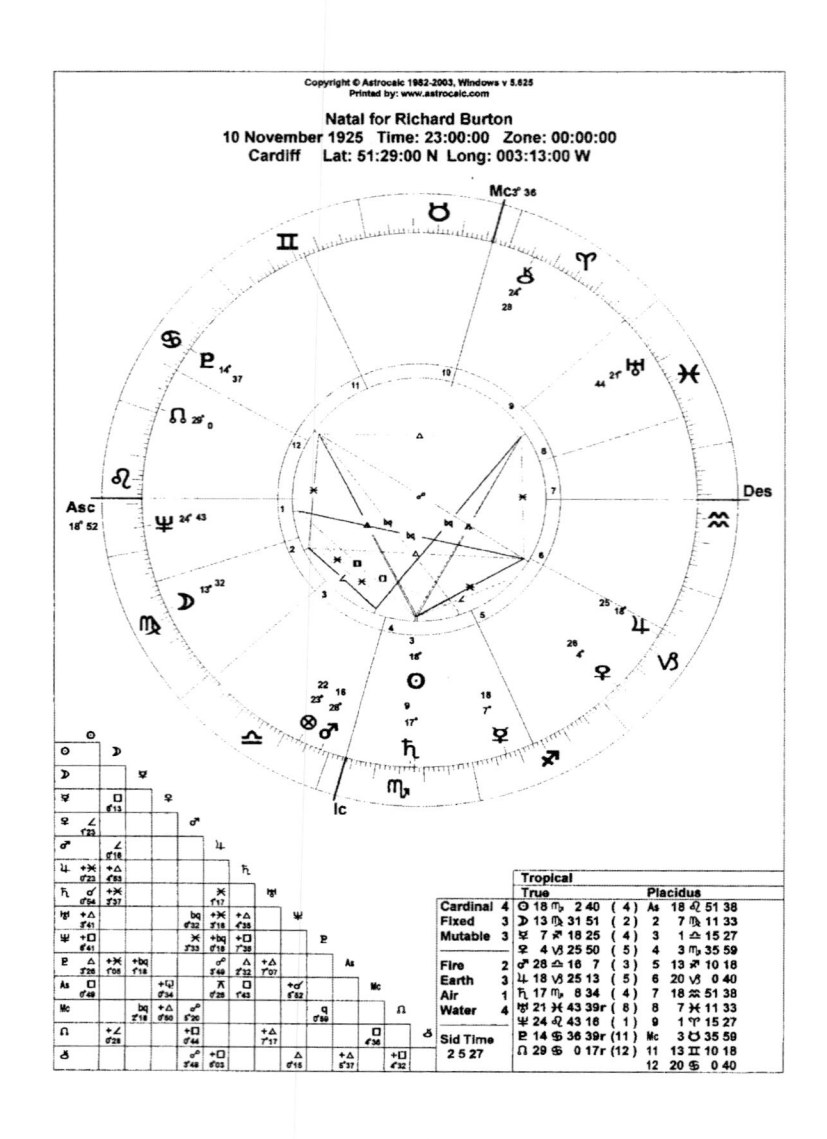

Natal for Richard Burton
10 November 1925 Time: 23:00:00 Zone: 00:00:00
Cardiff   Lat: 51:29:00 N Long: 003:13:00 W

Chart 21

146

Jupiter square Saturn

Saturn square North Node
Uranus sextile Saturn
Uranus inconjunct Neptune
Neptune opposition Mars
Neptune conjunction Neptune
Pluto square Venus
Pluto square Uranus
Pluto conjunction Pluto
North Node opposition Moon
North Node sextile North Node

Mercury opposition North Node
Venus trine Mars
Venus opposition Neptune
Venus inconjunct North Node
Mars inconjunct North Node
Jupiter sextile Venus
Jupiter square North Node
Saturn sextile Mars
Saturn square Uranus
Saturn trine Neptune
Saturn inconjunct North Node
Uranus trine Mercury
Uranus square Venus
Uranus trine North Node
Neptune trine Venus
Pluto trine Sun
Pluto sextile Moon
Pluto opposition Jupiter
Pluto trine Saturn
Pluto trine Uranus
Pluto conjunction Pluto

Not a pretty picture for either of them, especially for her, with all those very hard aspects from the composite to her natal horoscope. The most painful experiences for her were probably Sun square Uranus (although that is likely to have been exciting as well), Moon opposition Uranus (the needs of the relationship denying her freedom), Moon square Pluto (the needs of the relationship in conflict with her need to be in control), Mercury opposition Pluto (intense arguments),

147

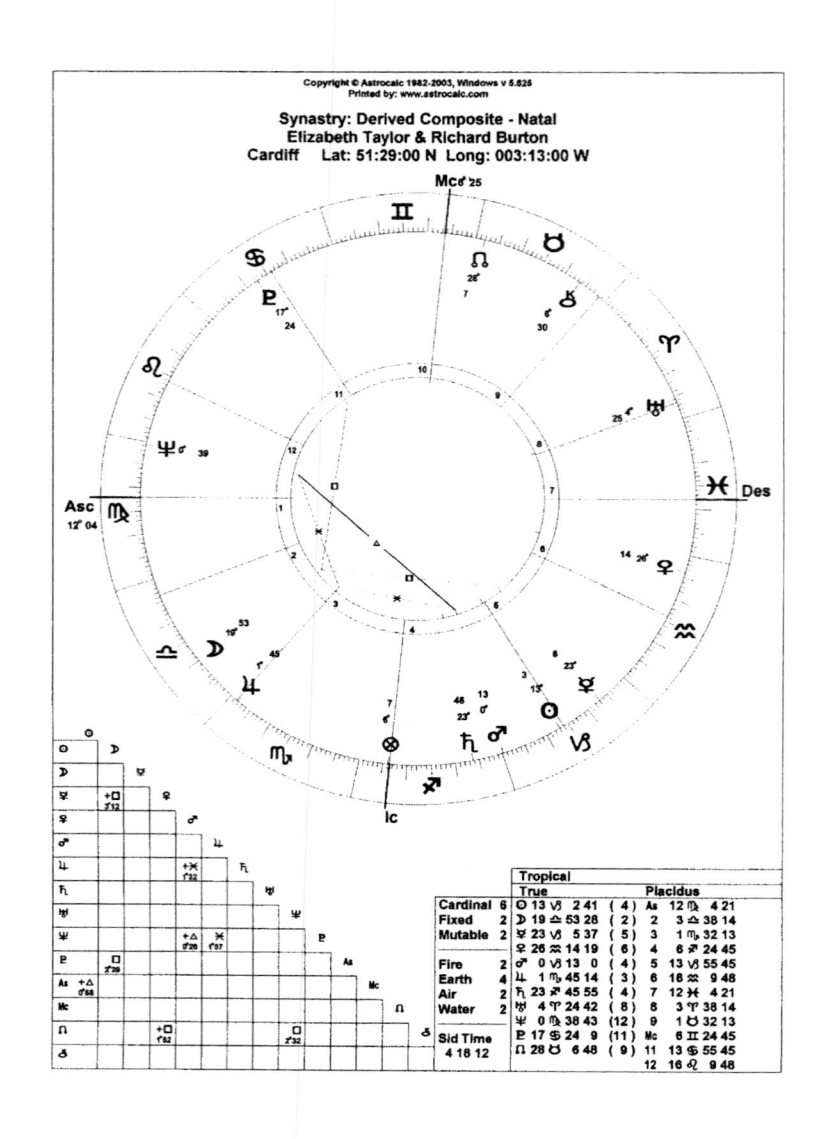

Chart 22

Saturn square North Node (the constraints of the relationship in conflict with her destiny), Neptune opposition Mars (the romance of the relationship in conflict with her need for self-assertion), Pluto square Venus (the pain of their passionate love).

He seems to have experienced the relationship somewhat more positively than she did, although it had plenty of pain for him as well. The most significant positive aspects from the composite to his natal horoscope were probably Sun conjunction Jupiter (heightened joy and optmism), Moon sextile Neptune (romance), Mercury conjunction Jupiter and sextile Uranus (communication that stimulated his intellect), Venus trine Mars (sexual fulfilment), Venus opposition Neptune (romance), Jupiter sextile Venus (love), Uranus trine Mercury (intellectual stimulation), Neptune trine Venus (romance). The relationship certainly invoked in him great romantic feelings and stimulating conversation.

But he, too, experienced plenty of pain in the relationship: Sun opposition Pluto (great power struggles), Moon square Jupiter and inconjunct Uranus (the needs of the relationship in conflict with his freedom), Moon square Pluto (more resistance to his need to be in control), Mercury square Mars (communication that incited him to aggression), Saturn square Uranus (the relationship severely restricted his freedom), Uranus square Venus (great excitement, but inharmonious with his love nature), Pluto opposition Jupiter (intense conflict over principles).

Overall, we can infer that the relationship was experienced by Richard Burton as a mixture of high romance and intense conflict; and the relationship was experienced by Elizabeth Taylor as almost wholly painful.

Elizabeth Taylor has 6 cardinal, 2 fixed, and 2 mutable planets; Richard Burton has 4 cardinal, 3 fixed, and 3

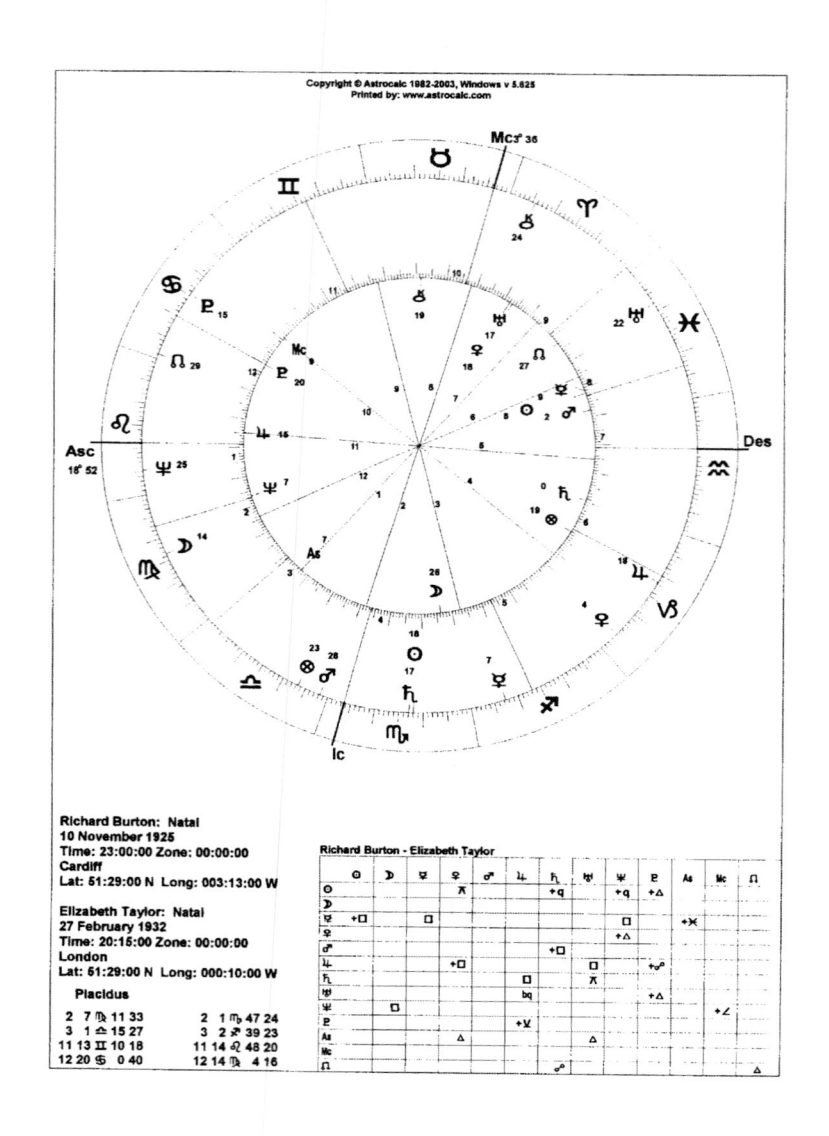

Chart 23

mutable planets. His 4 cardinal planets describe him as a generally forcefully initiating man, but this did not match her 6 cardinal planets, making her likely to be the "winner" in any power struggles between them.

Elizabeth Taylor has 2 Fire, 3 Earth, 1 Air, and 4 Water planets; Richard Burton has 2 Fire, 4 Earth, 2 Air, and 2 Water planets. The only noticeable feature of this comparison between them is her much greater emotionality than his (and his Sun in Scorpio also adds to the controlledness of his emotions).

Their Sun signs are trine
Their Moon signs are sextile
Their Mercury signs are square
Their Venus signs are square
Their Mars signs are inconjunct
Their Ascendant signs are sextile

Thus it is their everyday communication and their values and ways of expressing love that are likely to precipitate the most unhappiness between them.

There are 2 aspects to his Sun, 3 aspects to his Moon, and 2 aspects to his Saturn. There are 2 aspects to her Sun, 4 aspects to her Moon, and 1 aspect to her Saturn. Emotions (Moon) dominate the relationship and, with only one aspect to her Saturn (and that one is from his North Node rather than the energy of a planet), there is little chance of the relationship enduring for a lifetime.

The major aspects in the synastry between their natal horoscopes includes:

His Sun conjunction her Moon
His Sun square her Jupiter
His Sun trine her Pluto
His Sun opposition her Chiron
His Moon opposition her Sun
His Moon opposition her Mercury
His Moon conjunction her Neptune
His Mercury square her Sun
His Mercury square her Mars
His Mercury trine her Jupiter
His Mercury square her Neptune
His Venus trine her Neptune
His Mars trine her Mars
His Mars square her Saturn
His Jupiter square her Venus
His Jupiter square her Uranus
His Jupiter opposition her Pluto
His Jupiter trine her Chiron
His Saturn square her Jupiter
His Saturn trine her Pluto
His Saturn opposition her Chiron
His Uranus trine her Moon
His Uranus trine her Pluto
His Uranus sextile her Chiron
His Uranus conjunction her North Node
His Neptune trine her Venus
His Neptune opposition her Mars
His Neptune trine her Uranus
His Pluto trine her Mercury
His Pluto square her Venus

His Pluto square her Uranus
His Pluto conjunction her Pluto
His Pluto sextile her Chiron
His Chiron inconjunct her Moon
His Chiron square her Pluto
His North Node trine her North Node
His Ascendant square her Chiron

Their double-whammies are:

Sun-Moon (conjunction and opposition)
Moon-Neptune (conjunction and square)
Mercury-Mercury (square)
Venus-Neptune (trine and trine)
Mars-Mars (trine)
Uranus-Pluto (trine and square)
Pluto-Pluto (conjunction)
Chiron-Pluto (square and sextile)

His Sun conjunction her Moon is the most basic blending of man and woman - his strength and dominance, her emotional receptivity and nurturance. But this beautiful inter-aspect is spoilt by the other part of this double-whammie, his Moon opposition her Sun, which describes his feelings that her career goals were in conflict with his emotional needs. The loving and gentle aspects in their synastry include his Moon conjunction her Neptune and his Neptune trine her Venus. But these are heavily in competition with the extremely disharmonious aspects of Mercury square Mercury, his Mercury square her Mars, his Saturn square her Jupiter, and his Pluto square her Venus and square her Uranus.

153

We have now accumulated more than enough information about this relationship for all normal purposes. The important themes have been repeated several times and we have achieved a powerfull overall experience of the relationship. However, for the learning experience, we will complete our analysis of this relationship by reference to the planets in each other's houses and with a final check on how well the relationship matched the needs described in the individual horoscopes.

E.T's planet (in) R.B's house		R.B's planet (in) E.T's house	
Sun	8th	Sun	2nd
Moon	4th	Moon	11th
Mercury	8th	Mercury	3rd
Venus	9th	Venus	3rd
Mars	7th	Mars	1st
Jupiter	12th	Jupiter	4th
Saturn	6th	Saturn	2nd
Uranus	9th	Uranus	6th
Neptune	1st	Neptune	11th
Pluto	12th	Pluto	10th
Chiron	10th	Chiron	7th
Ascendant	3rd	Ascendant	11th
Midheaven	11th	Midheaven	8th
North Node	8th	North Node	10th

Elizabeth's Sun in Richard's 8th house suggests she was immediately attracted to his sexuality, and she had a desire to reform him (probably help him overcome his alcoholism). His Sun in her 2nd house suggests he was immediately drawn to her wealth and her beauty (both being her resources), but with his Saturn also in her 2nd house, he was probably critical of her extravagance (especially because of the poverty of his childhood), which she would have greatly resented. Her Saturn in his 6th house suggests that she seriously hindered him in the pursuit of his work, and she may also have had a negative effect on his health. The other obviously significant house placements are her Mars in his 7th and his Mars in her 1st - a real double-whammie of mutual aggression in the relaionship.

Looking to their individual natal horoscopes, Elizabeth's intimate relationship needs and expectations are overwhelmingly defined by the very close Venus-Uranus conjunction in the 7th house in Aries. Venus is the ruler of the Ascendant sign, and Uranus is the ruler of the 5th house of romance. Mars, the ruler of the 7th house of marriage, is in conjunction with the Sun in the 5th house, all making "love-and-marriage" the overwhelming central concern of her life, including much instability and demand for freedom and aggressive sexuality, which is all borne out in her numerous marriages, including the two she had to Richard Burton.

Richard Burton's 7th house of marriage has Aquarius on the cusp, ruled by Uranus in the 8th house of sexuality and transformation, describing his expectation of erratic and unstable intense sexual excitement in marriage. But this is made more complex by Pisces being on the 8th house cusp, ruled by Neptune in the 1st house, so he was also looking for high romance. He got all that he was looking for in his relationship to Elizabeth Taylor.

So the analysis of intimate relationships reminds us again and again that, ultimately, we all get what we want under the disguise of what we deserve. We are each dealt our hand of cards, which defines the limits of the possibilities of how we can play that hand. And yet we do learn from our mistakes,

155

and though we are bound to the core themes demanded by our horoscopes, and though, from the outside, we may just seem to repeat ourselves over and over again, from inside ourselves we know that the small progress we make in each successive falling down and picking ourselves up again makes us justly proud. For each of us in our quest to fulfil our own unique karma, the difference between heaven and hell is very small indeed.

Exercises

1) What is the name given to the analysis of planetary inter-aspects between two people?

2) In which house of your horoscope is another's Sun if he or she makes you feel he or she is:
    a) very romantically attracted to you?
    b) a very good friend to you?
    c) values your intellect?
    d) brings your "hang-ups" to the surface?

3) In what house of your horoscope is another's Moon if he or she makes you feel
    a) involved in his or her financial affairs?
    b) he or she responds to your status in the world?

4) In which house of your horoscope is another's Saturn if he or she
    a) restricts your spending?
    b) shares your work responsibilities?
    c) is unsympathetic to your sorrows?
    d) criticizes what you say?

5) In which house of your horoscope is another's Venus if her or she

    a) appreciates your values?

    b) shares your intellectual interests?

    c) likes your family?

    d) is very romantic towards you?

6) In which house of your horoscope is another's Mars if he or she

    a) generally spurs you to action?

    b) argues with you a lot?

    c) strongly disagrees with your religious beliefs?

    d) dominates you when you are with friends?

7 In which house of your horoscope is another's Jupiter if he or she

    a) enlarges your intellectual understanding?

    b) helps you further your ambitions?

    c) encourages you to buy things for yourself?

    d) makes you feel generally good about yourself?

8) In which house of your horoscope is another's Pluto if he or she

    a) has very deep conversations with you?

    b) helps you improve your health by controlling your bad habits?

    c) is obsessively jealous of his or her relationship to you?

9) Using their bi-wheel (Chart 19), delineate the house placements of John Lennon and Yoko Ono's planets in the

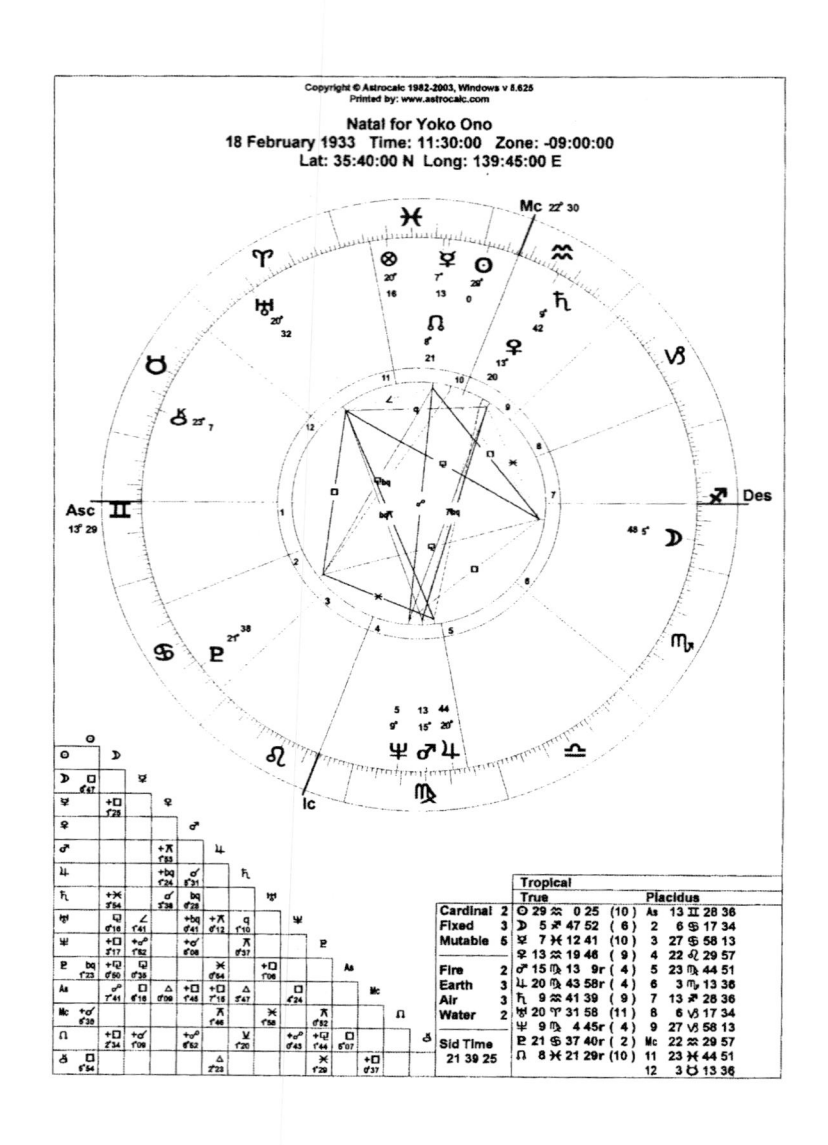

Chart 16

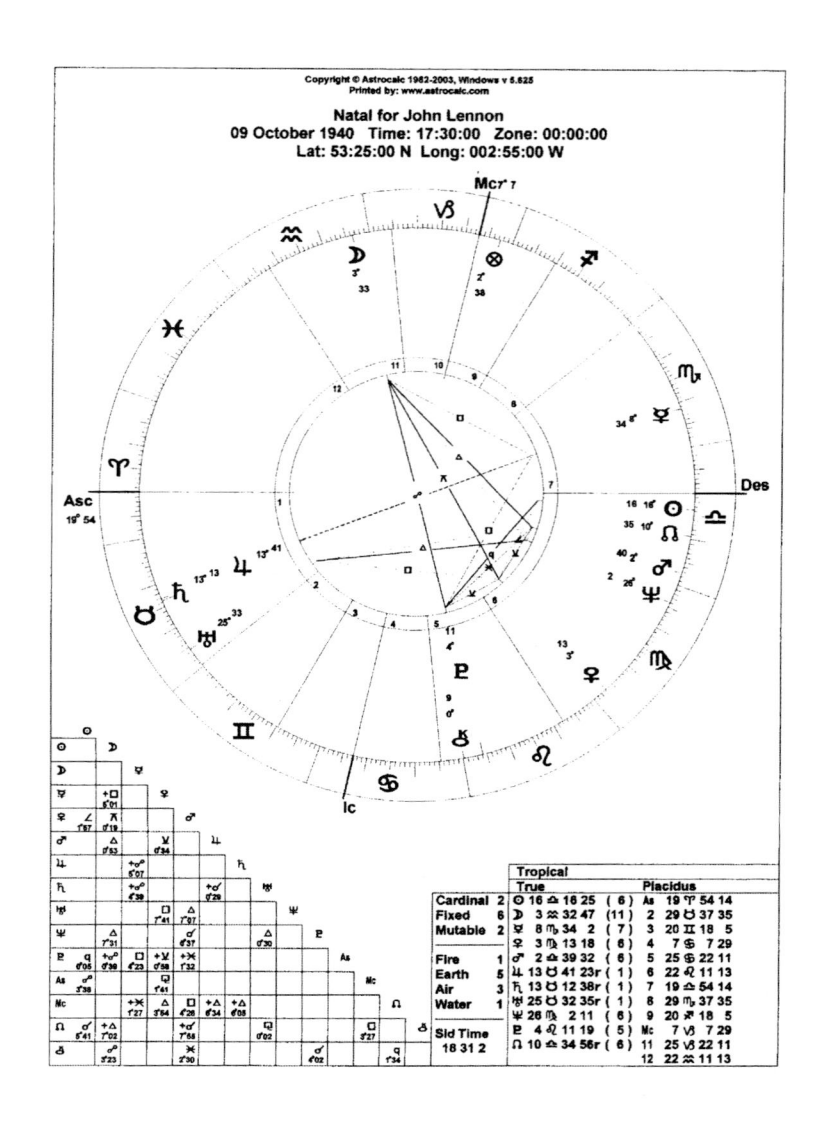

Chart 17

159

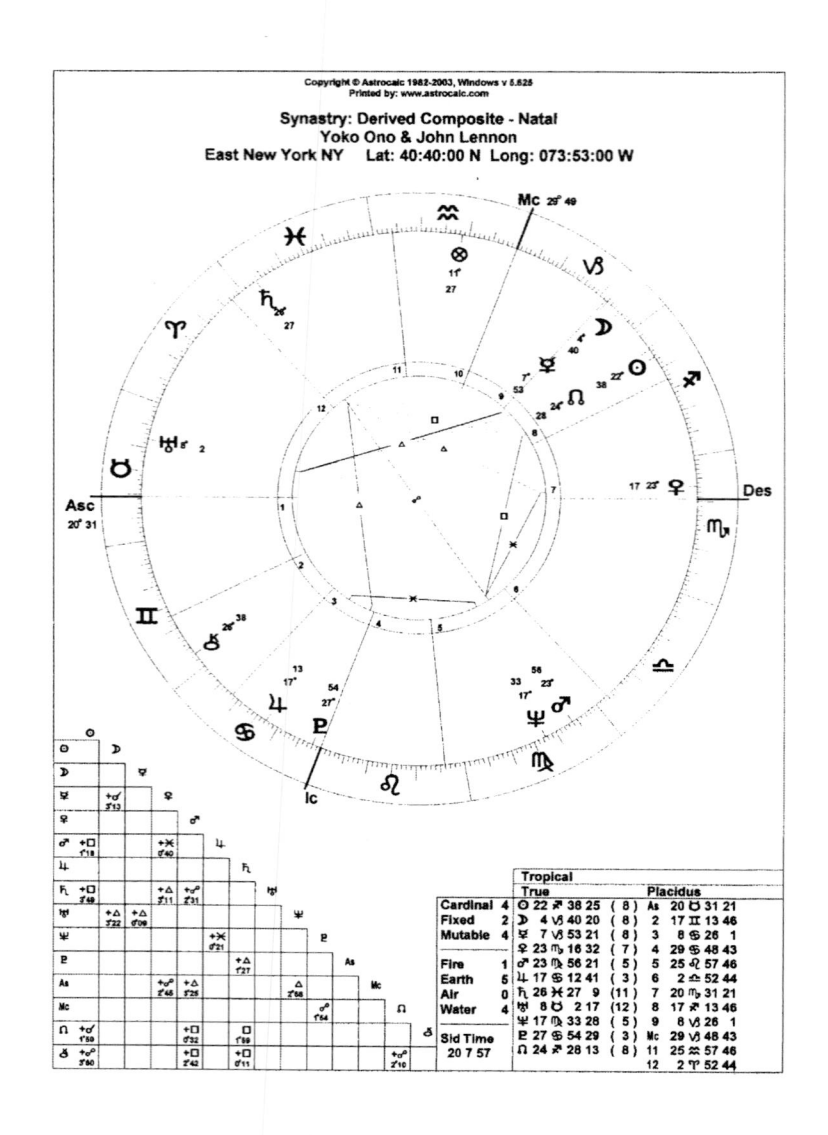

Chart 18

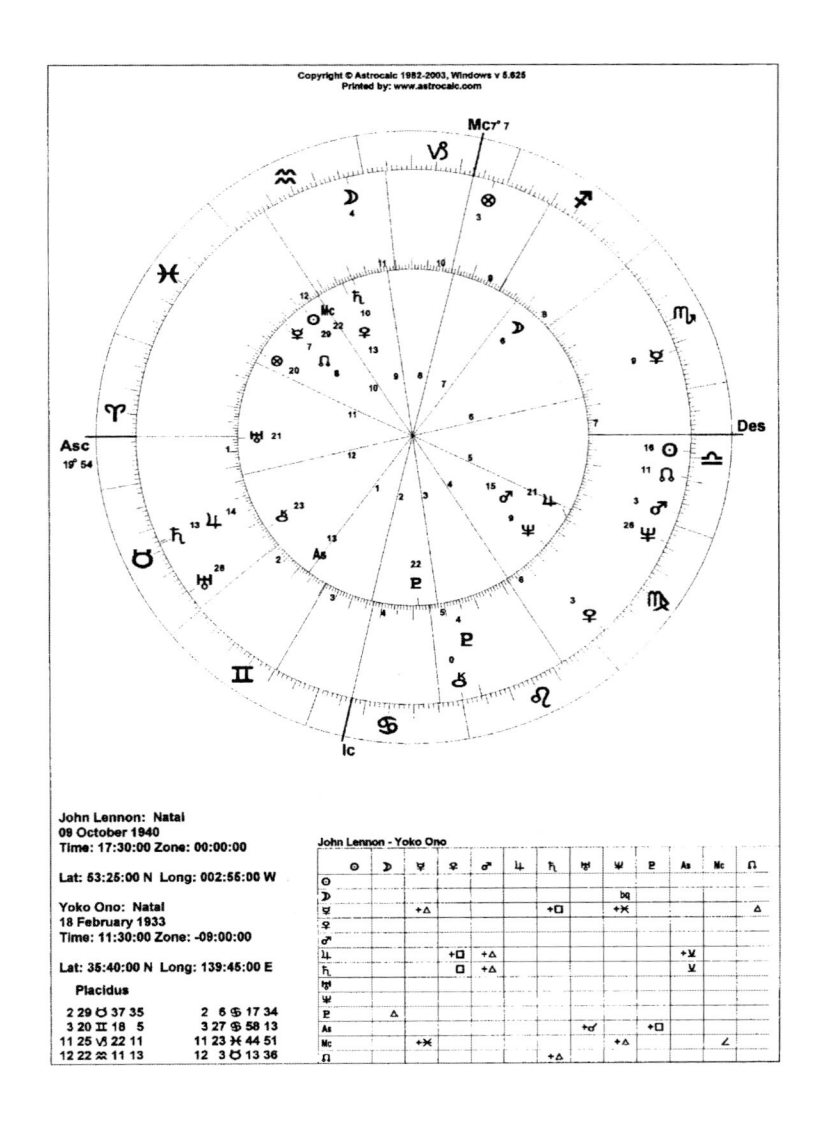

John Lennon: Natal
09 October 1940
Time: 17:30:00 Zone: 00:00:00

Lat: 53:25:00 N Long: 002:55:00 W

Yoko Ono: Natal
18 February 1933
Time: 11:30:00 Zone: -09:00:00

Lat: 35:40:00 N Long: 139:45:00 E

Placidus

2 29 ♉ 37 35   2 6 ♋ 17 34
3 20 ♊ 18 5   3 27 ♋ 58 13
11 25 ♑ 22 11   11 23 ♓ 44 51
12 22 ♒ 11 13   12 3 ♉ 13 36

Chart 19

161

houses of each other's horoscopes. How well do the implications of these placements match (or contradict) what you discovered through your previous analysis of their relationship?

Chapter 8
Love and Marriage Relationships

Summary: Intimate love and marriage relationships are very complex, involving, as they do more parts of each of the two people than any other kind of relationship. Broadly speaking, love and marriage relationships tend to be based on perceived samenesses and/or perceived complementarities between people. Three marriages are analyzed in detail.

Sameness and Complementarity in Love and Marriage Relationships

All love and marriage relationships are created out of the samenesses between people, which makes for the friendship component in the relationship; and out of the oppositenesses between people, which makes for the love component in the relationship. In heterosexual relationships, oppositeness is primarily contained in the gender oppositeness between the individuals, with all the magnetic attraction associated with this as well as the conflict understood as the timeless "battle of the sexes". In homosexual relationships, at a superficial level the couple seem to be seeking to bypass all the difficulties inherent in oppositeness in favour of sameness, but, however unconsciously, homosexual couples seem to re-create oppositeness in their relationships by polarizing their roles in their relationships into broadly "masculine" and "feminine" archetypes. It seems that sexual interest demands a degree of tension that total sameness cannot supply, as was the case for a woman who consulted me some time ago. She was married to her virtual twin, she and her husband having been born

163

within a few hours of each other. She confessed to me that although she felt "closer to her husband than she could imagine ever feeling towards any other person", she also felt terribly bored by him and had not been sexually aroused by him except before they were married, when sex between them was exciting by virtue of being illicit and furtive. So, in order to be fulfilling, any intimate relationship needs to have the dynamic tension of "hard" aspects between the individuals' horoscopes as well as the "soft" aspects of easy harmony, unless the couple are content to have an essentially a-sexual relationship. But even if a couple are content to have an a-sexual relationship, any relationship full of trines and sextile aspects and lacking squares and oppositions is likely to be stagnant and lacklustre because it goes against the basic human need to grow to the fulfilment of our potential through the challenges and conflicts that our relationships with other people offer us. Clearly, there can be no stereotypical "ideal relationship", although people instinctively but largely unconsciously choose to form intimate relationships with others who provide just the right blend of ease and difficulty that they need - at least at that time in their lives. Our job as astrologers is objectively to interpret what is the case, but never to have the arrogance to project our own values onto any relationship that is not our own.

Synastry in Love and Marriage Relationships

When we first meet another person towards whom we are romantically attracted, we all instinctively put our best Venus and Mars feet forward, and only later reveal our deeper Sun and Moon and Saturn selves. God (or the powers-that-be) in His wisdom rarely makes intimate relationships simple. Sometimes a relationship is wonderful at the Venus and Mars level and very difficult at deeper levels; and sometimes the opposite is the case.

Any long-term intimate relationship needs to be considered in all its complexity; but for a harmonious domestic relationship the synastry between the Moons and Mercurys of the two individual horoscopes will be very influential in determining the ease or difficulty with which the couple will get on with each other in everyday life. And without some aspects to the Saturns of each individual from the other's horoscope, the relationship is unlikely to endure, even if it is great fun while it lasts.

In considering love and marriage relationships we need to look at the 8th house and the sign placement of its ruler to reveal sexual needs and desires, the 5th house and the sign and house placement of its ruler to reveal the romantic nature, and the 7th house and the sign and house placement of its ruler for desires and needs in partnership. (Remember that, as well as marriage, the 7th house rules all partnerships of a contractual nature.)

In all intimate sexual relationships - whether heterosexual or homosexual - there is "masculinity" (Sun and Mars) in all women, and "femininity" (Moon and Venus) in all men. A fully heterosexual man may fall in love from the feminine parts of himself to the masculine parts in a fully hetersexual woman, as well as from the archetypal masculinity in himself to the archetypal femininity in her. Nevertheless, a man being a man and a woman being a woman, there are likely to be subtle but important differences in their experiences of the synastry between them, which you should take into account in an intuitive way.

A Lifelong Marriage

Esther and Mark (Charts 24 and 25) met when she was 14 and he was 19. They married in 1936 and stayed married until she died, just after their 60th wedding anniversary in 1996. She had a very volatile nature and struggled through-

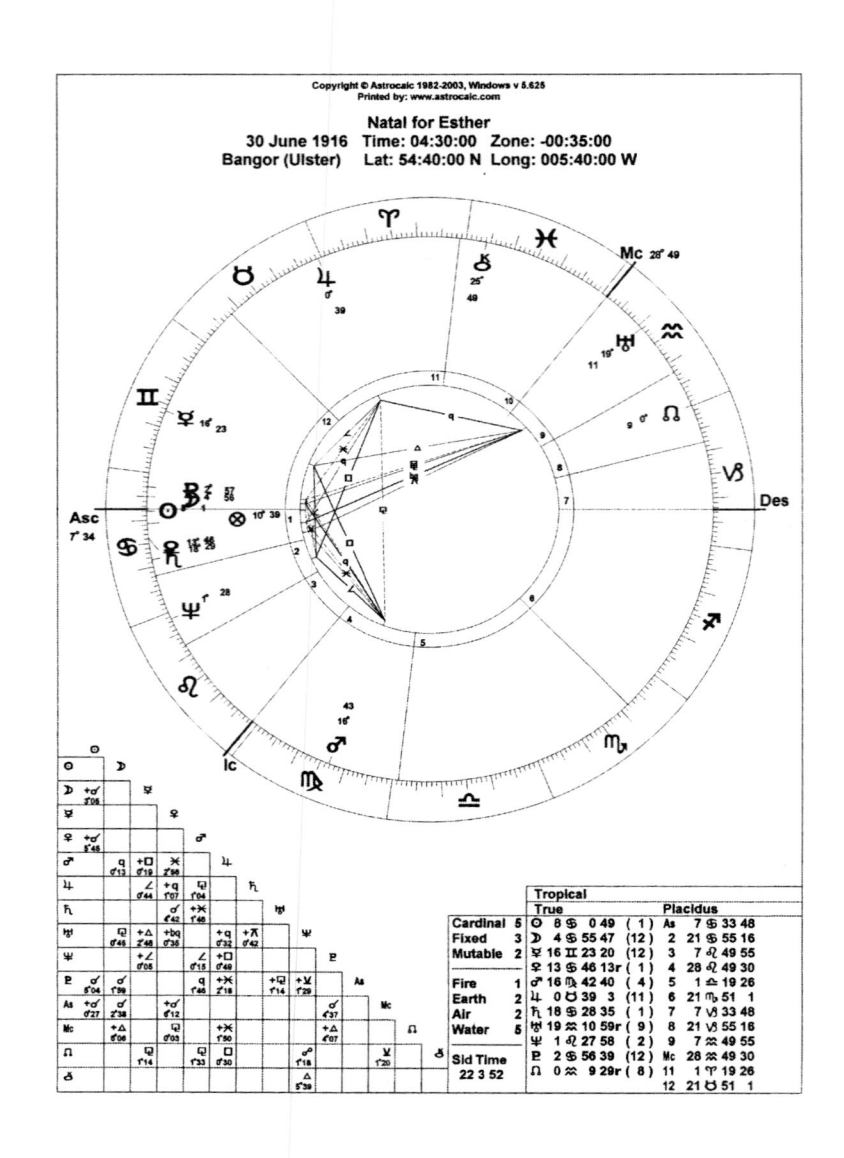

Chart 24

166

out her life to overcome a propensity to chronic depression and a propensity to express herself in a verbally aggressive way. She had literary interests and expressed a passionate love of poetry. She constantly criticized her husband, to which he responded with essential passivity, but with occasional bursts of stubborn refusal to do her bidding. He was a modestly successful businessman who retired in his 50's and was very happy to have done so, leaving him free to enjoy reading, walking, and other quiet leisure activities. Esther and Mark's birth times are not known.

Sun-Sun Comparison. Her Sun is in Cancer and his is in Pisces. They are basically compatible. She feels safely looked after by him, and he is gratified by her neediness of him. She tends to feel unresponded to by him, and he feels nagged and criticized by her.

Element and Mode Comparison. She has 1 Fire, 2 Earth, 2 Air, and 5 Water planets. He has 1 Fire, 2 Earth, 3 Air, and 4 Water planets. So, in the distribution of the elements they are alike rather than complementary, with an emphasis on feeling and communication. She has 5 cardinal, 3 fixed, and 2 mutable planets, while he has 4 cardinal, 3 fixed, and 3 mutable planets. They are both very dominant and initiating, although she somewhat more than he. He is somewhat more flexible than she is.

Inner Planet Comparison by Sign. Their Sun's are trine, their Moon's square, Mercury's square, Venus's square, Mars inconjunct (Ascendants unknown). While at the deepest (Sunsign) level they are profoundly well-matched, domestically this is a very tense relationship, both the Moons and the Mercurys being square to each other.

How Many Aspects to Each Sun, Moon, and Saturn? There are no major aspects to his Sun, 1 aspect to his Moon (square her Sun), and 3 aspects to his Saturn (trine Mercury, square

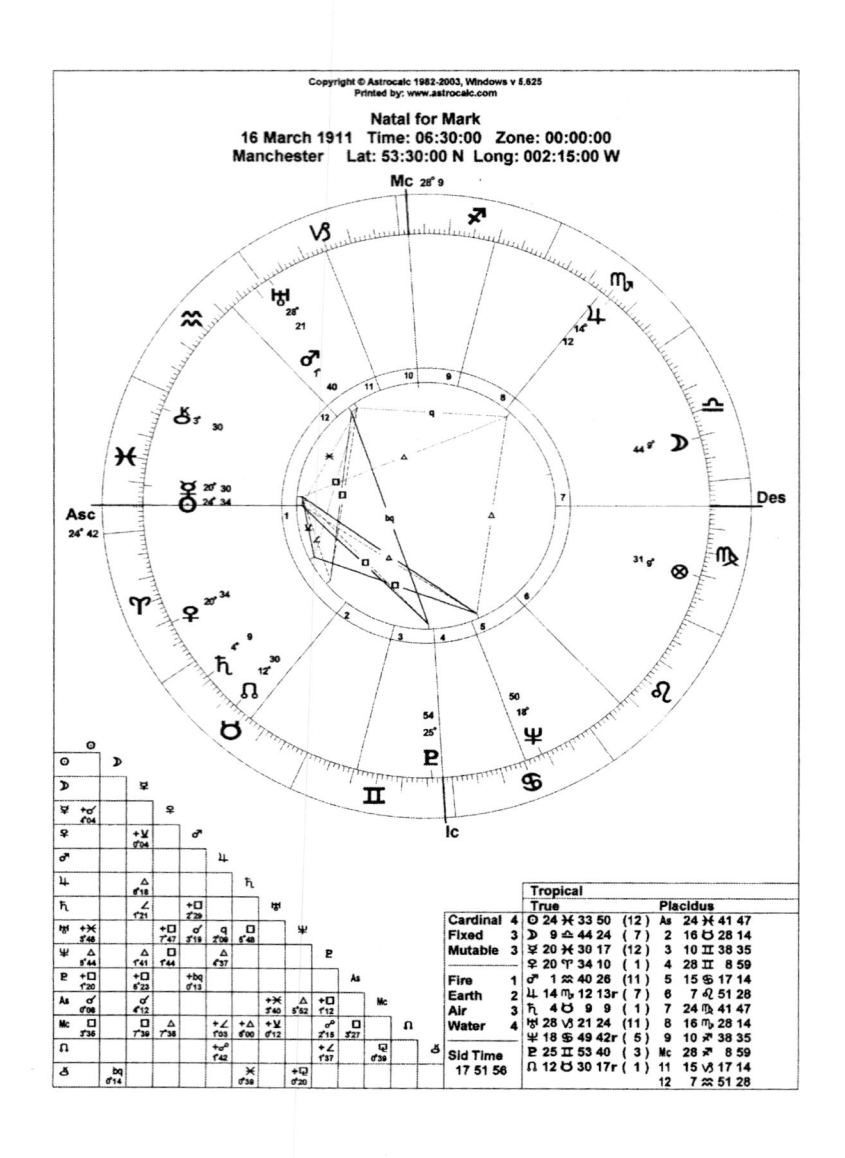

Chart 25

168

Venus, and conjunction his Neptune). From this we can infer that she plays no part in the furtherance of his ambitions, that his family background is in conflict with her ambitions, but his family conditioning is compatible with her principles and, with 3 aspects to his Saturn, he feels very bound to her.

There is 1 aspect to her Sun (square his Moon - at least by sign), (probably) 2 aspects to her Moon (square his Moon and sextile his Saturn), and 3 aspects to her Saturn (trine his Mercury, square his Venus, and conjunction his Neptune). From these we can infer that his emotional expectations of a woman were in conflict with her ambitions, that his emotions and hers were in conflict, but that she appreciated the structure he offered to her emotions, and that she was very bound to him.

Double-whammies. There is 1 double-whammie between their charts, his Saturn conjunction her Neptune and her Neptune square his Saturn. Thus, a central component of their relationship was consciousness of pragmatic reality, duty and responsibilities, versus imagination, dreaminess, and transcendance of reality. His sense of responsibility and practicality blended with her dreams, but she chronically challenged his pragmatism and discipline with her escapist dreams.

Outer to Inner Planet Aspect. Her Chiron is conjunction his Sun, making him very vulnerable to her and giving her the power to both soothe and wound him - which she did. Her Uranus is sextile his Venus, making him find her exciting but erratic, and prompting him to help her achieve order in herself. Her Neptune is opposition his Mars, square his Saturn, and opposition his Uranus, describing his difficulty in conquering her, his discouragement due to her lack of practicality and commonsense together with her perception of his reality as flat and boring and his difficulty in communicating with her elusive fantasies.

His Chiron is trine her Sun, her Moon, and her Pluto, enabling him to soothe and heal her at deep levels (notwithstanding the other tense aspects in their relaionship). His Uranus squares her Jupiter, describing her righteous criticism of him , and his defensive detachment. His Uranus also opposes her Neptune, describing his frustration of his progressive plans in the face of her nebulous dreams. And his Neptune is conjunction her Saturn, reflecting that he, too, tends to unrealism, which she controls with her pragmatism.

Other Aspects in the Synastry. Notwithstanding their conflicts, her Venus is trine his Jupiter and sextile his North Node, so he warms her and she helps him fulfil his destiny.

The Individual Horoscopes in Reference to the Relationship. Esther's 5 planets in Cancer forming a cluster of inconjuncts to her Uranus in Aquarius describes a very conflicted nature, full of great emotional dependency, challenged by a desire for freedom. Inasmuch as the dependency needs far outweigh the quest for freedom, Esther probably found as satisfactory a relationship as was possible for her in her gentle, tolerant, Pisces husband.

Mark's Pisces Sun and Libra Moon describe a man who finds his fulfilment in looking after another, and his Venus square Uranus square Neptune indicate his need for an unusual and exciting, if erratic, love relationship, in which he felt confused but, at the same time, able to maintain a degree of attachment. He got all this in his marriage to Esther.

A Fourteen Year Marriage

Miriam and Tony (Charts 26, 27, 28 and 29) met in high school in Australia. She was English-born, he Hungarian. They went to university together and their relationship developed into a sexually very passionate love affair, although they had tempestuous arguments from the start of their relationship. They married when she was 20 and he was 22, at which time he began his successful caeer as an academic scientist. After a few years of marriage her sexual feelings for him dissolved, but their tempestuous arguments continued. She left him after 13 years of marriage, taking their 2 children with her and returning to England. They were divorced 2 years later. Almost immediately after Miriam left him, Tony met another woman whom he has lived with ever since but whom he has never formally married. Miriam became a psychotherapist. She has not remarried.

Let us approach the analysis of this relationship in a holistic way rather than the step-by-step way in which we analyzed Mark and Esther's relationship. We will set out all the data and then selectively look for significant information in an intuitive way, scanning the data in no set order. In this way we will avoid being overwhelmed with information, some parts of which will be much more powerful and signficant than others.

Sun-Sun Comparison. Tony's Sun is in Sagittarius, Miriam's is in Libra.

The Composite Chart
The Sun is in the 5th house trine the Moon and the Midheaven.

The Moon is on the Ascendant trine Mercury, sextile Uranus, and trine the Midheaven.

Venus is in the 4th house, square the Ascendant. Mars is in the 7th house, trine Neptune.

Neptune is in wide conjunction with the IC. Saturn is in the 10th house, opposition Neptune and square Chiron

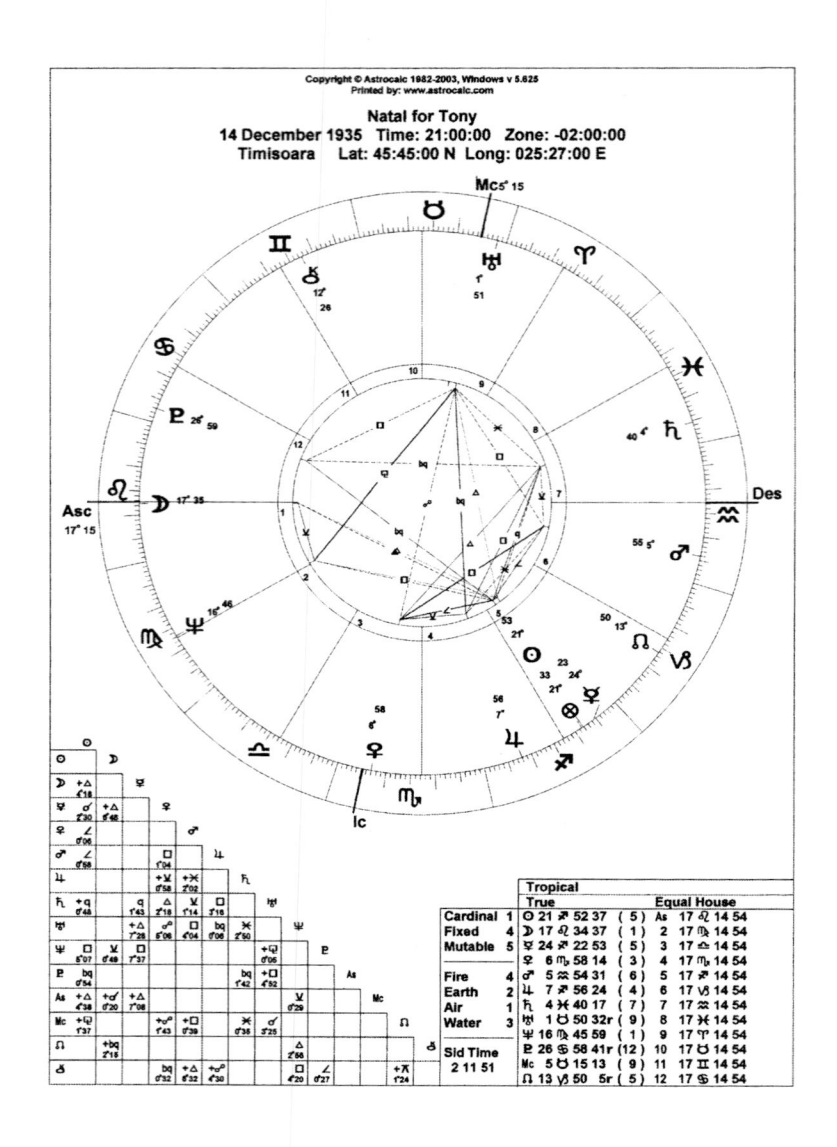

Chart 26

The Composite Chart in Relation to the Individual Horoscopes;

Composite to Miriam

Sun opposition Uranus
Moon inconjunct North Node

Mercury opposition Ascendant

Venus conjunction Sun

Mars conjunction Jupiter
conjunction MC
Jupiter conjunction Mars
North Node conjunction Mars
opposition Neptune
Uranus opposition Venus
square Mars sextile

Neptune square Sun
Pluto inconjunct Mercury

Composite to Tony

Sun sextile North Node
Moon trine Venus
inconjunct Jupiter trine Saturn
Venus trine Mars
inconjunct Uranus
Mars inconjunct Moon
trine Neptune
Jupiter conjunction
Sun conjunction Mercury
inconjunct Pluto
Saturn inconjunct Moon
inconjunct Ascendant

Saturn conjunction Midheaven

Inner Planet and Ascendant Comparison by Sign. The Suns are sextile; the Moons are square; the Mercurys are square; the Venus's are square: the Mars's are sextile; the Ascendants are square.

How Many Aspects to the Sun, Moon, and Saturn of Each Person? 3 aspects to Tony's Sun (conjunction Miriam's Mars,

173

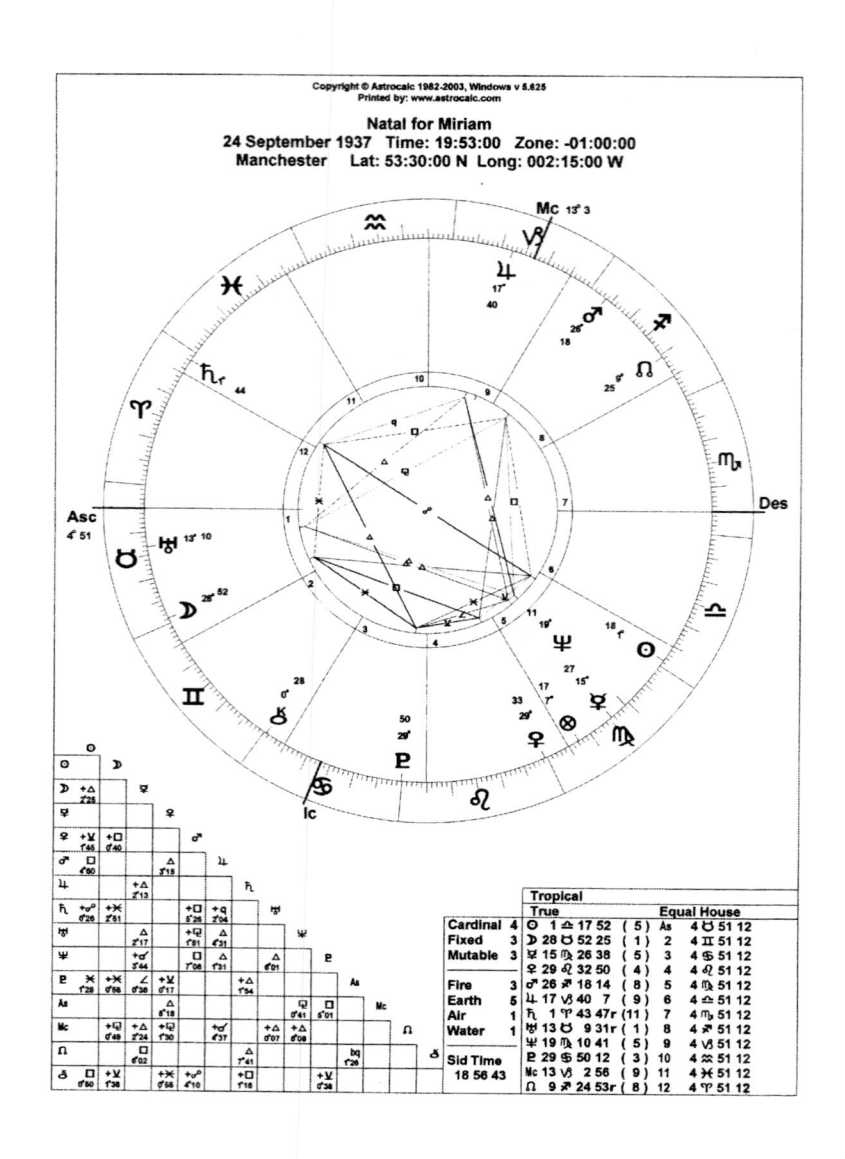

Chart 27

174

square Miriam's Mercury, and square Miriam's Neptune). No aspects to Miriam's Sun. No aspects to Tony's Moon. No aspects to Miriam's Moon.

No aspects to Tony's Saturn. No aspects to Miriam's Saturn.

Double-whammies. Venus-Uranus (His Uranus trine her Venus, her Uranus opposition his Venus. Neptune-Neptune (conjunction). Pluto-Pluto (conjunction).

Outer to Inner Planet Aspects. Miriam's Chiron trine Tony's Venus, inconjunct Tony's Mars. Miriam's Uranus opposition Tony's Venus. Miriam's Neptune square Tony's Sun. Tony's Chiron square Miriam's Mercury, inconjunct Miriam's Jupiter. Tony's Neptune conjunction Miriam's Mercury.

Planets in Houses

Miriam's in Tony's House

Sun	2
Moon	10
Mercury	2
Venus	1
Mars	5
Jupiter	5
Saturn	8
Uranus	10
Neptune	2
Pluto	12
Ascendant	9
Midheaven	5

Tony's in Miriam's House

Sun	8
Moon	5
Mercury	8
Venus	7
Mars	11
Jupiter	8
Saturn	12
Uranus	12
Neptune	6
Pluto	4
Ascendant	5
Midheaven	1

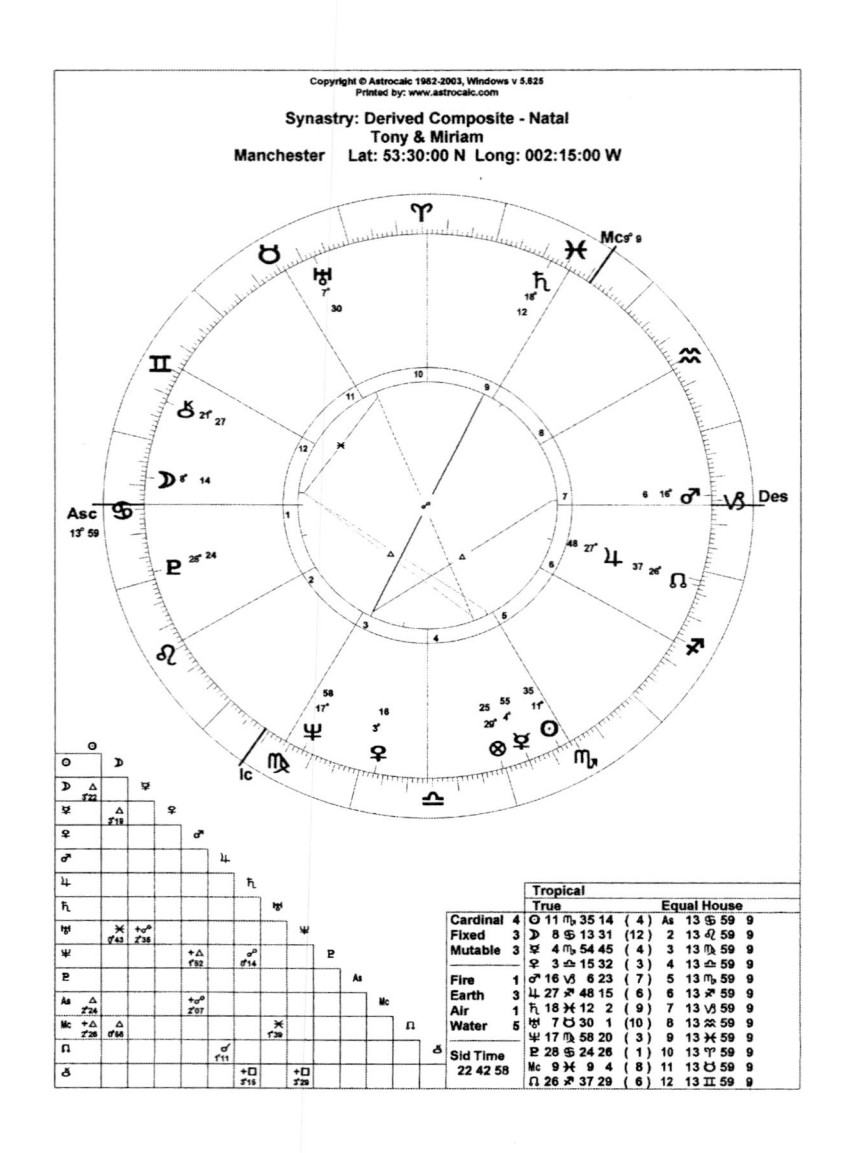

Chart 28

North Node	4	North Node	10
Chiron	11	Chiron	2

Other Aspects in Synastry. Miriam's Mercury trine Tony's North Node. Miriam's Mars conjunction Tony's Mercury. Miriam's Jupiter trine Tony's Neptune. Miriam's Uranus trine Tony's North Node. Miriam's Pluto square Tony's Uranus. Miriam's Ascendant square Tony's Mars. Miriam's Ascendant conjunction Tony's Uranus. Miriam's Ascendant conjunction Tony's Midheaven.

The Individual Horoscopes in Reference to the Relationship. Since the relationship is one of marriage, we refer to the 1st house (personality and appearance), the 5th house (romance and children), the 7th house (partnership and the contract of marriage), the 8th house (sexuality), and the 11th house (friendship).

Miriam's Ascendant is Taurus, its ruler Venus being in Leo in the 5th house. (Warm, romantic love, personal vanity, and self-expressive creativity, including children) are at the core of her needs. Her 5th house has Leo on its cusp, its ruler, the Sun, being in Libra in the 6th house. (Looking after other people in harmonious relationships is her natural way of expressing her creativity.) Her 7th house has Scorpio on the cusp, its joint rulers being Mars in Sagittarius in the 8th house and Pluto in Cancer in the 4th house. (She wants her one-to-one relaionships to be passionately sexy and to transform the deepest emotional roots of her being.) Her 8th house has Sagittarius on the cusp, its ruler, Jupiter being in Capricorn in the 10th house. (She is sexually attracted to men who are professionally concerned with intellectual and philosophical matters.) Her 11th house has Aquarius on the cusp, its ruler, Uranus, being in Taurus in the 1st house. (She is attracted to exciting and original people as friends she can identify with.)

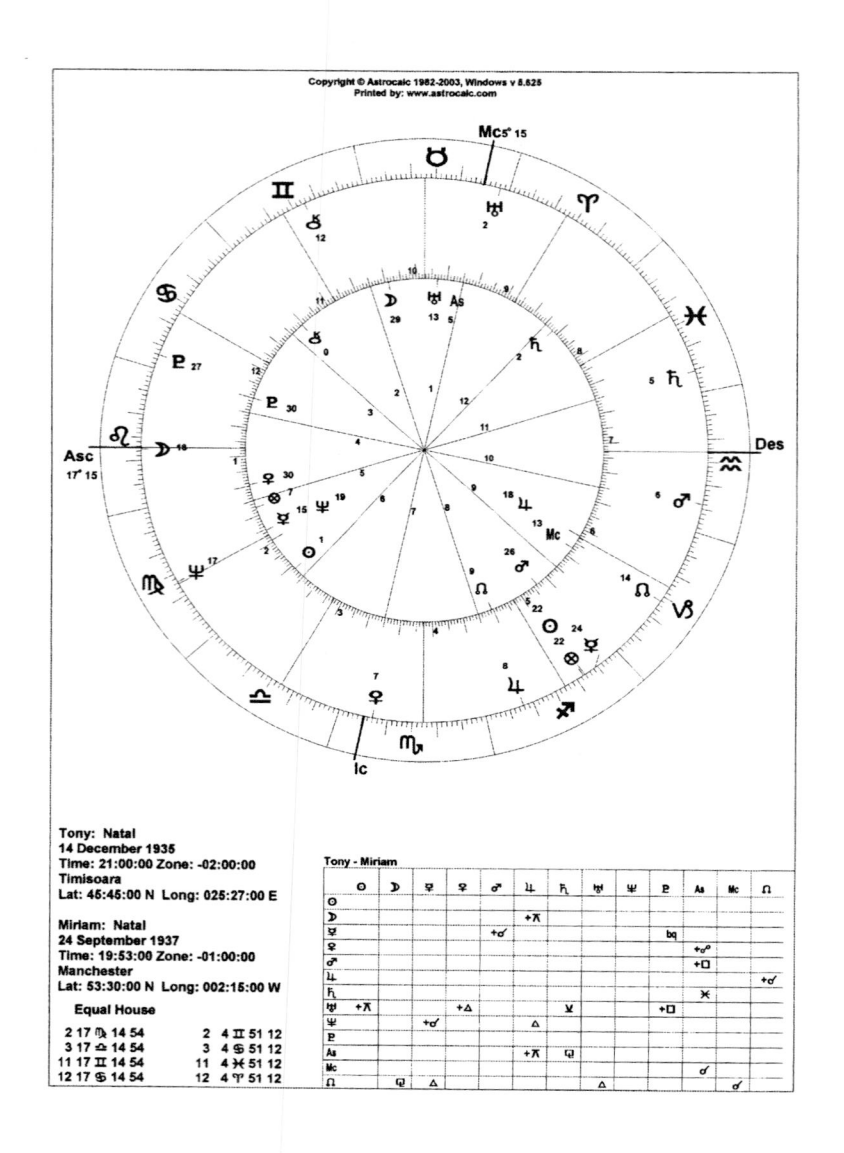

Tony: Natal
14 December 1935
Time: 21:00:00 Zone: -02:00:00
Timisoara
Lat: 45:45:00 N Long: 025:27:00 E

Miriam: Natal
24 September 1937
Time: 19:53:00 Zone: -01:00:00
Manchester
Lat: 53:30:00 N Long: 002:15:00 W

Equal House

2 17 ♍ 14 54   2 4 ♊ 51 12
3 17 ♎ 14 54   3 4 ♋ 51 12
11 17 ♊ 14 54   11 4 ♓ 51 12
12 17 ♋ 14 54   12 4 ♈ 51 12

Chart 29

Tony's Ascendant is Leo, its ruler, the Sun, being in Sagittarius in the 5th house. (His core need is to express himself intellectually and creatively, with high self-esteem.) His 5th house cusp is Sagittarius, its ruler, Jupiter, being in Sagittarius in the 4th house. (He wants to express his creativity and his romantic feelings in his home life, reflecting his deepest emotional conditioning.) His 7th house cusp is Aquarius, its ruler, Uranus, being in the 9th house in Taurus. (In his one-to-one relationships he seeks intellectually exciting people who are also down-to-earth in their thinking.) His 8th house cusp is Pisces, whose ruler, Neptune, is in the 2nd house in Virgo. (He is sexually attracted to imaginative, elusive women whose values he shares and who support him practically in his manner of earning a living.) His 11th house cusp is Gemini, whose ruler, Mercury, is in Sagittarius in the 5th house. (He wants his friends to be talkative and generally creatively communicative.)

The initial attraction between Miriam and Tony is represented by his Venus in her 7th house and her Venus in his 1st house. Her Mars conjunction his Sun makes for the lusty sexuality between them. The double-whammie Venus-Uranus adds to the excitement of the relationship for each of them. Since his Uranus is trine her Venus she enjoys his originality and unconventionality quite unambiguously, but her Uranus being opposition his Venus, he is disturbed and made insecure by her originality and need for independence even though he is very excited by her. This is reinforced by her Uranus being opposition the composite chart Sun. Although there are many more aspects from the composite chart to his horoscope than to hers, the essential spirit of the composite chart is the Sun in the 5th house, being about romance, creativity, and having children. (They shared great pleasure in their two children.) The composite chart Venus conjunction her Sun describes the love she felt for Tony, but her Uranus opposing the composite chart Sun, made her need for freedom from the marriage eventually stronger than her love.

Mars is prominent in the relationship. Tony's Mars is square Miriam's Ascendant, Miriam's Mars is conjunction Tony's Sun and Mercury, and Mars is in the 7th house of the composite chart. At the beginning of the relationship most of this Mars was expressed in the passionate sexuality between them, but as this passion inevitably subsided after the first few years of their relationship, it was increasingly expressed as very aggressive discord and unhappiness between them. (This discord existed at the start of the relationship as well, but then quarrels would be ended by falling into bed and making love!)

Miriam's need for deep emotional and psychological transformation as well as intense sexuality in marriage (Pluto co-ruler of the 7th house in Cancer in the 4th) prompted her, projectively, to expect Tony, too, to seek the transformation of the emotional roots of his being. Her Pluto in his 12th house sought to bring to the surface his unconscious hang-ups and deeply transform his consciousness. He, however, had no need for this, and he was profoundly resistant to and resentful of this attempt by her. Her Saturn in his 8th house eventually killed the sexual passion between them, and his Saturn and Uranus in her 12th house was experienced by her as an unsympathetic and oppressive attitude by him to her psychological hang-ups which he also stimulated.

She was the leader in the relationship (her 4 cardinal planets compared with his 1) and her practicality (5 planets in Earth) was appreciated by him as permission for him to concentrate on his career interests, leaving the everyday management of the household and money matters to her.

While intense sexual attraction was at the root of their relationship, they also fulfilled each other's needs for and expectations of intellectual stimulation in marriage, but her Neptune in close square to his Mercury (closer than his own Neptune square Mercury aspect) enabled him to project onto her his own difficulty in reconciling intuitive and logical thought, which caused many unhappy quarrels between them and which were exacerbated by the Mercury square Mercury in their synastry. So, notwithstanding the core compatibility of their Suns (sextile by sign), the squares (by sign) of their Moons, Mercurys, Venuses, and Ascendants makes them, on balance, incompatible, and the lack of aspects to both their Saturns made it relatively easy for the relationship to break up when the time was ripe. The fact that it was Miriam's Uranus that was opposition Tony's Venus, together with her greater cardinality, made it natural for her, rather than him, to take the initiative in the ending of the marriage. There are also many more aspects between the composite chart and his horoscope than there are between the composite chart and her horoscope, imlying that her was, overall, more involved in the relationship than she was.

The Marriage of Prince Charles and Princess Diana (Charts 6, 30, 31, and 32)

The marriage of Prince Charles and Princess Diana probably needs little introducion. She was the most photographed woman in the world, he was and is the heir to the British throne, and their marriage was a source of interest and speculation in the popular press throughout the world.

What was confidently known was that she was much more in love with him that he was with her and, in the scandalous months leading up to their separation and eventual divorce, he confessed to having loved another throughout his marriage and, indeed, having committed adultery.

It became well-known that Princess Diana suffered from the eating disorder, bulimia, and had suicidal tendencies, which were understood to derive from her mother having abandoned the family when Diana was a young child. Diana herself

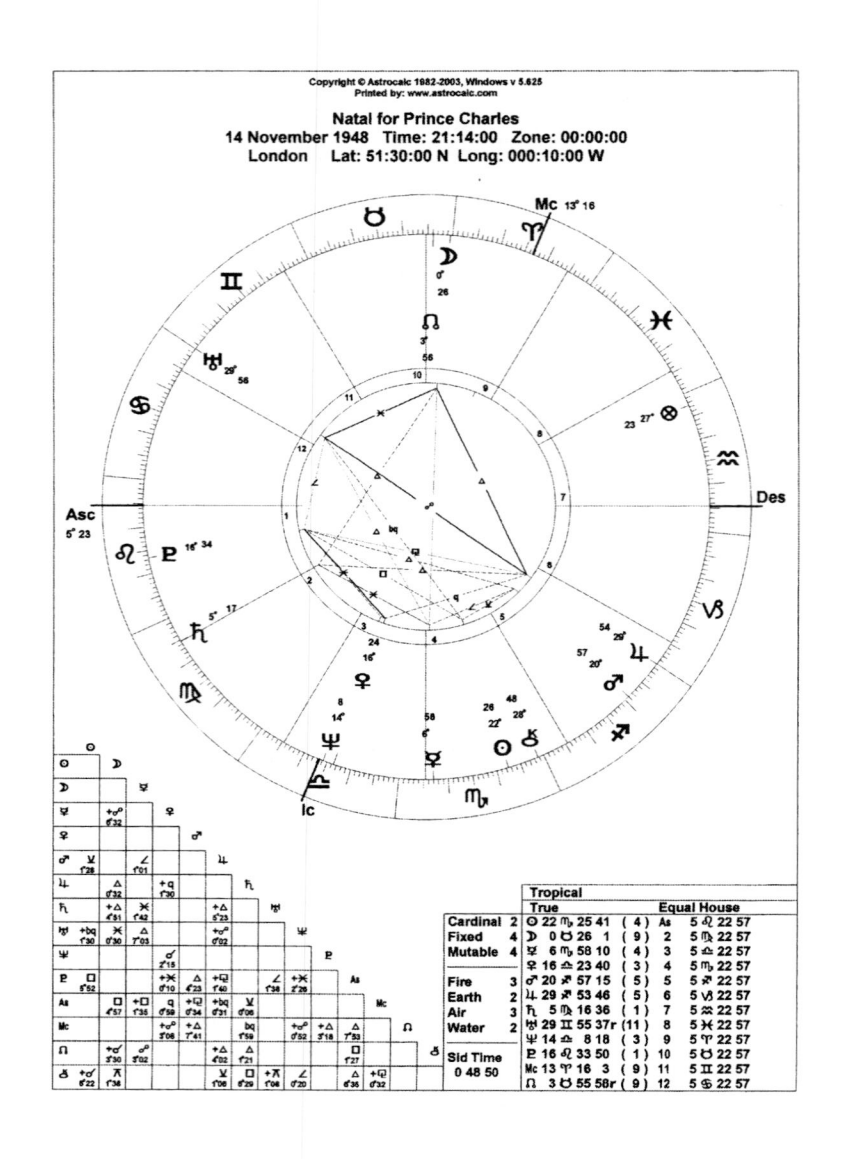

Natal for Prince Charles
14 November 1948 Time: 21:14:00 Zone: 00:00:00
London Lat: 51:30:00 N Long: 000:10:00 W

Chart 30

182

declared the one thing she would never do would be to abandon her children, which she poignantly did through her death.

Her Sun in Cancer and his Sun in Scorpio are trine, so they are, at core, alike in their emotionality. However she (Cancer) feels insecure in response to his self-sufficiency and he (Scorpio) feels overwhelmed by her demandingness.

The pain of their marriage is indicated by Saturn in the 7th house of their composite chart, but in the composite chart is also the public image of the relationship, and Saturn here is the ruler of the 10th house of their joint public career, making the dutifulness and the pain of the marriage evident to the public. However, Jupiter is conjunction Chiron in the 10th house, describing the huge popularity of this couple and the healing as well as the pain of their wounds that occurred through their public life together. This seems very obviously to apply to Diana who very much relished her status as a public icon and the love that millions of people avowed they felt for her. The value that Charles placed on this public approval was a lot more limited, but he undoubtedly became much more popular in his own right for becoming a married man rather than "a crusty old bachelor".

Charles' and Diana's everyday working responsibilities together was the essence of how the relationship expressed itself (Sun in the 6th house) and this is accompanied by the glamour - and the illusion and confusion - associated with Mars in an exact conjunction to Neptune (also in the 6th house). While their family life, as joint parents of their children, was probably where they expressed most loving harmony (Venus in the 4th house and ruler of the Ascendant), Uranus is also in the 4th house, describing the erratic instability of their home life. The ultimate goal of their relationship was clear communication (North Node in the 3rd house), but we can venture that this was never achieved,

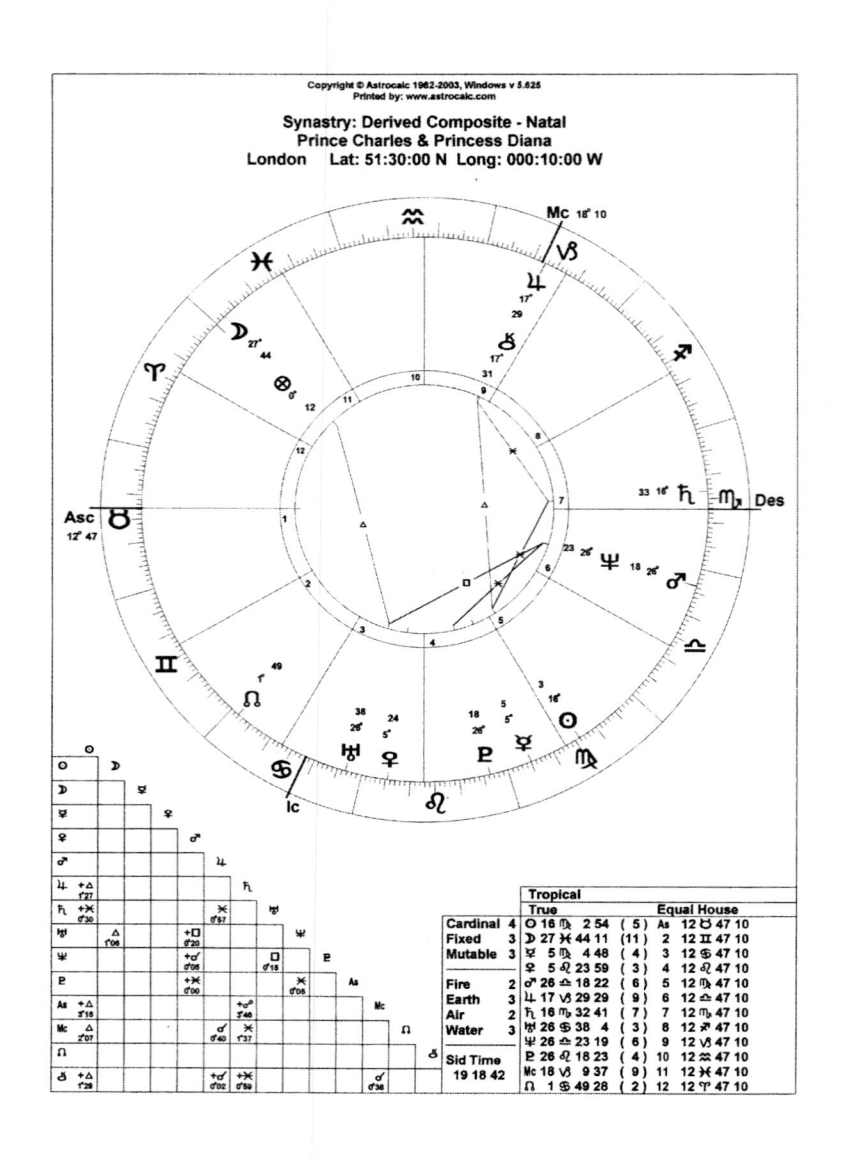

Chart 31

although they probably came closest to it through the transformation their children brought to both their lives (Pluto in the 5th house of children) and their communications about their children (Mercury in the 5th house). Her neurotic hang-ups (Moon in the 12th house) interfered with their everyday working duties (Moon in Pisces and ruler of Pisces, Neptune, in the 6th house).

How did they experience the relationship?

Composite to Diana	Composite to Charles
Sun square Ascendant	Sun square Mars
Moon sextile Saturn	Moon trine Sun square Jupiter square Uranus
Mercury conjunction Pluto	Mercury trine Moon, conjunction Saturn, trine Venus opposition Jupiter square North Node
Neptune Venus square	Mercury square North Node
Mars trine Moon square Saturn conjunction Ascendant conjunction Midheaven	Mars trine Uranus
Jupiter square Midheaven	Jupiter square Venus square Neptune square
Saturn opposition Venus Uranus opposition Saturn square	Midheaven Saturn conjunction Sun square Pluto
Midheaven	Uranus trine Sun

185

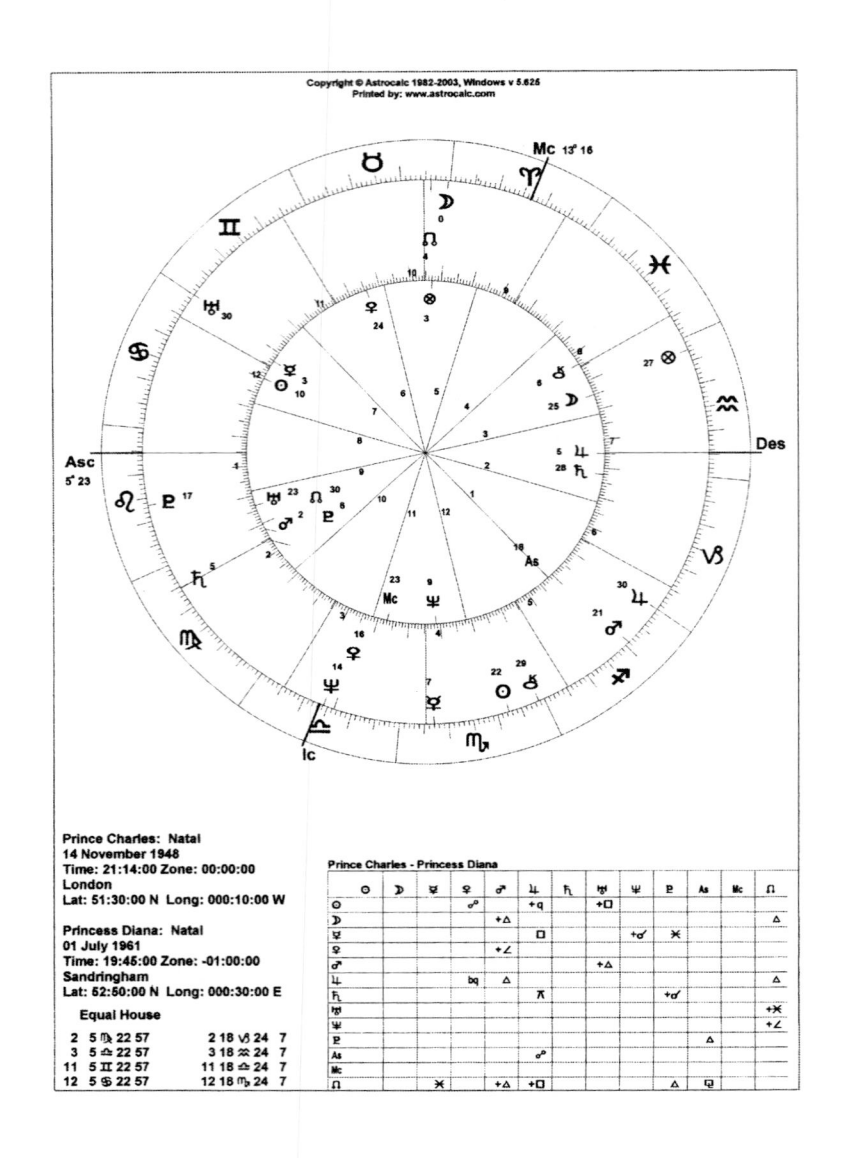

Chart 32

Neptune trine Moon square
Saturn

Neptune trine Uranus

Pluto opposition Moon square
Venus

Pluto square Sun trine
Mars trine Jupiter
conjunction Uranus,
conjunction North Node
trine Mercury

North Node conjunction Mercury

Here is enough to have kept Charles and Diana talking about their relationship for a lifetime! However, it is of the greatest importance in analyzing astrological data to see the essentials and not to lose sight of the wood for the trees. If you look at the horoscopes of any two people, even two strangers who pass in the street and would never dream of forming a relation-ship with each other (for any of a multitude of reasons that each would recognize instantly) you are still bound to see a large number of inter-aspects between them, some harmonious and some tense. Generally speaking, whether in our profoundly intimate relationships or in our fleeting encounters with strangers, we much more often notice the tense aspects between us than the harmonious ones. True, we might, for example, immediately like somebody whose Jupiter is conjunction our Moon, but, being human, we are much more likely to be aware of disliking somebody whose Saturn is conjunction our Moon. This is due to our fundamental propensity to believe our own ways of being to be "right", so that when we receive harmonious inter-aspects from another's horoscope which seem to endorse the "rightness" of our own way of being, we tend to take this for granted. But when we receive tense and challenging inter-aspects from another's horoscope, the equilibrium of our self-esteem is disturbed and we are very conscious of our discomfort.

In fleeting or brief encounters we have with other people, while we are pleased with the gentle inter-aspects between us, we mostly take them for granted; but the truly tense aspects between us prompt us to move away from that person as quickly as possible. But in committed intimate relation-ships such as marriage, while separation and divorce is possible, it is generally much more difficult to walk away from the tense inter-aspects between us. This is how and why, for all human beings, our most significant personal growth occurs in the context of committed intimacy.

So, returning to the specific relationship between Princess Diana and Prince Charles, let us look at the obviously powerful (because challenging) inter-aspects between their composite chart and their individual horoscopes.

The relationship forcibly propelled her into being at the centre of public attention and demanded of her that she overcome her shyness and inhibitions (Mars conjunction Midheaven and Mars square Saturn). It also very pleasantly fed her needy narcissism (Mars trine Moon). But in the pursuit of her career as a princess she found it very difficult to come to terms with the kind of dignity the relationship asked of her (Jupiter square Midheaven), and the relationship explicitly restricted her wish to democratize her love in the name of being "the Queen of Hearts" (Saturn opposition Venus). However, the relationship also liberated her from her inhibitions and gave her an excitingly new although challenging career (Uranus opposition Saturn square Midheaven). The relationship brought her glamour and great public adoration, which fed her emotional neediness, but which demanded that she overcome her shyness, which she did (Neptune trine Moon square Saturn conjunction Midheaven). Her emotions, her ways of relating to people, her life destiny, and her personality were totally transformed by the relationship (Pluto opposition Moon square Venus conjunction Uranus conjunction North Node trine Ascendant).

For Charles, the spirit of the relationship was in conflict with his sexuality - and we know he was in love with Camilla Parker Bowles throughout his marriage (Sun square Mars). The emotions of the relationship furthered his career, that is to become King of England, by bringing him two sons, but the emotions of the relationship were also deeply disharmonious with his beliefs and his need for freedom (Moon trine Sun square Jupiter square Uranus). The great enlargement and increase in popularity that the relationship brought him was in conflict with his values, his desire to fulfil his own quiet, spiritual pursuits, and the way he would personally have chosen to carry out his public duties (Jupieter square Venus square Neptune square Midheaven). His self-expressiveness and his need to be in control were severely restricted by the relationship (Saturn conjunction Sun square Pluto); and the relationship controlled and conflicted with his core self-expression (Pluto square Sun).

She has 3 cardinal, 5 fixed, and 2 mutable planets; he has 2 cardinal, 4 fixed, and 4 mutable planets. There is no great significance in their differences in this respect, although she is somewhat more go-getting and somewhat more persistent than he is, suggesting he felt he too often had to give in to her demands.

She has 1 Fire, 4 Earth, 2 Air, and 3 Water planets; he has 3 Fire, 2 Earth, 3 Air, and 2 Water planets. She was mostly practicality and feeling, he mostly inspirational and thoughtful. In this respect, "masculinity" and "femininity" were divided between them in a traditional way.

Their Sun signs are trine; their Moon signs are square; their Mercury signs are trine; their Venus signs are inconjunct; their Mars signs are square; their Ascendant signs are trine.

So it is the square Moons (emotions) and square Mars's (ways of asserting themselves) that describe the essential unhappiness of the relationship.

The major aspects of their synastry are: her Sun trine his Mercury, trine his Uranus, square his Neptune, square his Midheaven; her Moon square his Sun, square his Chiron; her Venus opposition his Sun, opposition his Chiron; her Mars trine his Moon, trine his Jupiter, conjunction his Saturn, trine his North Node; her Jupiter square his Moon, square his Mercury, opposition his Ascendant, square his North Node; he Saturn square his Moon, square his North Node; her Uranus square his Sun, trine his Mars, trine his Jupiter; her Neptune conjuncion his Mercury, square his Ascendant; her Pluto trine his Moon, conjunction his Saturn, trine his North Node; her Ascendant conjunction his Mars, trine his Pluto; her North Node trine his Moon, trine his Jupiter, trine his North Node, square his Chiron; her Midheaven trine his Uranus; her Chiron trine his Mercury, opposition his Saturn, inconjunct his Ascendant.

There are only 2 double-whammies in the synastry - Jupiter-Node (square and trine) and North Node-North Node (trine). His destiny was enlarged (Jupiter) by her at least to the extent that she bore him two sons and this was harmoniously (trine) in keeping with her own fulfilment (North Node).

They each found the other difficult to understand (her Sun square his Neptune, her Neptune square his Ascendant). Both her deep psychological problems and her unhappiness associated with them and her obverse exuberance and extravagance were greatly distasteful to him as being so unlike his mother - the natural prototype of womanhood for any man - (her Jupiter and her Saturn square his Moon). And the "little-girl" neediness through which she was sometimes able to court the public at large prompted rebuke rather than benevolent paternalism from him (her Moon square his Sun), and her erratic unpredictability likewise prompted him to rebuke her (her Uranus square his Sun). But, conversely, she felt he needed to be more freely expressive emotionally and she willfully and assertively attacked his propriety and stiff-upper-lipped inhibitions (her Mars and her Pluto conjunction his Saturn).

Overall, there are 4 aspects to her Sun (the relationship vastly enhanced her ambitions), but only 2 aspects to his Sun (his two sons?). There is only 1 aspect to her Moon (little connection to her childhood experiences in this relationship), but 3 aspects to his Moon (she aroused a lot of feeling in him). There are 2 aspects to her Saturn and 2 aspects to his Saturn, not enough, ultimately, to bind the relationship in the face of its difficulties.

Is there any further information about the relationship contained in their planets in each other's houses?

Diana's in Charles' House		Charles' in Diana's House	
Sun	12	Sun	11
Moon	8	Moon	4
Mercury	11	Mercury	10
Venus	11	Venus	9
Mars	2	Mars	1
Jupiter	6	Jupiter	1
Saturn	6	Saturn	8
Uranus	2	Uranus	7
Neptune	4	Neptune	9
Pluto	2	Pluto	8
Ascendant	5	Ascendant	8
Midheaven	4	Midheaven	3
North Node	2	North Node	4
Chiron	8	Chiron	11

She was deeply attracted to the reclusive, spiritual, introverted part of Charles' nature (her Sun in his 12th house) and, as is so often the case in human relaionships, what drew her to him was also what she eventually found most repugnant. She wanted to heal him through sex, but it turned out that she wounded and was wounded by his sexuality much more than healed (her Chiron in his 8th house, his Saturn in her 8th house).

He was first attracted to her as a friend (his Sun in her 11th house) and was emotionally drawn to her childlike vulnerability, which he wanted to help her overcome through their friendship, but which, in due course, became that part of her that he found himself least able to cope with (his Moon in her 4th house and his Chiron in her 11th house). He quarrelled with her general way of being (his Mars in her 1st house), although he also greatly enhanced her confidence and ability to be extraverted (his Jupiter in her 1st house). He was cold towards her sexually (his Saturn in her 8th house) and demanded a lot of freedom from her in their marriage (his Uranus in her 7th house).

What in their individual horoscopes explains how they came to choose each other?

She sought self-expression and power through a communicative and nurturing marriage (her Sun and Mercury in Cancer in the 7th house, with Gemini on the cusp). She wanted to be adored in a romantic way (Venus in the 5th house) in a bid to overcome the feeling of coldness in her childhood family life (Venus square Moon in Aquarius). (It often seems to be the case that women who have Moon square Venus are fulfilled either as mothers or lovers, but find it very difficult to be successful in both roles. They strenuously express warmth and love in a bid to get love in return, but often choose people who are precisely unwilling and/or unable to give them the love they crave.) She craved a glamourous career (Neptune in the 10th house). She was bound to have a highly tempestuous sex life, through which she would be profoundly transformed, and which would be the ultimate meaning of her life (Mars, Uranus, Pluto, and North Node in the 8th house).

He sought a coolly self-sufficient wife who would be his friend (Uranus in Aquarius in the 11th house), although there was also a strongly illusory romantic side to his nature (Venus conjunction Neptune) which also reflected the lack of clarity in his childhood conditioning (Neptune conjunction IC), which is known through the unhappiness he expressed concerning his harsh boarding school experiences and the resentment he later expressed towards his father for this brutalization of his sensitivity. While his ultimate destiny is about being a confidently self-assertive and pragmatic ruler of the people (Moon and North Node in the 10th house in Taurus, with Aries on the cusp of the 10th house), his Sun, Mars, Jupiter, and Chiron in the 5th house emphasize the importance of romance and/or children in his life - it might be said that having children to continue the royal line was the essential part of his career (Sun in the 5th house).

Thus, in an overall way, we have the impression of two people who each sought to heal the other, but through some deep incompatibilities in their natures were each wounded by their failure to make real contact with the other. Positively, her status in the world and the glamor she sought were fulfilled through the relationship, and she was happy in her role as a mother. He was emotionally and romantically profoundly unfulfilled in the relationship, but the relationship did bring him two sons, which was the fulfillment of a central part of his career responsibilities.

Exercises

1) Which aspects between planets are "soft"?

2) Which aspects between planets are "hard"?

3) Which aspect between planets is a mixture of "soft" and "hard"?

4) Which two planets most often refer to our sexual nature?

5) Which two planets most often refer to our deepest "true self"?

6) Which part of our horoscope is usually the first thing others notice about us?

7) What is the natural ruler of the 10th house?

8) What is the natural ruler of the 2nd house?

9) Which planets jointly rule the 11th house?

10) Which planets jointly rule the 8th house?

11) Which planets jointly rule the 12th house?

12) Which house is ruled by the Sun?

13) Which houses are ruled by Mercury?

14) Which houses are ruled by Venus?

15) Which houses are ruled by Mars?

16) Which house is ruled by the Moon?

17) Which 2 planets express the masculinity in all human beings?

18) Which 2 planets express the femininity in all human beings?

19) Which planet most expresses originality?

20) Which planet most expresses duty?

21) Which planet most expresses obsessiveness?

22) Which planet most expresses authority?

23) Which planet most expresses changeability?

24) Which planet most expresses imagination?

25) Which planet most expresses impulsive action?

26) Analyze in depth an intimate love or marriage relationship of your own.

Do appreciate that, in all intimate relationships, the two people's experiences of each other and of the relationship are not necessarily symmetrical. Check this by the inter-aspects between their individual horoscopes and the composite chart as well as by the synastry between their individual horoscopes.

Do appreciate that, however hidden or strange, all intimate relationships have come into being for some purposes that serve both people.

Don't judge any relationship as "good" or "bad"; only aim to understand its meanings.

Chapter 9
Family Relationships

Summary: The relationships between members of a family are genetic, and each horoscope of a human being may be looked at as a map of that person's genetic inheritance. For most people, parenthood is the most challenging and rewarding creative task of their lives. A family tree of four generations of one family is presented, together with individual horoscopes and the relationship horoscopes between many of the family members. The relationships of a father and daughter and two sisters in this family are analyzed. Also analyzed are the relationships of a grandfather and grandson, and a pair of twins from other families. Brief biographies of various members of a family, spread over four generations, are given, together with their horoscopes, for your study of the inheritance of astrological configurations and themes.

Parenthood

The horoscope of a human being can be understood as a map of his or her genetic inheritance and, in the not too distant future, it is possible and to be hoped, modern genetics and astrology will combine to delineate very specific physical and psychological characteristics and pre-dispositions from factors in a horoscope. But even without the help of genetics, astrological research on its own bears witness to the fact that communalities of many kinds occur in the horoscopes of parents and children far in excess of what would be predicted by chance. And, as in all relationships, communalities between people can reflect great affection or great disharmony between them, and very often, a mixture of both. Love and hate are two sides of the one coin of intimate involvement between people. The opposite of love is not hate, but indifference.

All young children believe their parents are the most wonderful people in the world; so do all older children, at the deepest level of their being, notwithstanding that they often declare the opposite in word and deed! Naturally, therefore, a child imitates her parents in her bid to be as wonderful as they are.

Children incorporate into their own selves the ways their parents are much more than the ways their parents exhort them to be. Ideally, parents' exhorations to their children match their ways of being, but if any of what you exhort your child to be or do has the flavour of "Do as I say, not as I do", you can be sure she will see through your hypocrisy and ignore your exhortations. Actions speak louder than words, and your actions are the model on which your child bases her own.

So long as he is not abandoned, the basic security of a child under the age of about five is vouchsafed by his belief in the God-like omniscience and omnipotence of his parents. Mummy and Daddy "know everything" and are capable of making everything all right, no matter what the difficulties. From about five onwards, Mummy and Daddy have to compete with other authorities - especially teachers - for "rightness" in matters of fact and opinion, but the child's emotional security goes on depending on his ability to perceive his parents as unambiguously powerful in their capacity to keep him safe and sound. And even when he is grown-up, as long as his parents are alive, a child is entitled to perceive his parents as always available, when the going gets rough, for the unconditional loving support that they alone are uniquely always willing to give him.

As well as implying enormous responsibility, there is no greater power on earth than that automatically bestowed on people when they (choose to) become parents: "the hand that rocks the cradle rules the world". Furthermore, becoming a parent is he natural final stage in human maturation. That is, it bestows on us, automatically, the joy of love - willingly making another person's well-being and happiness as important (if not more important) than our own. People who do not have children may have to work very hard to find for themselves commitments that will guarantee them the complete fulfilment in life that only comes from passionately serving others' as well as our own needs and desires; whereas, for as long as they are alive, parents are automatically granted this profound satisfaction by the mere existence of their children.

Parenthood is a constant tightrope act, a creative struggle to find and maintain the "just-right" balance between encouragement and constraint throughout the ever-changing developmental needs of children.

We also have to accept that in our creative struggles in rearing our children - as in all creative endeavours - we are not "perfect", but humanly frail. While we consciously determine not to commit on our children the sins that we believe our parents inflicted on us, we will inevitably - consciously or unconsciously - commit other sins which our children, in turn, will detemimedly avoid in the rearing of their children. And what of the genetically determined characteristics in both ourselves and our children that so obviously limit our own abilities to be all that we might want to be to our children, and limit our children's abilities to benefit from what we are able and willing to offer them?

In everything we do in our lives, and probably especially in the task of being a parent, we are bound to accept our impotence as well as our power, our badness as well as our goodness, our failures as well as our successes. And, ironically, it is in being "good enough" rather than "perfect" parents that we love our children best, because only by eventually perceiving their parents as good and powerful and loveworthy and humanly flawed, are grown-up children able to attain full self-esteem and confidence in the face of their awareness of their own flawed nature. Some of the most frightened and unhappy grown-ups are so by virtue of having been imbued with the idea of their parents' unassailable "perfection".

Yet, despite all its headaches and heartaches, for the vast majority of people, parenthood is still the most worthwhile task in the world and potentially the profoundest and most unassailable meaning we may give to our lives, and our ability to read our own and our children's horoscopes can enable us to add to our love for our children an ability to know them and to educate them in ways that nothing else could tell us. And so knowing them, we have the best possible chance of loving them and training them in ways that most positively enhance the fulfilment of their unique potential.

A parent is a child's first teacher, and in this role both Saturn and Jupiter are central energies in the parent to child relatioship. Saturn imposes limitations and structures, and Jupiter encourages expansion and freedom, and it is an appropriate balance between these energies that determines our well-being throughout our lives.

Not surprisingly, many people become parents for the first time around the age of twenty-nine when, for everybody, Saturn returns to its natal position, having made one complete circuit of the zodiac since birth. It is a critical time in everybody's life, denoting the beginning of true responsible adulthood, and the birth of a child is a profoundly appropriate marker of this turning point. It also means that the child and parent have Saturn in the same zodiacal place, and thus makes it relatively easy for the child to identify readily with the value of the parent's imposed structures and controls and so accept them easily.

Along with Saturnine restictions, loving parents also bestow on their children Jupiterian permissions.

Permissions are the opposite of inhibitions. Permissions are transmitted by parents to children through (Jupiterian) enthusiasm. While there is some value in explicitly and verbally giving a child various permissions, by far the most potent source of a child's lifelong capacity to enjoy life is the parents' own obvious enjoyment of life, which does not need to be reinforced with words. Permissions are essentially about the freedom to be emotionally expressive, and when a child is a witness to his or her parents' pleasure in cooking, reading, gardening, watching television, playing cards ... the child is likely to have an enhanced capacity for pleasure in these activities for the whole of his or her life. (Research has shown that the overwhelmingly most relevant factor in a five-year-old's ability easily to learn to read is that he or she has been a witness to his or her parents reading for their own pleasure.)

Permission appropriately to express unhappy feelings is also acquired by the child through being witness to his parents' unashamed and spontaneous expressions of grief, anger, disappointment, etc.

It is very important to distinguish between permissions and permissiveness. Permissiveness is a negatively excessive Jupiter and is the opposite of positively controlling Saturn. Parents' permissiveness towards their child usuaully derives from an immediate bid for expediency and/or a false desire to be liked by the child. Permissiveness is lazy, and it is also unloving because it denies the child the Saturnine structures and boundaries she so crucially needs to contain her impulses and thus feel safe in her interactions with the physical world and with other people. Children of permissive parents feel insecure.

Broadly speaking, the personal father in a horoscope is represented by the Sun and aspects to it, and the 10th house; and the personal mother in a horoscope is represented by the Moon and aspects to it, and the 4th house. These are generalizations that are usually, but by no means necessarily, the case. For example, a divorced or widowed mother, bringing up a child on her own is likely to be experienced by her child as both Sun and Moon, both 4th and 10th houses. And a father who looks after his child's basic daily needs for nurturance because his wife is too ill to do so is likely to be experienced by his child as Moon and 4th house as well as Sun and 10th house. Furthermore, the Moon in all horoscopes is not only the nurturing mother but also the needy and demanding baby. The complexities of all horoscopes (and life) are multifarious in their manifestations.

Practically speaking, in interpreting relationships between parents and children, look at the synastry between the two horoscopes, including aspects to the Ascendants. If the harmonious aspects are more numerous the relationship will be generally serene; if the conflicting aspects are more numerous there are likely to be tensions and difficulties. Most difficult are the squares between planets; and conjunctions between the Sun or Moon and Mars, Saturn, Uranus, or Pluto tend to create problems.

One interesting communality between the horoscopes of parents and children that is very common is that of planetary placements in houses. For example, a parent and child may each have Venus in the 12th house, even though there is no communality of sign or aspects to Venus. Such house equivalence seems often to represent a significant inheritance that the child receives from the parent. Similarly, a child may inherit an obvious chart shape or a singleton planet, say

Uranus as the "handle" of a bucket-shaped horoscope, depicting the inheritance of a propensity to have issues of "freedom" as a central issue in the life.

Mark and Miriam - Father and Daughter (Charts 25 and 27)

Miriam is the elder daughter of Mark. (Mark's birthtime is not known, so his horoscope is drawn for dawn.) As a child, Miriam was very much "Daddy's little girl" and attached herself to the calm security of his love for her in compensation for the very unstable and volatile love that was offered by her mother (Esther, Chart 24). Miriam's experience of her father was of a very kind and gentle man. She was aware that her father sought to protect her from her mother's volatility, but was also aware that her father's first priority was to look after his psychologically disturbed and deeply depressed wife. (See A Lifelong Marriage, Chapter 8). Miriam knew she had to accept this and "not upset Mummy" in order to sustain her father's love for her.

Let us analyze the relationship between Mark and his daughter Miriam and also see what we can discern Miriam has astrologically inherited from her father.

His Sun is in Pisces, her Sun is in Libra, so they appreciate each other's core gentleness, but she experiences him as too passive and he experiences her as too bossy. They both have 4 planets in cardinal signs, 3 planets in fixed signs, and 3 planets in mutable signs. They both have the majority of planets in feminine signs, she having 5 Earth and 1 Water, he having 2 Earth and 4 Water. He is more emotional than she is, she is more practical than he is.

Their Sun signs are inconjunct; their Moon signs are inconjunct; their Mercury signs are opposition; their Venus signs are trine; their Mars signs are sextile. Thus they are most harmoniously united in their warm (Fire) ways of loving and relating to people.

Their synastry includes: Mark's Sun sextile Miriam's Moon, square her Mars, and trine her Pluto; his Mercury is square her Mars, opposition her Neptune; his Venus is trine her Mars, square her Jupiter; his Mars is trine her Sun, sextile her Saturn, square her Ascendant; his Jupiter is sextile her Mercury, sextile her Jupiter, opposition her Uranus, and sextile her Midheaven; his Saturn is inconjunct her Sun, conjunction her Ascendant; his Uranus is trine her Sun, trine her Moon, inconjunct her Venus, opposition her Pluto; his Neptune is sextile her Mercury, opposition her Jupiter, and sextile her Neptune; his Pluto is sextile her Venus, opposition her Mars; his North Node is trine her Mercury, conjunction her Uranus, and trine her Midheaven; his Chiron is sextile her Ascendant.

The double-whammies between them are: Sun-Mars (square, trine), Mercury-Neptune (opposition, sextile), Jupiter-Jupiter (sextile), Neptune-Neptune (sextile). These are represented in their relationship as a shared interest in literature (Mercury-Neptune), a shared valuation of orthodox religious observance and a very good teacher-pupil relationship between them (Jupiter-Jupiter), and a shared detached dreaminess in their approaches to life (Neptune-Neptune).

There are a considerable number of quite aggressive aspects between them that were never expressed openly, probably because each of them in their essentially gentle natures, were careful never to overstep the boundaries that could lead to hostility between them. Miriam was very conscious of being obedient to her father's spoken and unspoken requirement of her that she avoid upsetting her mother (his Saturn conjunction her Ascendant) in order to retain her father's love, which she valued very highly. Later in life, when she was grown-up and married and had children of her own,

Miriam found release for the suppressed pain of her childhood family life by becoming a (group) psychotherapist. Gradually, as an adult, she refused to capitulate to her mother's hysterical demands, which enraged her mother and prompted her father to express his Sun square Miriam's Mars and his Mars square Miriam's Ascendant. Thus she felt the loss of a portion of her father's gentle love for her as the price she eventually decided to pay in order to release herself from the pain of her own suppressed needs.

All of this points to the reality that young children are acutely aware (without being able to articulate their awarneness in words) of the parts of themselves and the aspects between themselves and their parents that they must avoid expressing in the interest of their self-preservation within the family. Children are entirely at the mercy of their parents, so if there are aggressive aspects in the synastry between children and parents, the parents' power over the child will always be manifest in the expression of such aggressive aspects. Some children are more capable than others of expressing the care necessary to avoid the aggression (emotional as well as physical) that their parents might wield against them, and Miriam was particularly capable of appropriate self-restraint through the very close Sun-Saturn opposition in her own horoscope and her father's Saturn in close conjunction to her Ascendant. The happiest part of Miriam's synastry with her father is the 4 aspects from his Jupiter to her Mercury, Jupiter, Uranus, and Midheaven, through which her father taught her many skills in a very encouraging way. Jupiter conjunction the Midheaven of her own horoscope confirms her experience of one of her parents being a benevolent teacher to her. Her father's Chiron sexile her Ascendant was a mixed blessing, gently soothing her hurt feelings and reassurring her when her mother was violent; but also hurting her very much when he was so absorbed in caring for his sick wife that he did not notice Miriam's needs or pain.

What aspects does Miriam inherit from her father, and what do they represent in their characters and personalities? The major planetary inter-aspects they share are; he has Sun square Pluto, she has Sun sextile Pluto; he has Mercury trine Jupiter, she has Mercury trine Jupiter; he has Mercury trine Neptune, she has Mercury conjunction Neptune; he has Mars square Saturn, she has Mars square Saturn; he has Jupiter trine Neptune, she has Jupiter trine Neptune.

These confirm the dominance in their communality of the "soft" energies of Mercury-Jupiter, Mercury-Neptune, and Jupiter-Neptune; but there is also, in both of them, a lot of controlled violence (Mars square Saturn and Sun-Pluto aspects) around which they both tread very carefully for the sake of maintaining the peace between them that they both so value.

It is noteworthy that in Mark's own horoscope Sun square Pluto, Mars square Saturn, and Mars conjunction Uranus speak of a great deal of violence in his nature, which was never overtly expressed. Such violence is very much in conflict with his core Pisces Sun, which has "won" over the other, aggressive parts in him. However, it is probably the case that he found "displaced" expression of his own violence in the very explicit violence of his wife. And he also, in subtle (Pisces) ways expressed a considerable amount of "passive aggression" in his refusing often to be responsive to his wife's desperate bids to incite a full-blooded emotional response from him. In this respect, it is noteworthy that Mark's Moon (in Libra, the sign of marriage) is probably (irrespective of his time of birth) unaspected, giving him the ability, and possibly the necessity, to isolate his own feeling responses from the rest of his nature. Neither are there any aspects from his Moon to his daughter, Miriam's planets (although, depending on his time of birth, his Moon may be in conjunction with her Sun) so, notwithstanding that they both sensitively "make the most" of their relationship, and she is grateful for what he has

205

given her, she experiences a lack of sufficient nurturing care from him.

Finally, one interesting connection between this father and daughter is that his Moon is in Libra, which is the sign of her Sun. I have noticed (but not put to any statistical test) that this kind of connection between a parent and child occurs more often than would be expected by chance. That is, there seems to be a tendency between a parent and child for a cross-gender connection between their Suns and Moons, a non-random propensity for a father's Moon to be in the same sign as his daughter's Sun, and a mother's Sun to be in the same sign as her son's Moon. You might like to collect some data on this hypothesis from amongst your own family and friends.

Grandparent-Grandchild Relationships

As is well-known, without reference to astrology, children sometimes seem more like their grandparents than their parents, and such communalities represent the complex ways in which "regressive genes" manifest through the generations. These are often fascinatingly depicted in comparisons of children's and their grandparents' horoscopes. And, of course, a child may seem more like an aunt or uncle than his or her own parents. All of these most interesting genetic facts can be discerned astrologically.

Generally speaking, Jupiter is often associated with the relationship between grandparents and their grandchildren, representing the universal acceptance that grandparents are traditionally allowed to benevolently indulge their grandchildren in ways that are not appropriate between parents and children.

Sigmund Freud and Lucien Freud - Grandfather and Grandson (Charts 33 and 34)

Sigmund Freud is one of the outstanding geniuses of the twentieth century. His theories of human nature, child development, and psychopathology have permeated the cultural consciousness of Western thinking in every domain of life, and they are implicitly understood in many ways even by people who have never heard of him. At core, Sigmund Freud has bequeathed us a systematic awareness of how our unconscious minds function and, in so doing, has enabled us to accept the reality that, beneath the veneer of civilized behaviour, we are all motivated by powerful impulses of self-centred aggression and sexuality that, however well-camouflaged, direct our lives.

Lucien Freud, although born in Germany, came to live in England while still a child and is considered British by adoption. He is generally thought of as the greatest living British painter. His paintings are all of naked people, powerfully presented in all the vulnerability of their less-than-perfect bodies, and they bear the power of their deep, unmasked truthfulness.

Sigmund and his grandson Lucien seem to see human truth in very similar terms, one in the language of words, the other in the language of paint. What representation of Lucien's genetic inheritance from his grandfather can we see in their two horoscopes? (We do not have Lucien's time of birth, so his horoscope is drawn for dawn.)

One day, it is to be hoped in the not too distant future, astrologers and geneticists will have joined hands and mapped known human genes against particular planetary placements and aspects in a person's horoscope. However, without yet having this theoretical knowledge, we do have a great deal of accumulated empirical evidence that overall

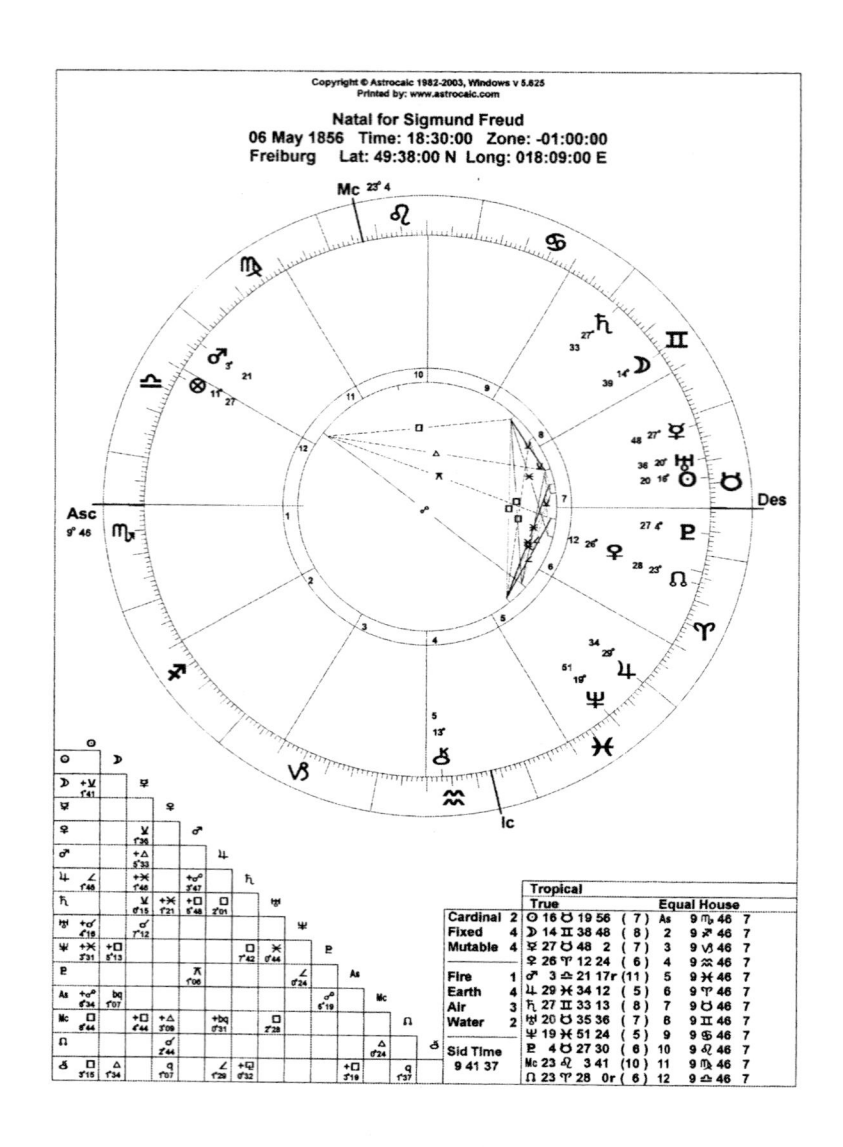

Chart 33

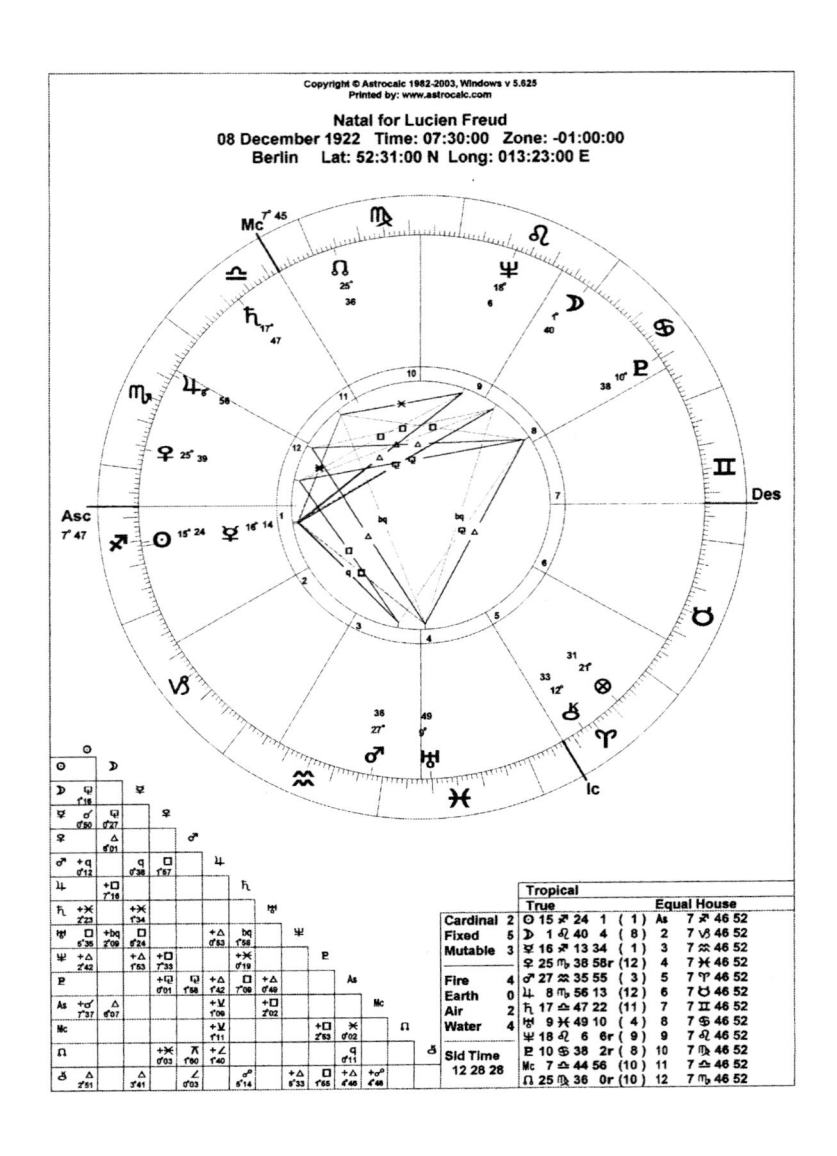

Chart 34

chart patterns, planets in houses, and planetary aspects testify to human inheritance with remarkable vividness.

We might have expected the overall shape of Lucien's horoscope to resemble Sigmund's in some way, but it does not. (Sigmund's horoscope is very tightly packed into a small section of the Western hemisphere, except for the singleton planet, Mars; Lucien's horoscope is a much more all-round "splash" shape, with no obviously dominating planet.)

There may well be some planetary placements in houses that Lucien has inherited from his grandfather, Sigmund, but without the datum of Lucien's birthtime we cannot investigate this.

So we are left with planetary aspects to describe the talent (that has made them both so famous) and the depiction of humanity in its raw vulnerability (that is the central message they have both communicated). Here are the compound planetary energies they share, that is the interactions between like planetary energies, irrespective of what particular asspects (which are much less important than the planetary energies themselves).

Sigmund	Lucien
Sun conjunction Uranus	Sun square Uranus
Sun sextile Neptune	Sun trine Neptune
Sun square Chiron	Sun trine Chiron
Mercury semi-sextile Saturn	Mercury sextile Saturn
Venus conjunction North Node	Venus sextile North Node

What a magnificently convincing array of communality! Three powerful, shared outer-planet aspects to their Suns (driving spirit, ambition, masculinity), to Uranus (shocking originality), to Neptune (imagination that reaches the deepest essence of things), and to Chiron (pain and vulnerability transmuted into fame).

They share Mercury-Saturn and Mercury-Uranus aspects, which together describe the shared subject-matters of their communications to the world: Mercury-Saturn (depicting the core pain and burden of humankind's mortal nature), and Mercury-Uranus (the shockingly original and enlightening way in which they both express themselves).

Their shared Venus-North Node aspects bear witness to the multiplicity of meanings carried by all the planetary energies. Sigmund's ultimate destiny was fulfilled in his overall theory of how human beings relate to each other (Venus); Lucien's ultimate destiny is fulfilled in his art (Venus).

Brothers and Sisters

The horoscopes of brothers and sisters can be compared in the same way as other horoscopes, but there is one non-astrological factor that is immensely important to take into consideration, namely birth-order. Much psychological research confirms that a child's position in his or her family is an extremely important factor in determining his or her temperament, character, and general outlook on life, with only genetics and gender being more powerful influences.

The personalities of oldest children are almost always over-emphatically responsible and sensible; of youngest children over-emphatically dependent and compliant. Only children tend to acquire personalities that contain elements of both too great self-sufficiency and too great compliant dependency. In families of three children, the first child often welcomes the third child as an ally against the second child of whom he is typically very jealous, and, over the years, the second child may easily be made, by the first child's manipulation, to have a personality that proclaims, "I am the odd one out". How distorted an individual's natural propensities are through negative experiences associated with his or her position in the family depends, of course, on how insightfully and lovingly parents modify these tendencies. However, it is always worth knowing an individual's position in his or her family and bearing in mind the general implications associated with this in interpreting his or her horosocope.

The horoscopes of twins (whether identical or fraternal) are a very interesting and special challenge to astrological understanding. From the testimonies of parents of twins, it is often the case that they develop markedly dissimilar personalities and characters. How can we understand this astrologiclly when there horoscopes are, in the vast majority of cases, virtually identical? In some cases, it may be that characteristics that non-astrologers see as hugely different are, in fact, different manifestations of one and the same astrological factor. For example, say a pair of twins have Neptune conjunction Midheaven trine Mercury and one of them becomes a photographer and the other a sailor. Astrologically speaking, each of their chosen careers is entirely apposite to the same symbols, even though, in ordinary, non-astrological perception, they could hardly be more different.

Another possibility in consideration of the horoscopes of twins is that when they dislike their identity as twins and desperately seek to establish differences between themselves in order to avow their unique individualities, they consciously or unconsciously "divide their horoscope up between them", one living out one half of their horoscope's potential and the other living out another half. (This hypothesis is supported by the mother of now grown-up genetically identical twins who have developed very contrasting personalities. She told me that when the twins were five she heard one say to the other, "You learn to read and I'll learn to write.")

Anita and Stella - Sisters (Charts 35, 36, 37, and 38)

Anita and Stella have markedly dissimilar temperaments.

Anita is introverted, quietly self-absorbed, single-mindedly devoted to her professional art as a painter and print-maker. She feels strained by conventional social demands, although she is loyally devoted to a few close women friends.

Stella is extraverted and boisterous, very interested in people and their motives, and easily charms people with her exuberant warmth.

Stella has always been jealous of the attention and praise Anita has been given from early childhood for her artistic talent. Anita has always been jealous of Stella's charm, and the responsive praise she gets from other people for it.

They are both loyal and kind towards each other but say that they would almost certainly not choose to be friends with each other if they were not related. Let us see what astrology reveals about their relationship.

Their Sun signs, Aquarius and Taurus, are square, which immedialy tells us of core conflict between their ways of expressing themselves, which is enhanced by the fixity of these signs and which means neither is likely to capitulate to the other for the sake of peace.

Saturn right on the Ascendant in their composite chart speaks of he burden of constraint that their relationship demands of them, but it also ensures the endurance of the relationship, which is confirmed by 7 planets being in fixed signs.

The Moon in the 7th house in the context of this relationship is probably their mother (the intimate other) for the sake of

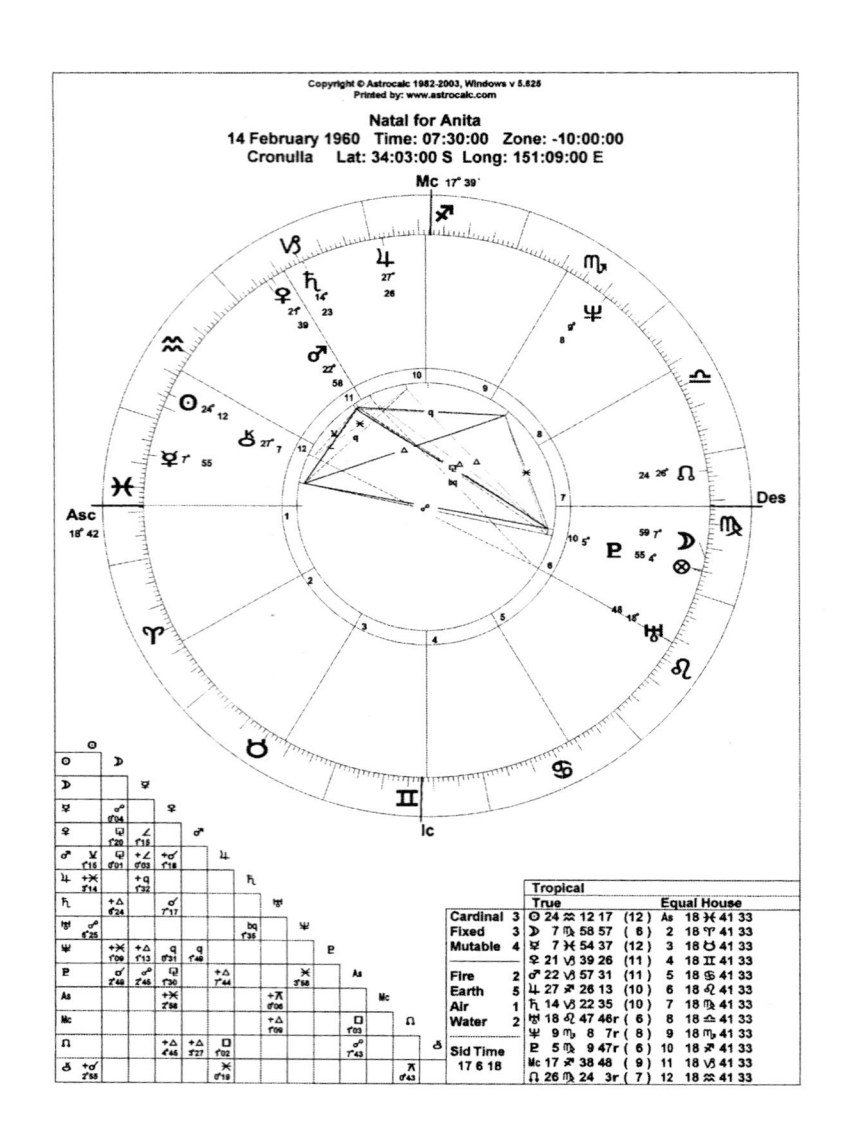

Natal for Anita
14 February 1960   Time: 07:30:00   Zone: -10:00:00
Cronulla   Lat: 34:03:00 S   Long: 151:09:00 E

Chart 35

214

whom they accepted the Saturnine difficulties of their relationship, and for which they were rewarded with their mother's happy love (Jupiter in the 1st house opposition Moon).

The core spirit of the relationship is the Sun, which is in the 3rd house, which rules both everyday communication and brothers and sisters. In the sign of Aries it refers to the self-assertiveness that they each express in their commumications with each other.

Anita has 3 cardinal, 3 fixed, and 4 mutable planets; Stella has 3 cardinal, 5 fixed, and 2 mutable planets. When it is a matter of who can hold out longest in a battle of wills between them, Stella wins.

Anita has 2 Fire, 5 Earth, 1 Air, and 2 Water planets; Stella has 3 Fire, 4 Earth, 1 Air, and 2 Water planets. In this distribution they are very alike, both highly practical (Earth), although Anita slightly more so, and Stella is more impetuous than Anita (Fire).

Their Sun signs are square; Moon signs are sextile; Mercury signs are sextile; Venus signs are square; Mars signs are inconjunct; Ascendants are square. Thus their Moon-Moon and Mercury-Mercury relationships are easy, which very much helped them to share a domestic environment when they were children, without many disputes, despite the many incompatibilities between them.

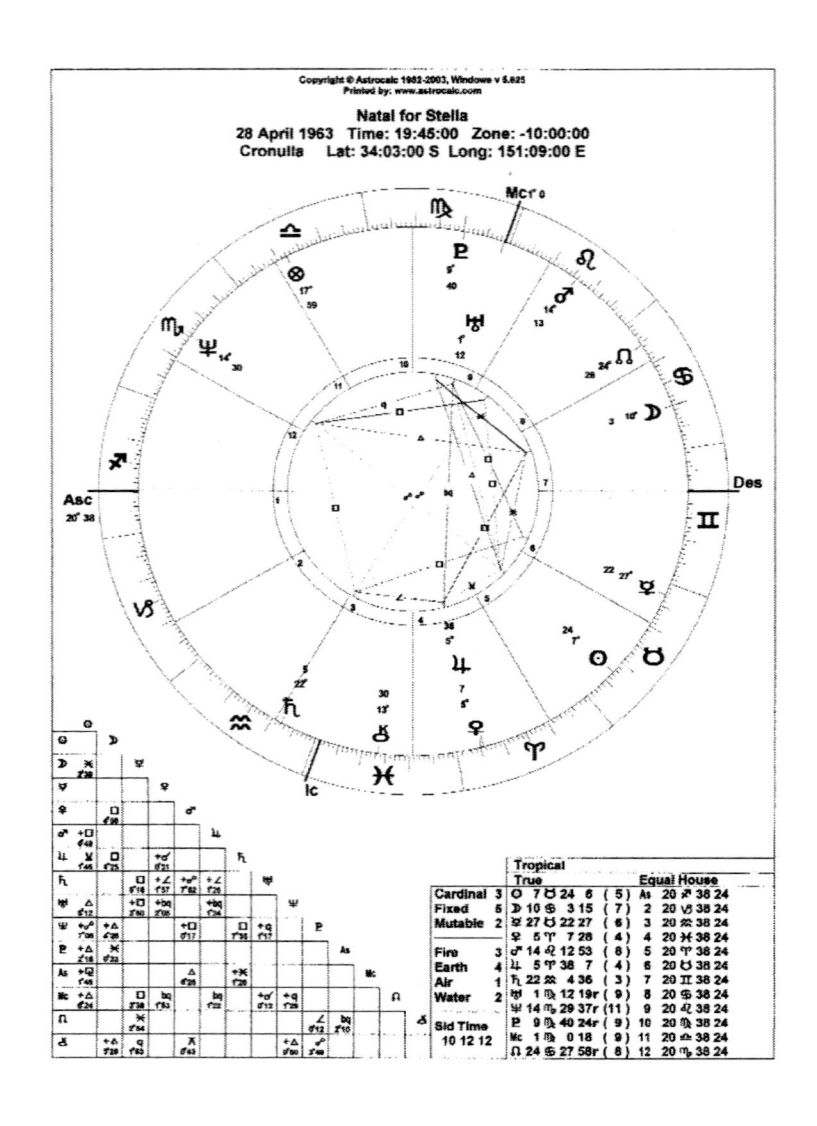

Chart 36

The synastry between them is:

Anita's		Stella's
Sun	square	Mercury
Sun	conjunction	Saturn
Moon	trine	Sun
Moon	sextile	Moon
Moon	conjunction	Pluto
Moon	conjunction	Midheaven
Mercury	sextile	Sun
Mercury	trine	Moon
Mercury	trine	Neptune
Mercury	opposition	Pluto
Mercury	opposition	Midheaven
Venus	trine	Mercury
Venus	opposition	North Node
Mars	trine	Mercury
Mars	opposition	North Node
Jupiter	sextile	Saturn
Jupiter	conjunction	Ascendant
Saturn	opposition	Moon
Saturn	inconjunct	Mars
Uranus	conjunction	Mars
Uranus	opposition	Saturn
Uranus	square	Neptune
Uranus	trine	Ascendant
Neptune	opposition	Sun
Neptune	trine	Moon
Neptune	square	Mars

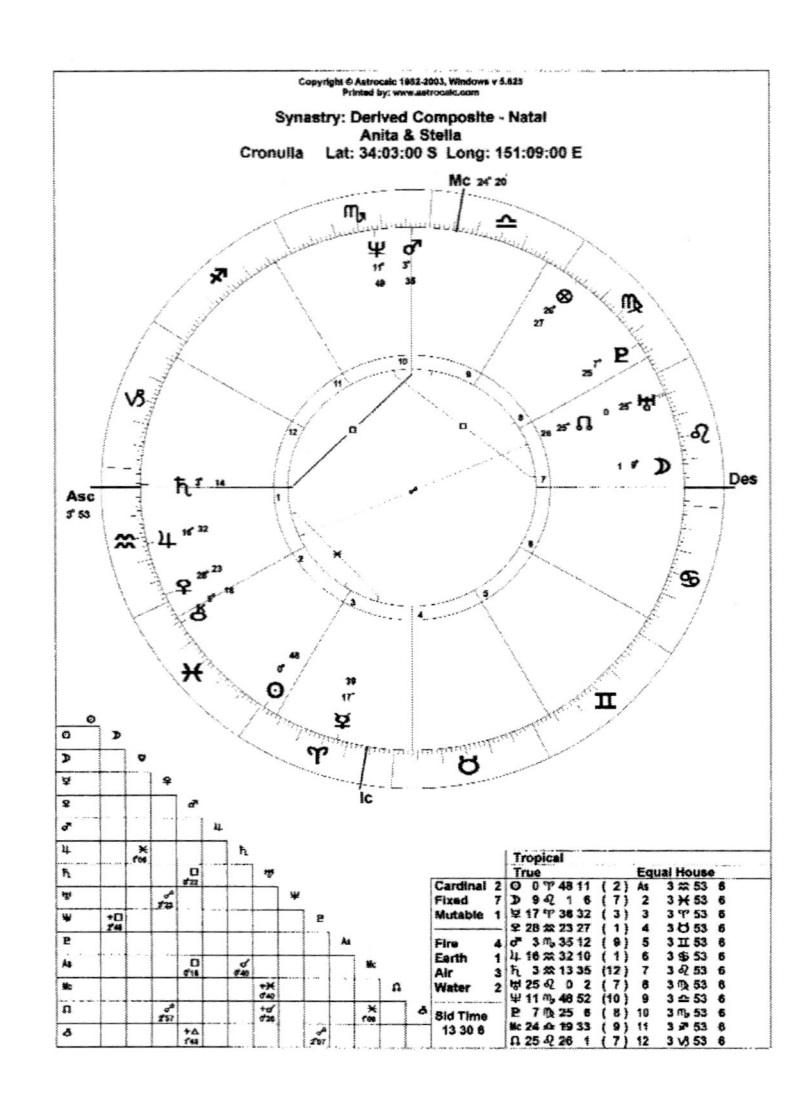

Chart 37

Neptune	conjunction	Neptune
Neptune	sextile	Pluto
Pluto	trine	Sun
Pluto	inconjunct	Venus
Pluto	inconjunct	Jupiter
Pluto	conjunction	Uranus
Pluto	conjunction	Pluto
Pluto	conjuction	Midheaven
Chiron	square	Mercury
Chiron	conjunction	Saturn
Chiron	inconjunct	North Node
Ascendant	trine	Nepune
Ascendant	square	Ascendant
Midheaven	trine	Mars
Midheaven	sextile	Saturn
Midheaven	conjunction	Ascendant
North Node	trine	Mercury
North Node	square	Ascendant
North Node	sextile	North Node

The most powerful inter-aspects between them are Anita's Sun conjunction Stella's Saturn which, combined with Anita's Uranus opposition Stella's Saturn, speak of Stella's ability to intimidate Anita and Anita's rebellion against that intimidation.

Anita's Moon conjunction Stella's Pluto and her Mercury opposition Stella's Pluto describe Stella's ability powerfully to control Anita, but Anita found her defence in her Saturn opposition to Stella's Moon, by which she was able to hurt Stella with cold withdrawal from her.

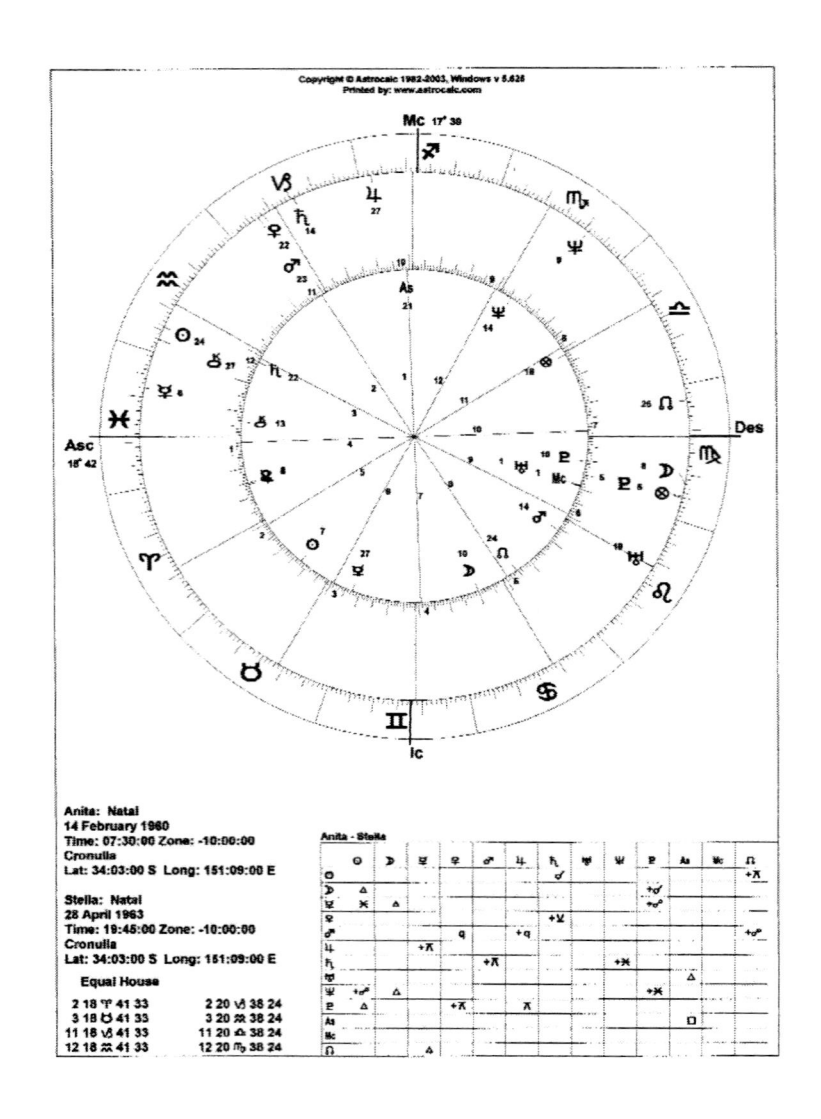

Chart 38

Anita's Jupiter conjunction Stella's Ascendant was a benevolent aspect of their childhood relationship in which Anita, as the elder child, looked after Stella and was a teacher to her. But she also got delight out of teasing Stella and inciting Stella to an aggressive response (Anita's Uranus conjunction Stella's Mars).

Anita's Mercury conjunction Stella's IC describes their ability to talk to each other about their parents, which is supported by Anita's Moon and Pluto in Stella's 10th house and her Mercury and Ascendant in Stella's 4th house. Likewise, Stella's Moon is in Anita's 4th house and her Ascendant is in Anita's 10th house.

The double-whammies between them are:

Sun-Mercury (square, sextile)

Moon-Moon (sextile)

Neptune-Neptune (conjunction)

Pluto-Pluto (conjunction)

Thus the foreground of their relationship is assertively talking to each other, peaceful domestic harmony associated with their joint relationship to their mother, and the sameness of their generational influences described by their Nepune and Pluto conjunctions.

In their individual horoscopes, they both have Sun-Uranus, Moon-Neptune, and Moon-Pluto aspects, which describes the inheritance they share of powerful needs to experience their lives in the context of the transcendance of the personal in favour of the challenge of deeply probing their psyches and transforming themselves through so doing.

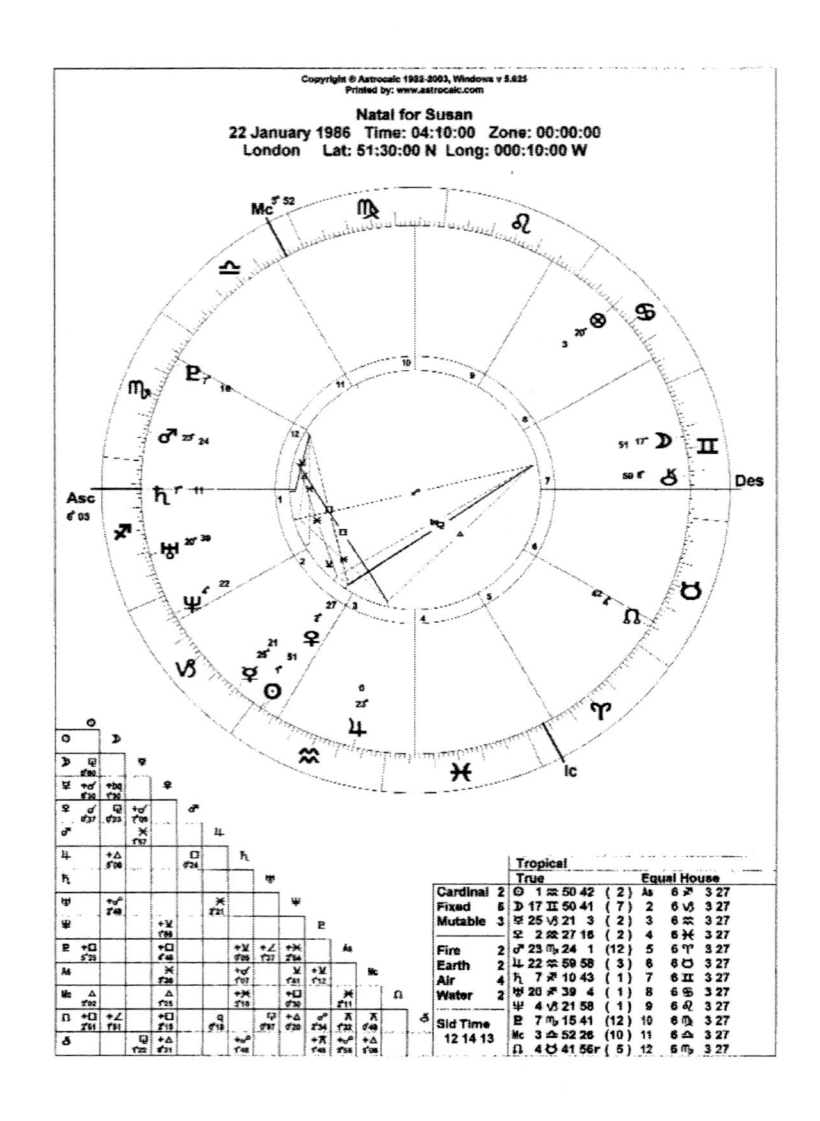

Chart 39

Twins - A Divided Horoscope (Charts 39 and 40)

Susan and Helen are (non-identical) twins. They have always wanted to be different from each other. Susan is generally demure, thoughtful, and pleasing. She is very conscientious and neat and sensible, and does very well at school. She is blond and left-handed. Helen is angry and selfish. She has always said she wants to be a boy and has refused to wear dresses. She does as little work at school as possible, although she is obviously intelligent. She is very dominant in her relationship to Susan. She is dark and right-handed.

Sometimes twins, although usually born only a few minutes apart from each other, have their Ascendants or Midheavens or even their Moons in different signs, which may account for significant differences in their characters and personalities. However, in the case of Susan and Helen, their horoscopes are virtually identical, so we need to look for ways in which they have - consciously or unconsciously - "divided up their horoscope" between them. We do not have to look very far to see the way their horoscope is naturally split between the "bucket" of all the planets except the Moon and Chiron and the "handle" formed by the Moon and Chiron, the essential link between the two parts being the close opposition between the Moon and Uranus, supported by the opposition of Chiron to Saturn. It is clear that Susan has chosen to live out the "bucket", and Helen has chosen to live out its "handle".

Susan's part of the horoscope is dominated by Saturn right on the Ascendant which, irrespective of anything else, accounts for her controlled, obedient, demure nature. And Helen's part of the horoscope is Moon opposition Uranus, accounting for her emotionally volatile, willful, unorthodox nature, exemplified in her expressed desire to be a boy, that is, to choose her own persona in defiance of the ways conventionally attributed to girls. Chiron opposition Saturn supports this, to the extent that Chiron's nature is a mixture of Saturn and

223

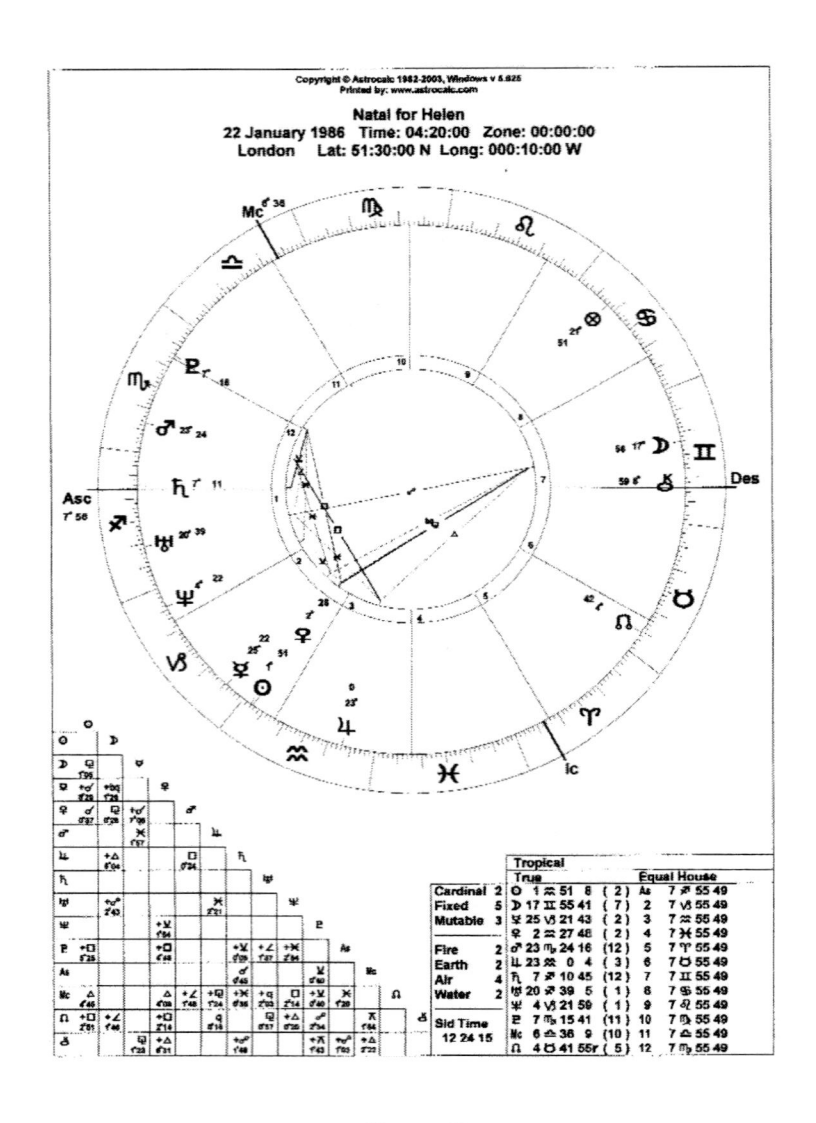

Chart 40

Uranus qualities, from which we can infer that she "projects" the Saturn quality of Chiron onto her sister and scorns this with the Uranian component of Chiron that she claims for herself.

One slight difference between Susan and Helen's horoscopes might account for the fact that Susan rather than Helen chose the Saturn-dominated part of their horoscope to live out, and Helen rather than Susan chose the Moon opposition Uranus part of the horoscope to live out. Susan's Saturn is definitely in the 1st house of her horoscope and virtually on the Ascendant, so it would be very difficult for Susan not to present herself to the world as the controlled and self-disciplined personality that she is. Helen's Saturn, although also virtually conjunction the Ascendant, is technically in the 12th house, where it is much more able to hide itself.

Ultimately, of course, the whole horoscope belongs to both Susan and Helen and it is likely that, in due course, when these twins are grown up and probably no longer living with each other, they will have to acknowledge and find expression for the parts they have, up till now, projected onto the other. Susan will need to acknowledge and release the volatile, rebellious, unstable part of her nature; and Helen will need to acknowledge and find expression for the conventional and disciplined part of her nature. Meanwhile, their horoscope and its obvious division by them is a wonderfully precise match for the description of their present natures as told me by their father.

Four Generations (Chart 41)

Chart 43 is the "family tree" of four generations of one family. You have met most of them already! Here is some information about the members of the family you have not yet met, together with some information about various relaionships

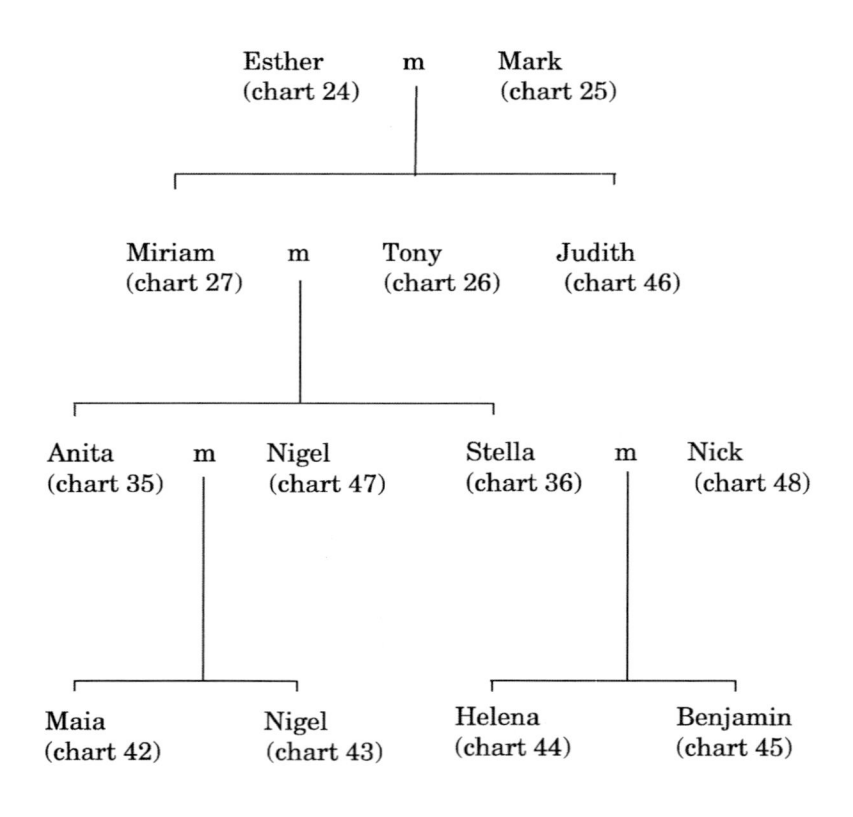

```
                    Esther    m    Mark
                   (chart 24)      (chart 25)
         ┌─────────────────┼─────────────────┐
      Miriam     m     Tony             Judith
     (chart 27)       (chart 26)       (chart 46)
    ┌──────────────────┴──────────────────┐
  Anita   m   Nigel           Stella   m   Nick
 (chart 35) (chart 47)       (chart 36)  (chart 48)
    ┌────────┴────────┐        ┌────────┴────────┐
   Maia           Nigel      Helena          Benjamin
 (chart 42)    (chart 43)   (chart 44)      (chart 45)
```

Chart 41. Four Generations

within the family. The horoscopes of the individual members of this family tree, together with the bi-wheels and composite charts of many of their relationships, are presented to you here as material for further study. You can use them to practise analyzing various kinds of intimate family relationships and also exploring the fascinating realm of inherited characteristics delineated in people's horoscopes.

Maia (Chart 42) is the elder daughter of Anita and Nigel. She is talented at music, playing both the piano and cello, and at imaginative writing, but she is, as yet (aged 16) not markedly ambitious, although she occasionally professes to wanting to be prime minister!

She has shown a marked propensity to flirtatious behaviour since she was very young. Notwithstanding her Mars conjunction Uranus conjunction Ascendant in Sagittarius, all square Sun, she is not at all boisterous or obviously aggressive, and, indeed, tends to be quite timid and a physical coward, but she hopes to be a prefect in her school next year. She reads voraciously and is extremely interested in the nuances of human relationships, in which she shows considerable maturity.

Leila (Chart 43) is the younger daughter of Anita and Nigel. She has sometimes been a worry to her parents because of her proneness to obsessive behaviour and morbid thoughts which she struggles to keep to herself. She is very sensitive to and considerate of other people's feelings but demands a lot of privacy and is reluctant to express her own deepest thoughts and feelings to others. She communicates most easily with her sister, Maia.

Leila is very talented at drawing and increasingly good at mathematics. From infancy, she has demonstrated great willful independence and unwillingness to be led by others.

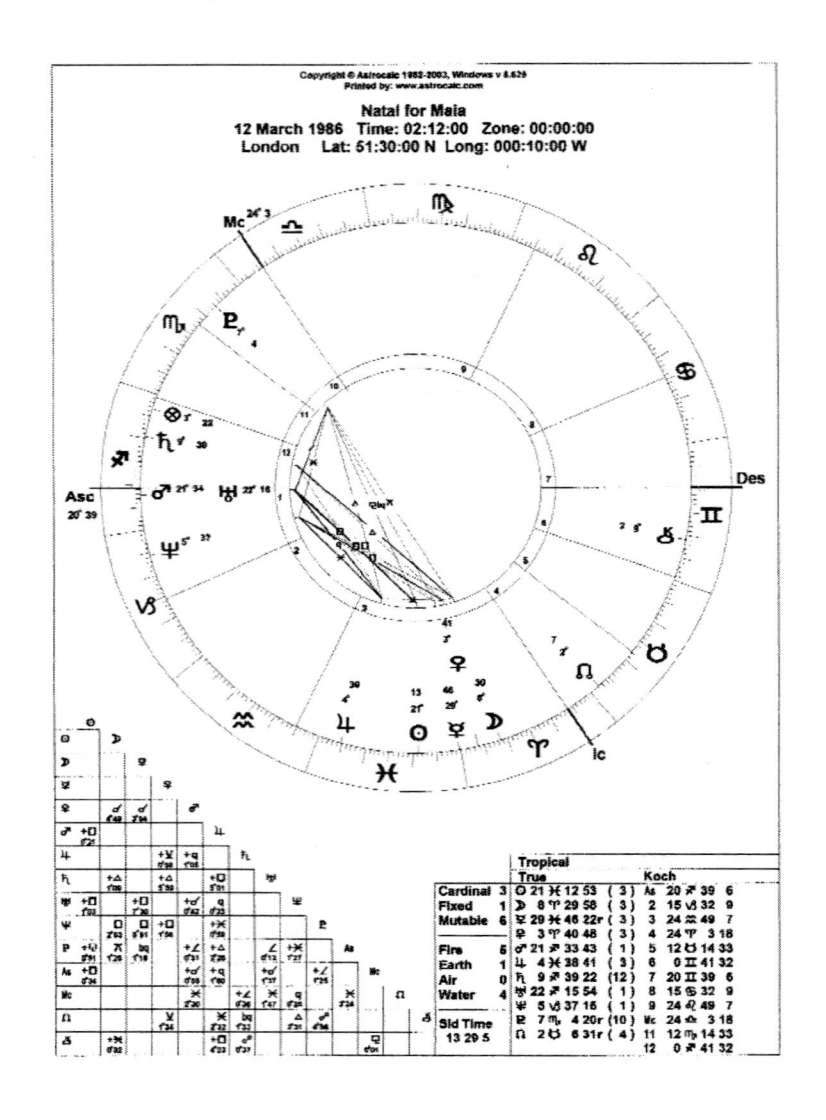

Chart 42

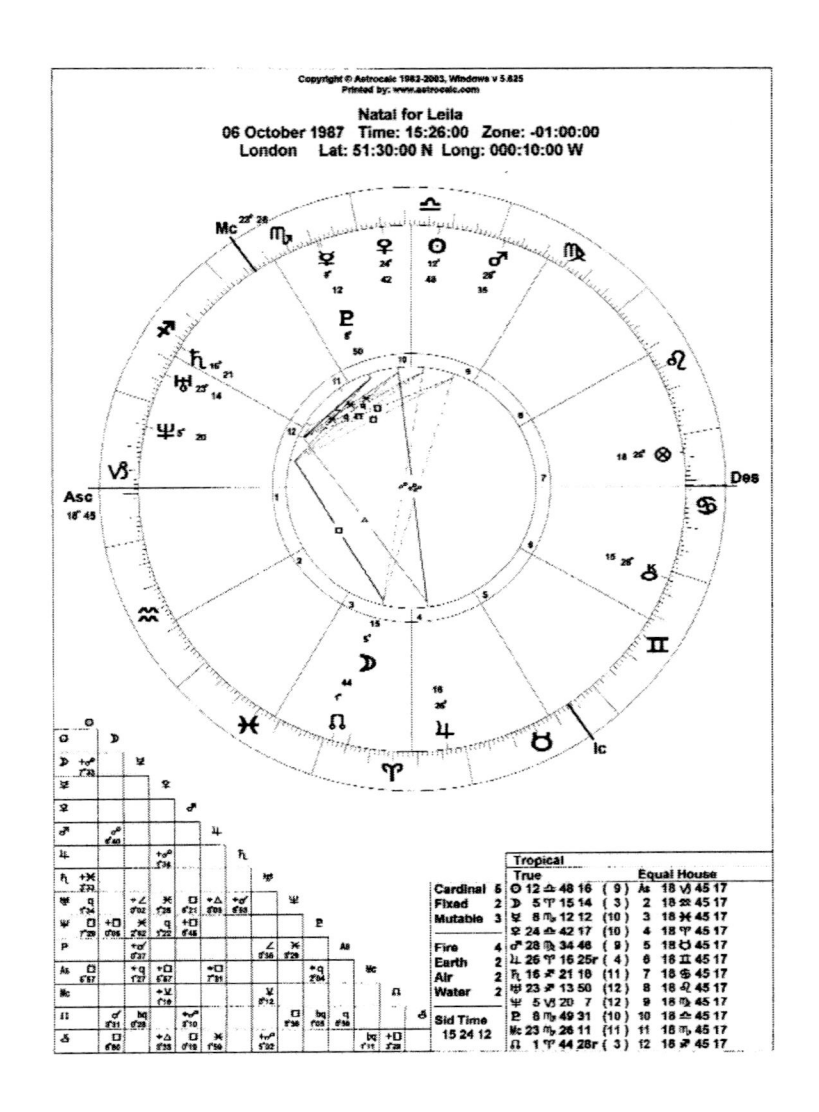

Chart 43

229

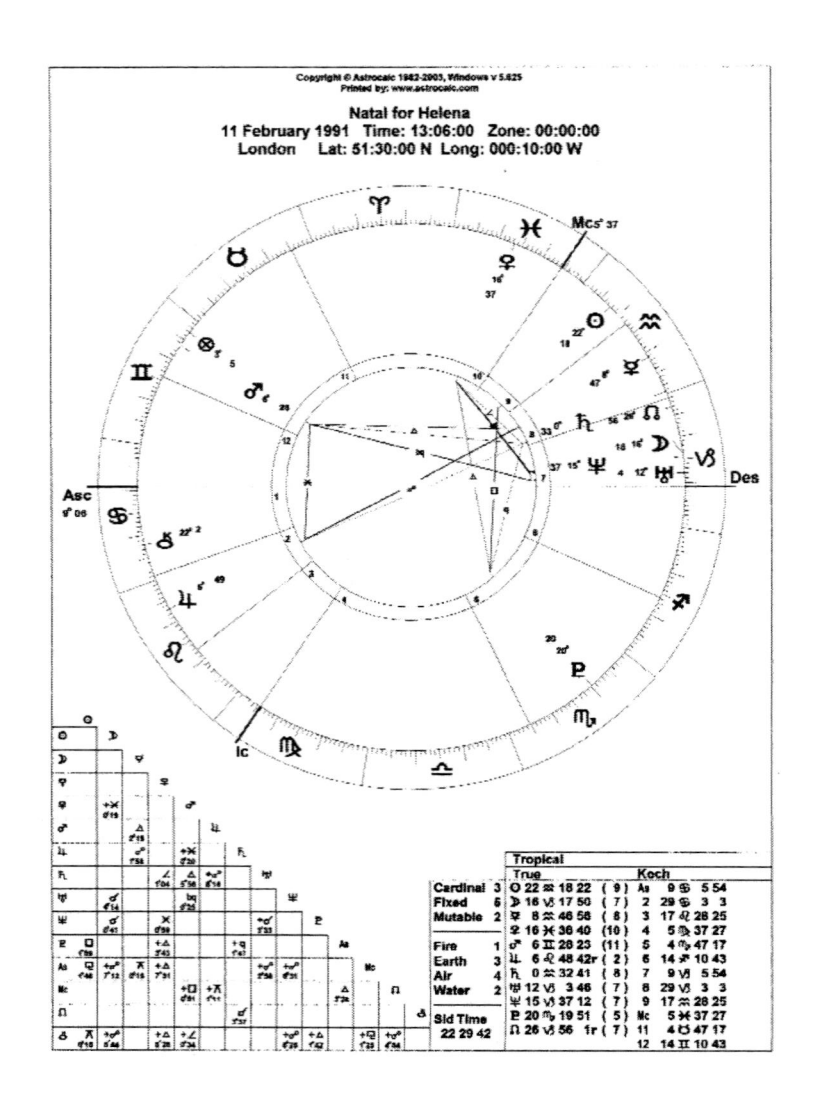

Chart 44

Helena (Chart 44) is the elder child of Stella and Nick. She is reserved in the expression of her emotions and extremely sensitive to criticism. She needs a lot of encouragement to think well of herself. She has started learning to play the violin which seems to be a very good medium for her to express the emotional poignancy that seems to be bottled up inside her. Physically, however, she is very robust and daring, loves climbing trees, roller- blading, and playing football. She generally gets on well with her brother, Benjamin, although she is manifestly jealous of his easy extraversion and quick responsiveness that does not come naturally to her.

Benjamin (Chart 45) is extraverted and a natural leader, articulate, and interested in everything. He is constantly "inventing" devices and games and asking questions, particularly of a scientific and factual kind. He is enthusiastically learning the piano. He often defers to his sister, Helena, rather than fight with her.

Judith (Chart 46) is the younger daughter of Esther and Mark and the sister of Miriam. In response to the unhappiness of their childhood family life, Judith defended herself against pain by "not noticing", in contrast to Miriam who wanted to talk about the family pain constantly. Miriam and Judith got on very badly, each professing to hate the other. As adults, despite the best intentions of both of them, they still rub each other up the wrong way and struggle to maintain amiable communication. Recently, in her fifties, in response to problems she was experiencing in her relationship to her own daughter, Judith embarked on a course of psychotherapy which enabled her to bring to the surface all her repressed pain from childhood, and resulted in her having some very hostile confrontations with her parents who, she now feels, were both very unloving, for which she feels very resentful.

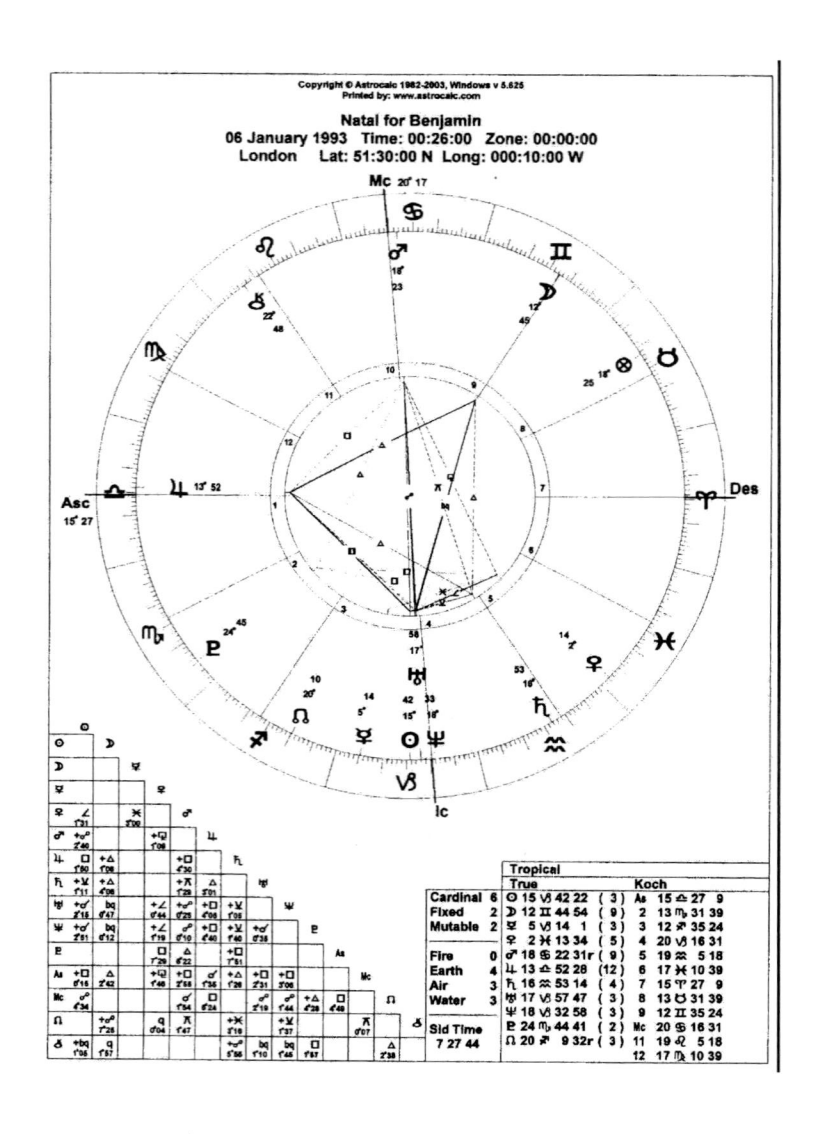

Chart 45

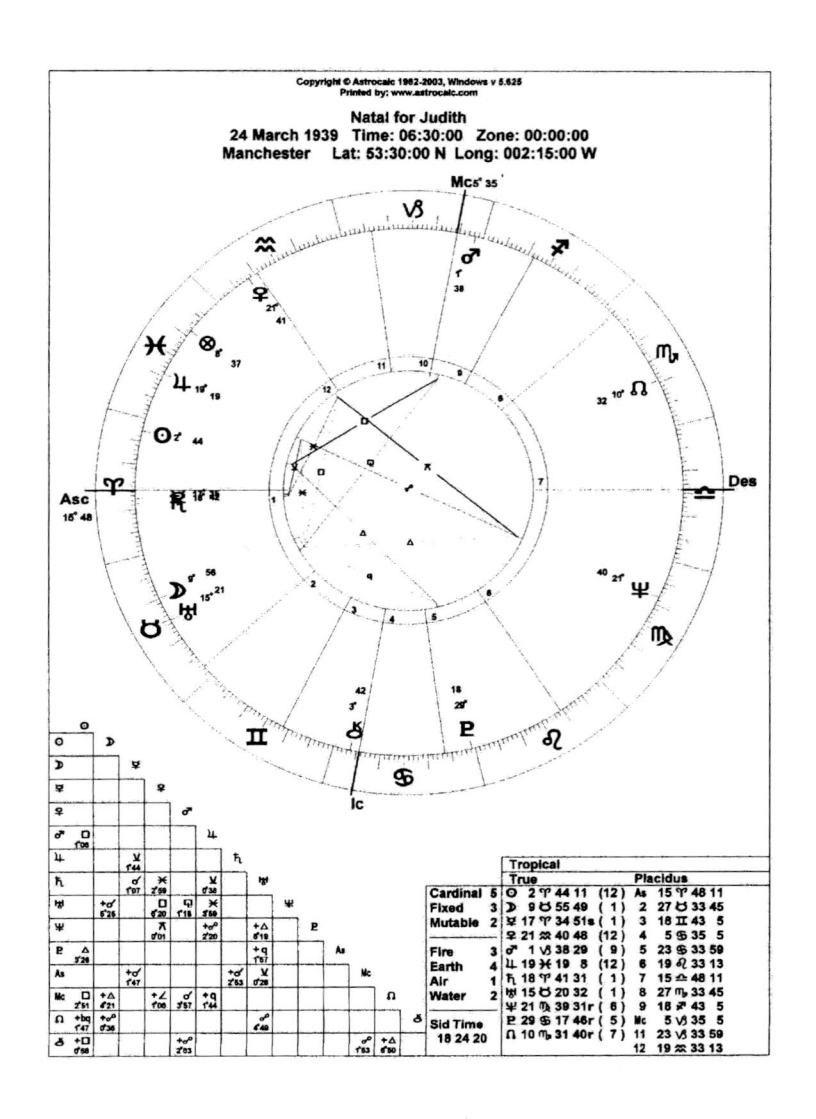

Chart 46

233

Exercises

1) Which 2 planets most represent the teaching of a parent to a child?

2) Which planet most represents a mother?

3) Which planet most represents a father?

4) Which planet most represents a baby?

5) Which planet most represents a young child?

6) Which planet is often associated with grandparents?

7) When does true adulthood begin?

8) Which planet is most used by parents to control their children?

9) Which planet is most used by parents to encourage their children?

10) Which houses of a horoscope are associated with parents?

11) Which birth position tends to make a child overly responsible?

12) Which planet is most associated with rebellion against parental authority?

13) Which 2 planets are most associated with compliance to parental authority?

14) Which planet is most associated with power struggles between family members?

15) Which planet is most associated with quarrelling in a family?

16) Which planet on the MC most tends to make a child loved by teachers?

17) Which planet on the IC or MC suggests an absent or sick parent?

18) Which planet on the IC or MC suggests an unstable parent?

19) Which planet on the IC or MC suggests a harsh parent?

20) Which planet on the IC or MC suggests an overly controlling parent?

21) Which house refers to relationships with brothers and sisters?

22. Using the facts you have been given, together with the horoscopes included in this book, you may like to practise analyzing any of the following relationships.

Parent-Child Relationships
Esther and Miriam (Charts 24 and 27)
Esther and Judith (Charts 24 and 46)
Mark and Judith (Charts 25 and 46)
Miriam and Anita (Charts 27 and 35)
Miriam and Stella (Charts 27 and 36)

Tony and Anita (Charts 26 and 35)
Tony and Stella (Charts 26 and 36)
Anita and Maia (Charts 35 and 42)
Anita and Leila (Charts 35 and 43)

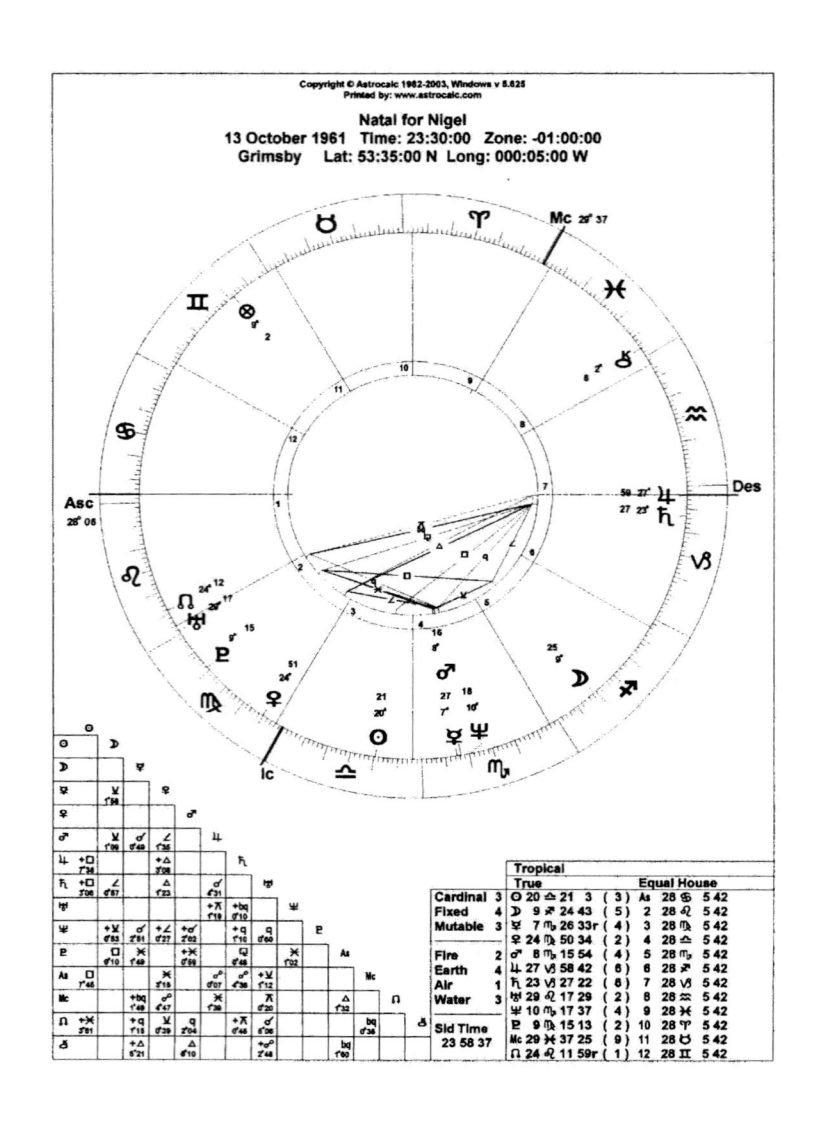

Chart 47

Nigel and Maia (Charts 47 and 42)
Nigel and Leila (Charts 47 and 43)
Stella and Helena (Charts 36 and 44)
Stella and Benjamin (Charts 36 and 45)
Nick and Helena (Charts 48 and 44)
Nick and Benjamin (Charts 48 and 45)

Sibling Relationships
Miriam and Judith (Charts 27 and 46)
Maia and Leila (Charts 42 and 43)
Helena and Benjamin (Charts 44 and 45)

Cousin Relationships
Maia and Helena (Charts 42 and 44)
Maia and Benjamin (Charts 42 and 45)
Leila and Helena (Charts 43 and 44)
Leila and Benjamin (Charts 43 and 45)

Grandparent-Grandchild Relationships
Esther and Anita (Charts 24 and 35)
Esther and Stella (Charts 24 and 36)
Mark and Anita (Charts 25 and 35)
Mark and Stella (Charts 25 and 36)
Tony and Maia (Charts 26 and 42)
Tony and Leila (Charts 26 and 43)
Tony and Helena (Charts 26 and 44)
Tony and Benjamin (Charts 26 and 45)
Miriam and Maia (Charts 27 and 42)
Miriam and Leila (Charts 27 and 43)

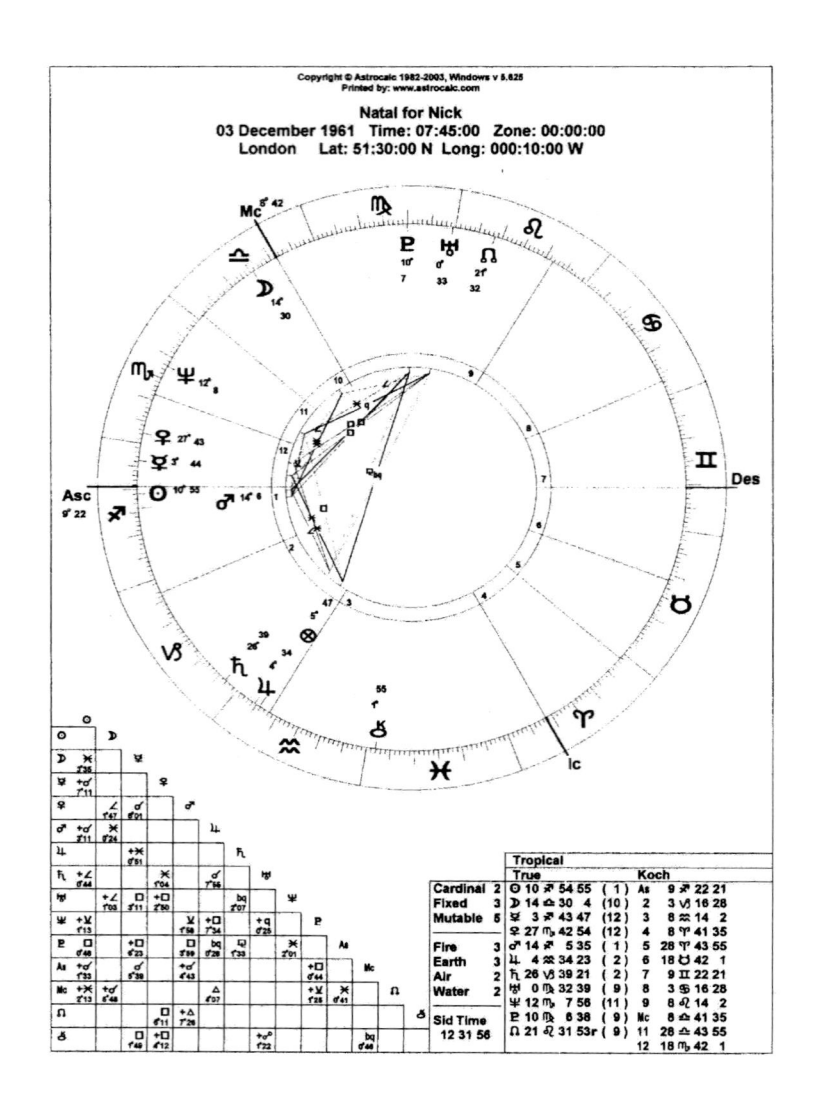

Chart 48

Miriam and Helena (Charts 27 and 44)
Miriam and Benjamin (Charts 27 and 475)

23) With the help of the family tree (Chart 41), write an essay (about 1,000 words) on the themes that run through the four generations of this family (excluding reference to Tony, Nigel, or Nick). Mention any interesting astrological factors that particularly link any of the individuals to any of the other individuals? What talents and what neuroses do you think are endemic to this family? Mention any relationships between any two members of this family that you think will be particularly harmonious and any that you think will be particularly inharmonious, giving your reasons.

Do realize that well-functioning families are not static but, through the tensions between their horoscopes, they dynamically help each other to grow throughout their lives.

Do remember that a brief analysis based on a few powerful key factors is much more meaningful than an attempt to say "everything".

Don't overwhelm and confuse your mind with too much detail.

Chapter 10
Friendship and Work Relationships

Summary: Friendship and work relationships are simpler than intimate love and family relationships. Friendships are usually chosen for the communalities (rather than complementarities) betweeen people. Successful work relationships are those which bring rewards to both parties. They may contain elements of brother and sister relationship, friendship, and parent-child relationships. One friendship and two work relationships are analyzed.

Friendship

Whereas our intimate love relationships, including family relationships, inevitably include challenges for us to extend the boundaries of our being to accommodate other people's different ways of being, we choose our friends precisely because they approve of and endorse the way we are. Thus friends tend to be very like each other in their beliefs, their interests, and their emotional responses to life. We feel comfortable with out friends especially because we know that we can rely on them to "be on our side" whenever other people or the world make us miserable. Very occasionally, we may be willing to accept some challenging confrontations from our "best friends" but, by and large, if it gets to the point where we feel an important part of ourselves is disapproved of by a friend, the friendship is likely to end.

Of course, people who are friends do not necessarily agree with or endorse all the characteristics of each other. But it is implicit, if not explicit, in the idea of friendship that we interact with our friends from the parts of ourselves and them that do agree with each other. Thus, most of us feel the need of a number of friends with each of whom we feel different parts of ourselves are enjoyed and approved of. So even if there are aspects between our own and a friend's horoscope that are potentially volatile, we tend just to keep those aspects between us out of sight and more or less out of action while we are with our friend. This is possible because, unlike our intimate loving relationships, we spend relatively little time with our friends and so can "be on our best behaviour" with them; whereas with intimate others with whom we share a home it is virtually impossible to avoid our more difficult inter-aspects with them coming to the surface at least from time to time.

Friendships are most common between near-contemporaries who, by definition, share a great many cultural and age-related assumptions, as described by the close identity between them of the positions in the zodiac of the outer planets in their horscopes. Apart from this, friends are generally chosen for the the obvious sympathy described by harmonious inter-aspects between the Ascendant, Venus, Moon, Mercury, Jupiter, and Sun aspects.

With inter-aspects between any two people's Jupiter and Ascendant, Jupiter and Sun, or Jupiter and Moon, these people will simply like each other, and no further justification for their friendship needs to be sought.

To the extent that it is possible to find some communalities between our own and any other human being's nature as described by our horoscopes, it is in principle possible for us to extend friendly goodwill to all other people, so long as the time we spend with them is short, and we can therefore readily only interact with them from however limited a number of positive aspects there are between us.

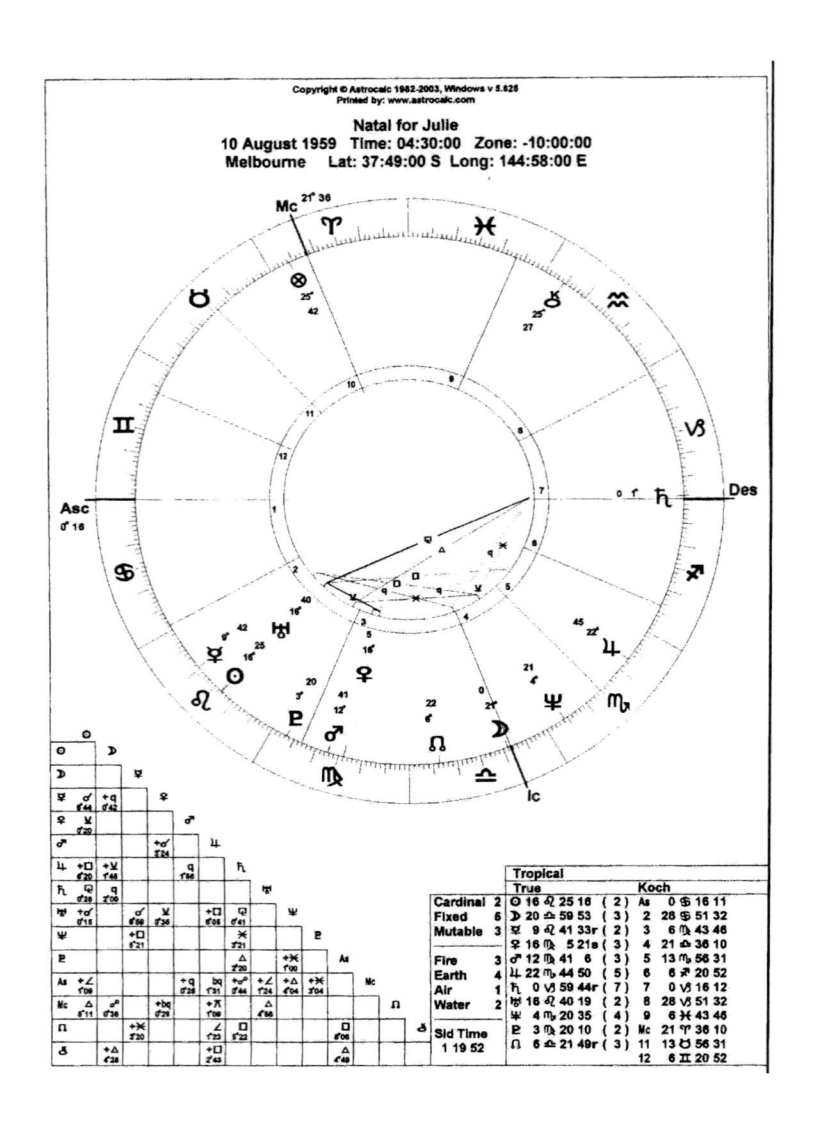

Chart 49

Anita and Julie (Charts 35, 49, 50, and 51)

Anita and Julie have been friends since they first met at school when they were five years old. Even though they now live thousands of miles apart they are in regular contact with each other and feel very loving towards each other. They agree that a core meaning of their friendship is the empathetic identification they have towards the painful family lives they both experienced in childhood. Julie's life was marred by her father's manic-depressive illness - he was many times hospitalized - and Anita's life was marred by the great unhappiness of her parents' marriage and their separation and subsequent divorce when she was 11 years old. (See "A Fourteen Year Marriage", Chapter 8.)

What are the parts of Anita and Julie that define the loving friendship between them?

Anita's Sun sign is Aquarius, Julie's is Leo. Julie appreciates Anita's cool detachment, Anita appreciates Julie's warmth, although, being a same-sexed friendship, they might also feel their "oppositeness" as dislike or rivalry.

Their composite chart is very powerful, having planets on all the angles, and the 6 planets in fixed signs testify to the durability of the relationship. The Sun-Mercury conjunction in the 1st house describes their general mutual interest in expressing themselves to each other, which is linked to the North Node conjunction Moon in the 5th house in Virgo, Mercury being the ruler of Virgo. So it is the creative (5th house) expression of their feelings (Moon) which is the deepest purpose of their relationship (North Node) and what they most often choose to talk about (Mercury). Uranus on the IC describes the volatile instability of their family backgrounds that they share. Venus, Mars, and Neptune conjunction the Descendant describes their willingness to share the experiences of their sexual relationships with each other.

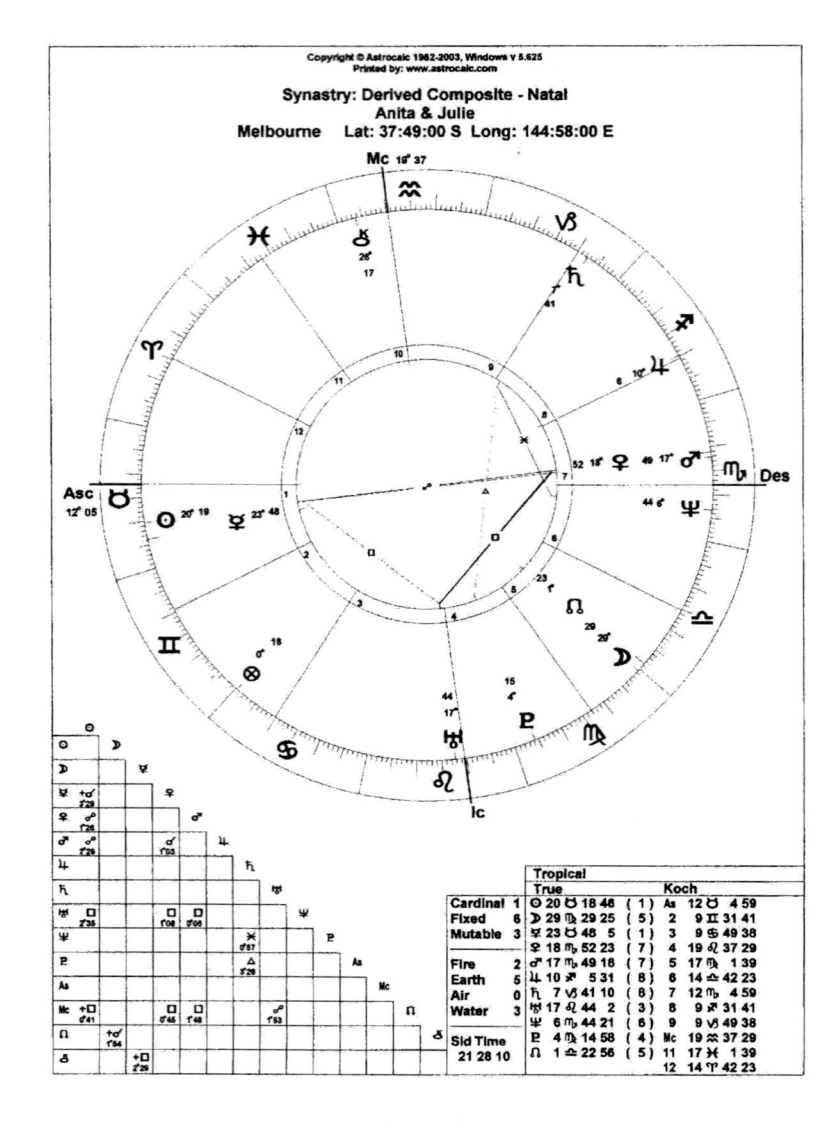

Chart 50

244

Chiron in the 10th house reflects their mutual need to heal their wounds as a "purpose" of their relationship and, being in Aquarius which is ruled jointly by Saturn and Uranus, links this purpose to the painful instability of their childhood family lives.

How do they each experience their relationship?

Composite to Julie	Composite to Anita
Sun trine Venus	Sun square Sun
Sun trine Mars	Sun trine Venus
Sun opposition Jupiter	Sun trine Mars
Sun square Uranus	Sun trine Saturn
Moon square Saturn	Sun square Uranus
Moon conjunction North Node	Sun trine North Node
Moon square Ascendant	Moon conjunction North Node
Mercury opposition Jupiter	Mercury square Sun
Mercury square Uranus	Mercury trine Venus
Venus square Sun	Mercury trine Mars
Venus conjunction Jupiter	Mercury square Uranus
Venus square Uranus	Mercury trine North Node
Mars square Sun	Mercury square Midheaven
Mars conjunction Jupiter	Venus square Sun
Mars square Uranus	Venus square Uranus
Jupiter trine Sun	Venus trine Ascendant
Jupiter trine Mercury	Mars square Sun
Jupiter square Venus	Mars square Uranus
Jupite square Mars	Mars trine Ascendant
Jupiter trine Uranus	Jupiter square Moon
Saturn trine Mars	Jupiter square Mercury
	Jupiter square Pluto

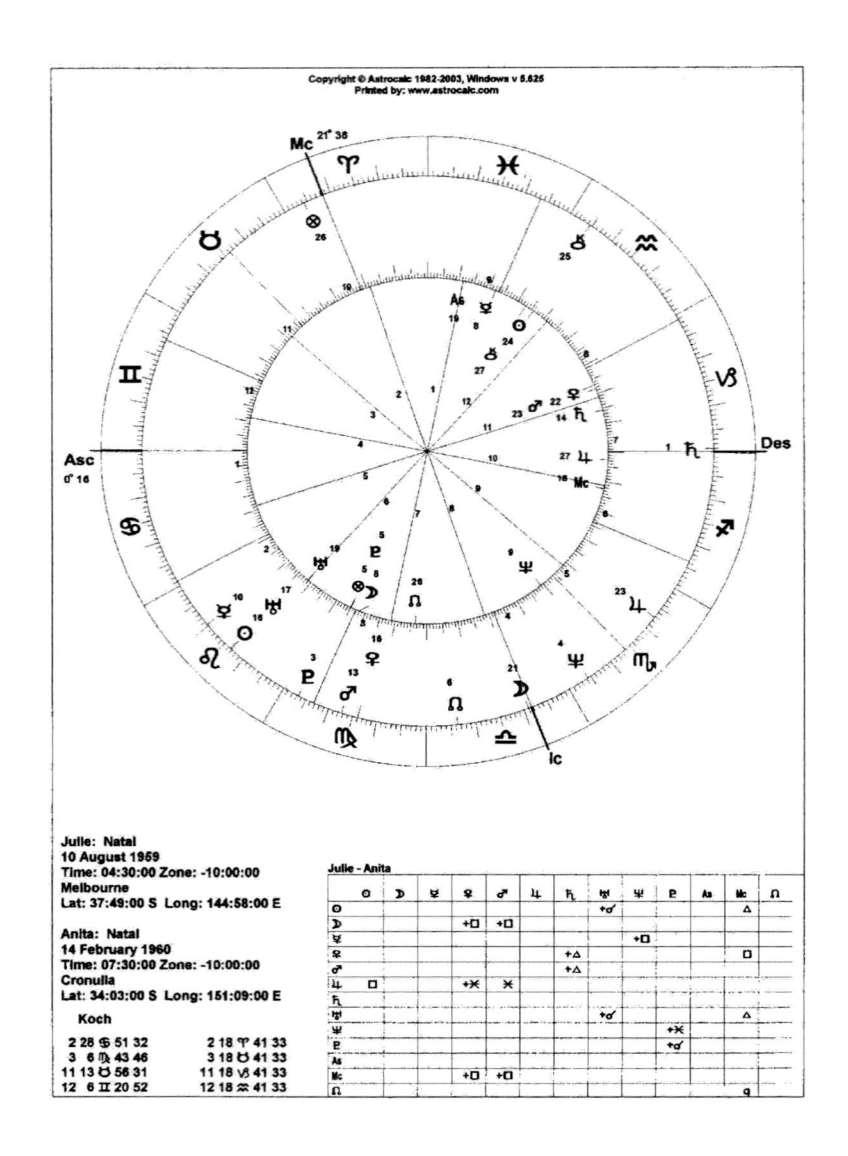

Chart 51

Jupiter square Ascendant
Jupiter conjunction Midheaven

Because they are near-contemporaries, the outer planets of the composite chart are so close to conjunction with the same outer planets in each of their individual horoscopes as to merely reinforce the aspects that each already experiences as an individual. So these aspects from the composite chart do not reveal anything significant and are not included in the list above. However, it is worth remembering that so many people tend to form relationships with their near contemp-oraries precisely for the fact of the communality of their outer planets which, of course, provides a background of many shared deep assumptions.

The most significant aspect in Julie and Anita choosing each other as friends is probably the Moon of the composite chart being conjunction the North Node in each of their individual horoscopes, confirming the deep purpose of the relationship as the sharing of feelings associated with their early childhood conditioning. Julie feels particularly joyfully expanded through the relationship, with the double-whammie of composite Venus conjunction her personal Jupiter and composite Jupiter square her personal Venus; and composite Jupiter also trines her personal Sun and personal Venus. Anita also feels expanded under the influence of the relationship through the composite Jupiter aspecting her personal Moon, Mercury, Pluto, Ascendant, and Midheaven, but four out of these five aspects are squares, suggesting she experiences some challenges to her ways of being through the relationship even while being enlarged by it.

Anita has 3 planets in cardinal, 3 planets in fixed, and 4 planets in mutable signs; Julie has 2 planets in cardinal, 5 planets in fixed, and 3 planets in mutable signs. There seems to be an absence of significance in this comparison.

Anita has 2 planets in Fire, 5 planets in Earth, 1 planet in Air, and 2 planets in Water signs; Julie has 3 planets in Fire, 4 planets in Earth, 1 planet in Air, and 2 planets in Water signs. In these distributions they are remarkably similar, and probably take for granted their shared practical, down-to-earth orientation to life.

Their Suns are opposition by sign; their Moons are semi-sextile by sign; their Mercurys are inconjunct by sign; their Venus's are trine by sign; their Mars's are trine by sign; their Ascendants are trine by sign. Thus it is their values, their ways of projecting themselves, and their general approaches to life that are particularly easeful in their relationship.

The major aspects of their synastry are:
Julie's Sun opposition Anita's Sun
Julie's Sun conjunction Anita's Uranus
Julie's Sun trine Anita's Midheaven
Julie's Moon square Anita's Venus
Julie's Moon square Anita's Mars
Julie's Moon square Anita's Saturn
Julie's Mercury square Anita's Neptune
Julie's Venus trine Anita's Saturn
Julie's Venus opposition Anita's Ascendant
Julie's Venus square Anita's Midheaven
Julie's Mars conjunction Anita's Moon
Julie's Mars trine Anita's Saturn
Julie's Mars conjunction Anita's Ascendant
Julie's Jupiter square Anita's Uranus
Julie's Saturn trine Anita's Moon
Julie's Saturn trine Anita's Pluto
Julie's Ascendant opposition Anita's Jupiter

The most significant friendship aspects in their synastry are probably Julie's Sun conjunction Anita's Uranus, making for excitement for Julie and a general sense of liberation for both of them; Julie's Venus trine Anita's Saturn making Julie lovingly understanding of Anita's inhibitions and pains; Julie's Venus on Anita's Descendant, making Julie like the intimacy between them; Julie's Mars conjunction Anita's Moon, making Anita feel energized in the expression of her deepest feelings by Julie; Julie's Saturn trine Anita's Moon, describing Anita' understanding sympathy for Julie's inhibitions and pain.

There are 4 aspects to Julie's Sun, 3 aspects to Julie's Moon, and 2 aspects to Julie's Saturn (apart from those Saturn aspects that are already present in her own horoscope). There are 2 aspects to Anita's Sun, 1 aspect to Anita's Moon, and 2 aspects to Anita's Saturn (apart from those Saturn aspects that are already present in her own horoscope). Thus, overall, while they both value their friendship highly, Julie seems to value it significantly more than Anita.

The double-whammies between them are:
Moon-Mars (conjunction, square)
Mercury-Neptune (square, trine) (although Anita has Mercury trine Neptune in her own horoscope).

So the central consciousness between them in their interactions with each other is the energetic encouragement of the other to express her feelings; and imaginative and compassionate verbal communication.

249

Anita's in Julie's House		Julie's in Anita's House	
Sun	8	Sun	5-6
Moon	3	Moon	4
Mercury	8	Mercury	5
Venus	7	Venus	6-7
Mars	7	Mars	6
Jupiter	6-7	Jupiter	9
Saturn	7	Saturn	6
Uranus	2	Uranus	5-6
Neptune	4	Neptune	8
Pluto	3	Pluto	6
Chiron	8	Chiron	12
Ascendant	9	Ascendant	4

Overall, the placement of planets in each other's houses confirms the deeply emotional nature of their relationship, the 4th, 8th, and 12th houses being the deeply emotional (Water) houses. The 4th refers to our deepest emotional conditioning, the 8th to our deepest transformative growth, and the 12th to our neurotic hang-ups. For Anita, her Sun in Julie's 8th house describes the essence of the relationship to her to encourage emotional transformation, which is supported by her Mercury also being in Julie's 8th house (and transformation is what they talk about a lot), and by Chiron in Julie's 8th house (by which transformation they are healed). Anita's Neptune in Julie's 4th house describes the overall confusion of Julie's childhood emotional experience, to which Anita is sensitively responsive.

Julie has her Moon in Anita's 4th house (responsiveness to Anita's childhood experiences), her Neptune in Anita's 8th house (sensitivity to Anita's quest to transform herself), her Chiron in Anita's 12th house (helping her heal her hang-ups), and her Ascendant in Anita's 4th house (identification with her childhood experiences).

Their straightforward liking of each other is described by Anita's Venus and Jupiter in Julie's 7th house, and Julie's Venus in Anita's 7th house.

Finally, what can we see in their individual horoscopes that throws light on their friendship?

Interestingly, their individual horoscopes reflect some profound complementarity between them that has not been obvious from any of our previous analytical techniques (except for their Suns being in opposition). Anita's planets are mostly above the horizon, emphasizing her life focus on her career and associations in the outer world; and the only three planets below the horizon are Moon, Uranus, and Pluto, all in the 6th house of work, which clearlly relate to all the other career-oriented planets.

Julie's planets, in contrast, are all, excepting Saturn, below the horizon, emphasizing the focus of her life being on private and personal rather than career relationships (although Julie is a professional doctor).

Thus each of them represents the fascination of the other's quite different focus on life, and enables them to extend the boundaries of their own consciousness of life's possibilities.

Anita's Sun is in Aquarius and her 11th house of friendship contains Venus and Mars in Capricorn, describing the importance of friendship to her and, being in Capricorn, that her friendships are very deep and serious. Julie's house of friendship contains no planets, but is ruled by Venus which is conjunction Mars in the 5th house of pleasure, so they share a Venusian and Martian attitude to friendship. And Julie's 11th house has Taurus on the cusp, an Earth sign, as is Capricorn on Anita's 11th house cusp.

Work Relationships
Like friendships, work relationships are more limited than intimate love and family relationships, but they are not as freely chosen as friendships. Work relationhips also encompass more of our time than friendships and usually tend to involve many of the houses of our horoscopes.

The main purpose of work relationships is material gain for both parties, so the position of Jupiter in the comparison between the charts is of special importance. Saturn is also important, representing as it does the responsibilities and duties entailed in a work relationship. Particularly relevant houses are the 2nd (money), the 6th (everyday work), the 8th (other people's money), and the 10th (career). When a work relationship takes the form of some kind of partnership, the Ascendant and Descendant become important as well. Work relationships may contain elements of brother-sister interactions (3rd house), parent-child interactions (IC-MC axis) and friendship (11th house). In all work relationships particular attention should be given to interactions between Mars, Saturn, Moon, Mercury, and the Sun in the two horoscopes. Difficult aspects between any of these planets are likely to be problematic in the relationship.

The Relationship Between Sigmund Freud and Carl Jung (Charts 33, 52, 53, and 54)

The relationship between Sigmund Freud and Carl Jung is a good one to analyze because it is known quite explicitly to have been a working relationship, a friendship, and a (quasi-) parent-child relationship, all of which is reliably recorded in the annals of history. Let us analyze it in a systematic way.

1. Sun-Sun. Freud's Sun is in Taurus, Jung's in Leo. This is a square aspect and therefore tense. While Jung respected Freud's Taurean depth, he was also irritated by Freud's fixity

in his points of view. Furthermore, Jung's Leo Sun wanted to shine in his own right, which it ultimately did after the two men's bitter quarrel and separation. With their Suns in fixed signs, both of them were stubborn.

2. The Composite Chart. The Sun, Mercury, and Uranus are all in the 7th house of partnership, describing the core of their relationship as purposeful, ambitious (Sun) excitingly innovative (Uranus) communication (Mercury). The Sun and Mercury are in Gemini, which is also on the cusp of the 7th house, reinforcing the communicative nature of the relationship, but the rulership of their partnership (7th house) is shared by Cancer (in which Uranus is also placed), pointing to the importance of childhood conditioning (Moon) in the theories they espoused. The Moon itself is in Taurus (Freud's Sun sign, bearing witness to him being the originator of the theory) in the 6th house (of everyday work). Psychoanalysis is, at core, a theory of human emotions, including their origins in childhood conditioning (4th house), the neuroses produced by childhood conditioning (12th house), and the potential transformation of these neuroses into healthy - especially sexual - functioning (8th house). Neptune, Saturn, and the North Node all in the 4th house respectively describe confusion and self-undoing through childhood conditioning, pain and inhibition through childhood conditioning, and achieving a deep understanding of these matters as the ultimate goal of the relationship. All of these being in the sign of Aries describes the assertive self-expression which is at the core of psychoanalysis as therapy. The 12th house (of neurotic inhibitions) has Scorpio on its cusp, and its ruler, Pluto, is in Taurus in the 5th house, describing the deep (Taurus - Freud's Sun sign again!) utterly transformative (Pluto) creativity (5th house) that the relationship was about. The 8th house (of transformation) is jointly ruled by the Moon and Sun (Cancer and Leo), respectively in the 6th house (of their everyday work) and the 7th house (of the partnership).

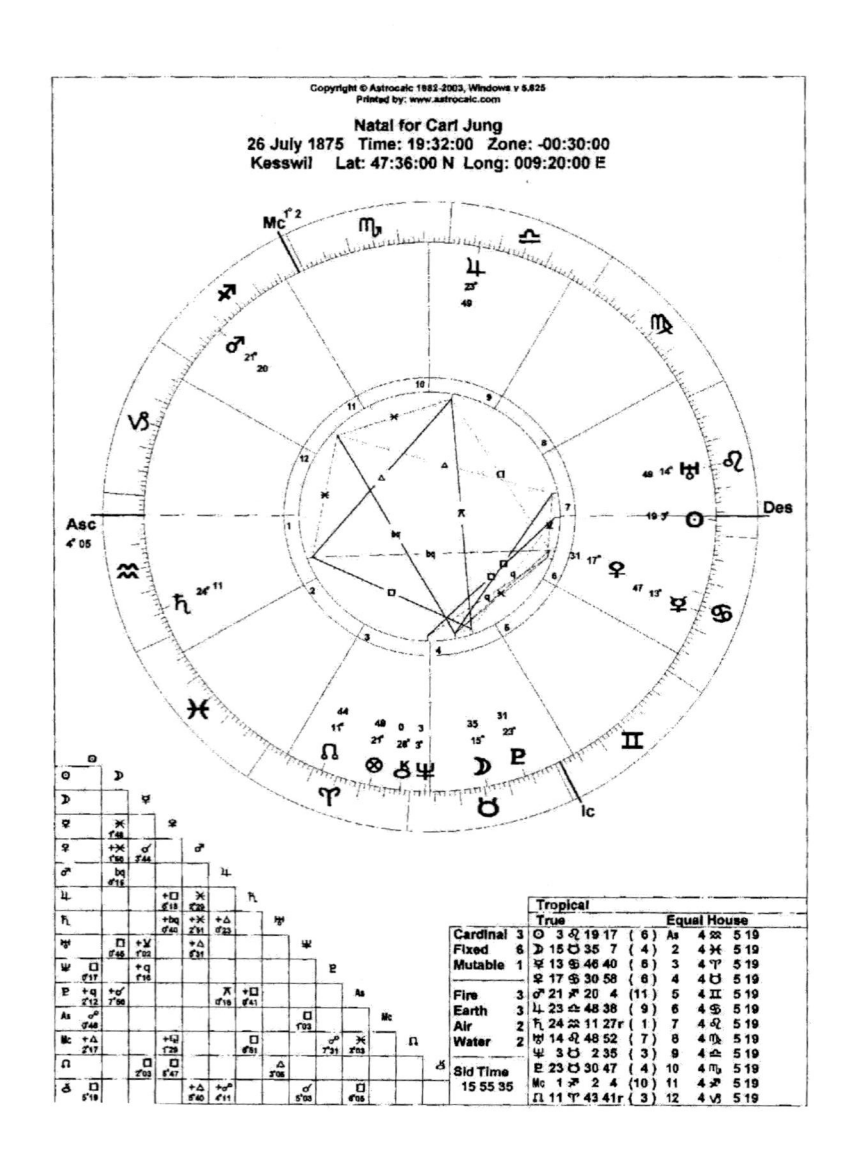

Chart 52

While cooperation was the goal between these two men (Libra Midheaven), Mars in the 11th house (of friendship) in close opposition to Pluto eventually overthrew that cooperation. With Sagittarius on the Ascendant, the "personality" of the relationship was intellectual, but the Ascendant ruler, Jupiter, is in square aspect to Neptune, making for tension and confusion between Freud's atheistic intellectuality and Jung's inclination to irrational religious thinking (Neptune).

Chiron in the 3rd house in Pisces describes psychoanalysis as the free-association (Neptune ruler of Pisces) talking (3rd house) that is the means of healing our wounds (Chiron), which is the essence of psychoanalytic therapy.

There are a number of powerful aspects from the composite chart to Freud's horoscope, describing how Freud experienced the relationship. He probably valued the energy the relationship brought to his own ambitions and self-discipline and deep probing of his goals (composite Mars opposition natal Sun, composite Sun conjunction natal Saturn, and composite Pluto conjunction natal Sun). But he was probably also disturbed by the challenge to his masculine assertiveness from the composite Uranus square his natal Mars.

For Jung, the relationship very harmoniously energized his intellectual ideas and the structuring of them (composite Sun trine his Jupiter and trine his Saturn), but the controlled assertiveness of the relationship was undoubtedly in conflict with his need to express his own ideas freely (composite Mars square natal Uranus, composite Jupiter opposition natal Mercury, and composite Saturn opposition natal Jupiter).

3. Element and Mode Comparison. Freud has 4 planets in fixed signs and 4 planets in mutable signs; Jung has 6 planets in fixed signs, and 1 planet in a mutable sign, making them both extremely stubborn. However, Jung is ultimately considerably more stubborn than Freud and a great deal less

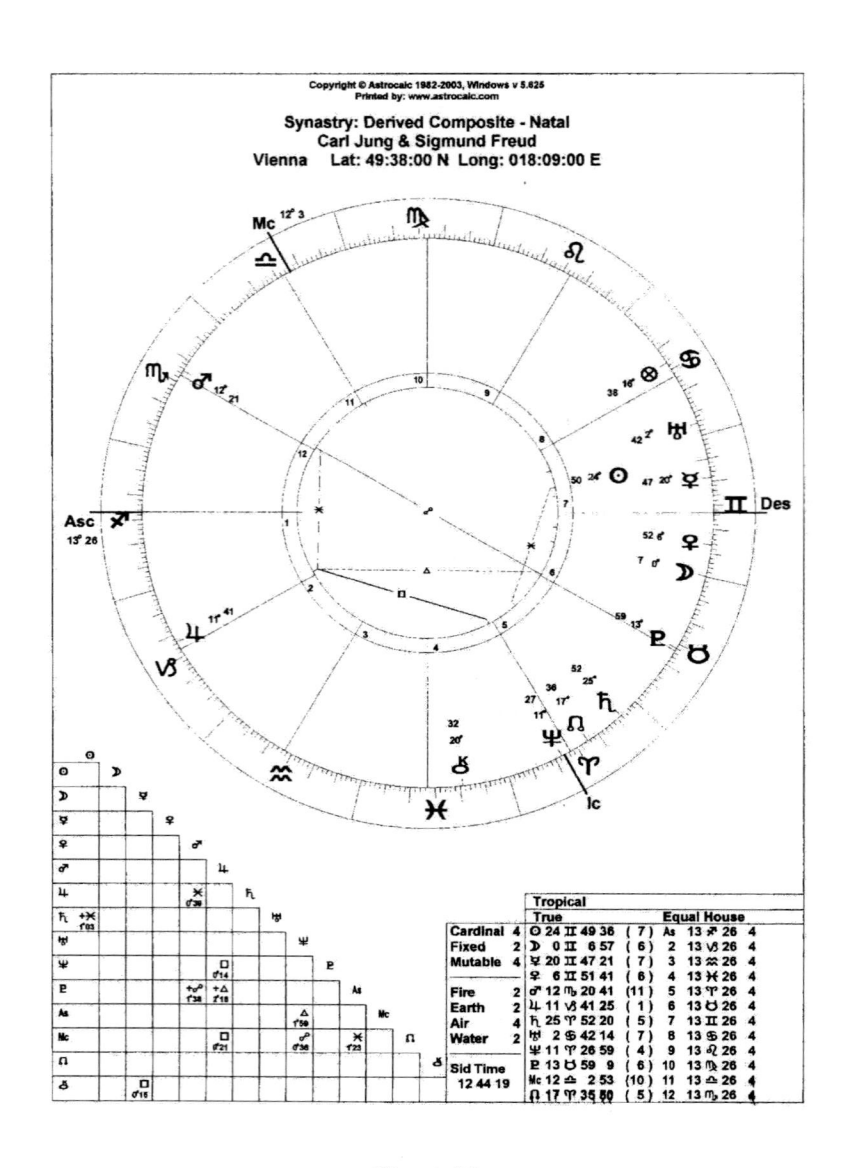

Chart 53

responsive (mutability) to other people's ideas (although Jung projected his own stubborn inflexibility onto Freud in his accusations against Freud). Jung has 3 planets in Fire signs compared with Freud's 1 planet in a Fire sign, confirming Jung's greater religiosity and inclincation to act on impulse and inspiration.

4.Inner Planet and Ascendant Comparison by Sign. The Suns are square; the Moon's are semi-sextile (similar in effect to inconjunct); the Mercurys are sextile; the Venus's are square; the Mars's are sextile; the Ascendants are sextile. Overall, compatibility and incompatibility are about even.

5. Aspects in Synastry to the Sun, Moon, and Saturn of Each. There are 3 aspects to Freud's Sun, 1 aspect to Freud's Moon, and no aspects to Freud's Saturn. There are 3 aspects to Jung's Sun, 2 aspects to Jung's Moon, and 1 aspect to Jung's Saturn.

The 3 aspects to each of the Sun speaks of the considerable mutual purposefulness of their relationship, but the total absence of aspects to Freud's Saturn and only 1 aspect to Jung's Saturn depicts the lack of durability of the relationship (if problems arise within it).

6. Double-whammies. There are no double-whammies in their relationship, so no particular issues dominate their consciousness of their relationship.

7. Outer to Inner Planet Synastry Aspects. Freud's Neptune square Jung's Mars describes Jung's felt need to fight what he experienced as Freud's deceptive and unfair subordination of his, Jung's, self-assertiveness. Freud's Pluto square Jung's Sun describes Freud's obsessive bid to control Jung, but Jung's ultimate triumph (Sun) over this is supported by Jung's insistent battle for freedom from Freud's domination (Jung's Uranus square Freud's Sun).

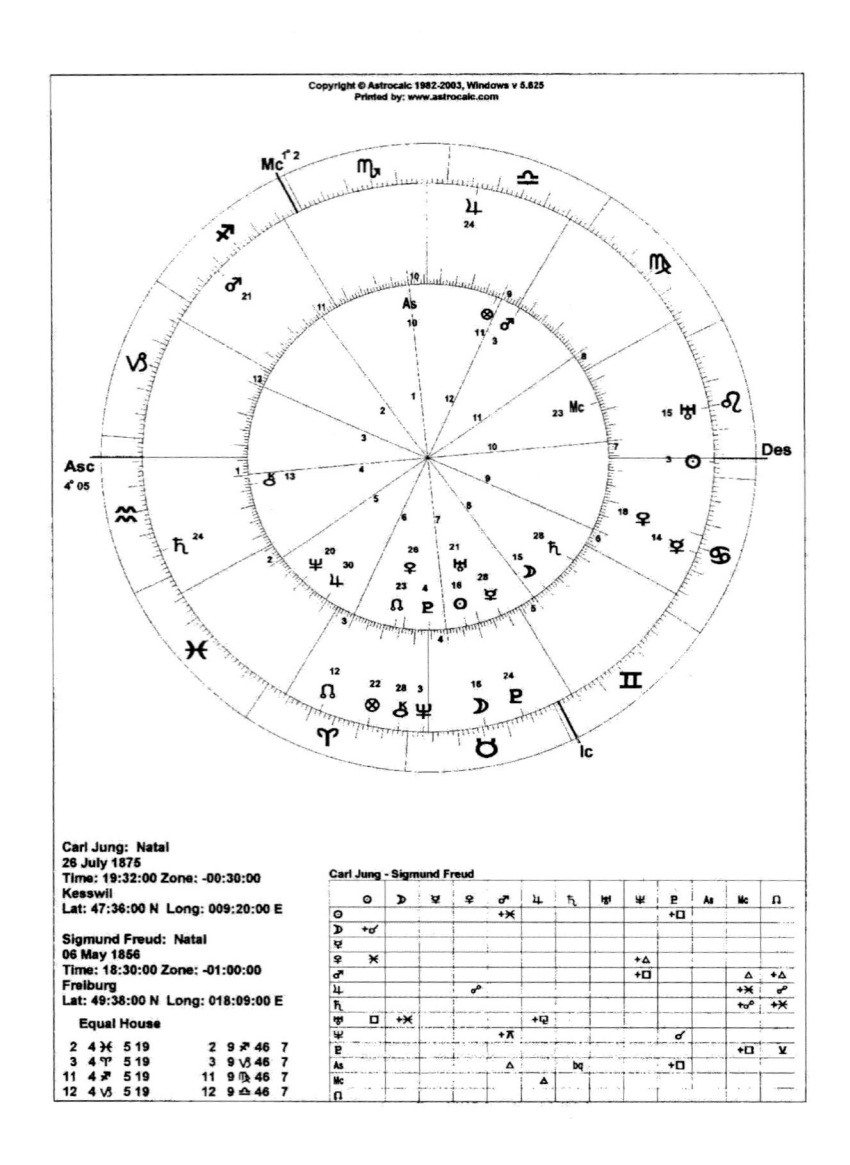

Carl Jung: Natal
26 July 1875
Time: 19:32:00 Zone: -00:30:00
Kesswil
Lat: 47:36:00 N Long: 009:20:00 E

Sigmund Freud: Natal
06 May 1856
Time: 18:30:00 Zone: -01:00:00
Freiburg
Lat: 49:38:00 N Long: 018:09:00 E

Equal House

2	4 ♓	5 19	2	9 ♐ 46	7
3	4 ♈	5 19	3	9 ♑ 46	7
11	4 ♐	5 19	11	9 ♍ 46	7
12	4 ♑	5 19	12	9 ♎ 46	7

Chart 54

258

8. Planets in Houses. Jung's Sun is in Freud's 9th house, describing his ambitious attraction to Freud's intellect and philosophy; but his Uranus is conjunction Freud's Midheaven, describing both his attraction to Freud's originality and his need to express his own autonomous originality in relationship to Freud. Freud's Sun and Uranus are in Jung's 3rd house, indicating Freud's attraction to Jung as somebody with whom he could freely communicate.

9. Other Aspects in Synastry. The closest and by far the most significant aspect between Freud and Jung is Freud's Sun in virtually exact conjunction with Jung's Moon. Freud was the father (Sun) and Jung was the obedient child (Moon) until "the child" rebelled against the dominant authority of "the father", as he was bound to do with all the strength of the power struggles contained in the other inter-aspects between their horoscopes, especially Jung's Sun square Freud's Pluto and Jung's Uranus square Freud's Sun.

10. The Individual Horoscopes in Reference to the Relationship. The Sun, Mercury, Uranus, and Pluto all in Freud's 7th house can be seen to describe the focus of his life's work being on intimate relationships. However, it also suggests his personal need for partnership in order to fulfil his ambitions. He did, of course, have many acolytes, but Jung was that special intimate other who fulfilled his 7th house needs. Jung also had Sun and Uranus in his 7th house, and this is perhaps the greatest communality between them, making for the friendship side of their relationship. However, this communality also united them in their contradictory needs for partnership (Sun in the 7th house) and freedom within any partnerships they each formed (Uranus in the 7th house).

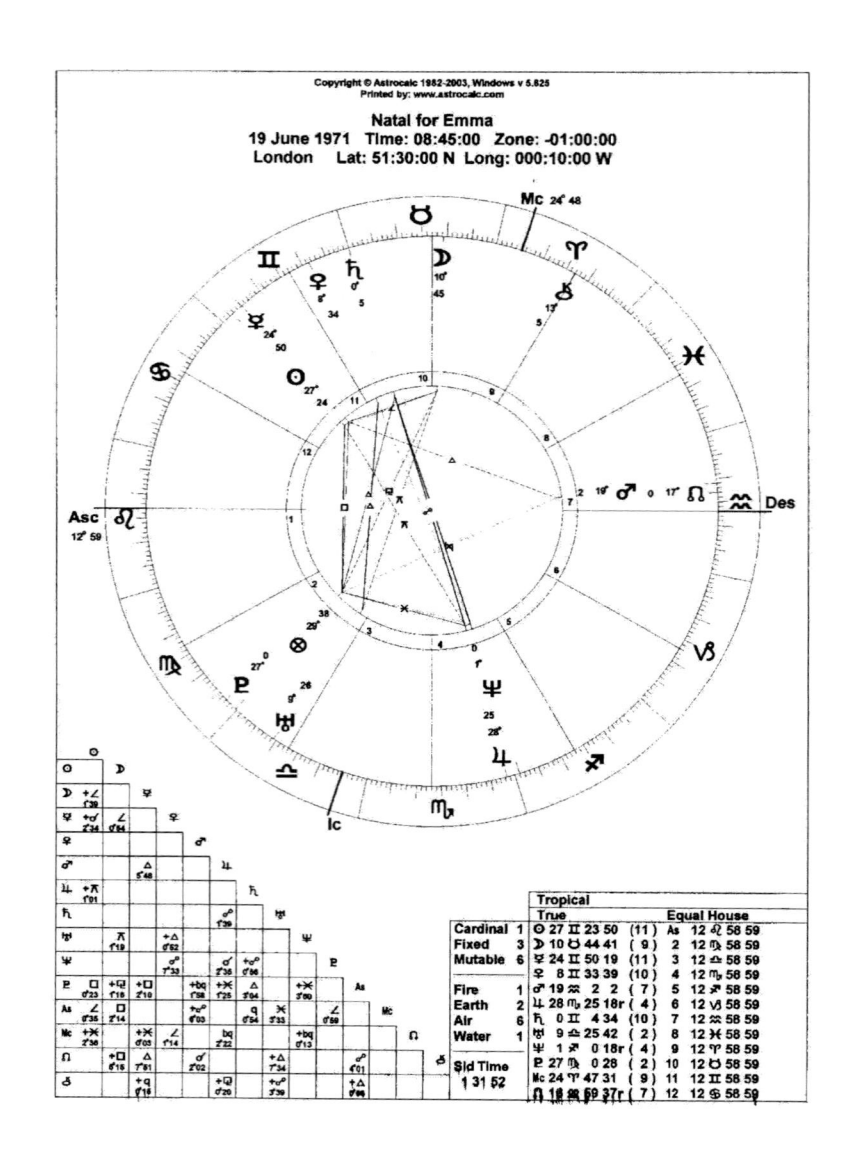

Chart 55

The Relationship Between Emma and Her Boss (Charts 55, 56, 57, and 58)

Emma works in a printing and photocopying shop. Her boss is the owner of the shop. She says they get on very well. Why?

Her Sun in Gemini and his in Aquarius are exactly trine by degree as well as sign. They are in communicative Air signs, which describes both the core harmony between their essential natures and the communicative ease with which they both relate to their customers, and also their liking for the communicative nature of the work they actually do.

In their composite chart, Uranus (technology) is dominant in the third house of communication, is the ruler of the Midheaven (career), is in the sign of Cancer (looking after people's needs), and the ruler of this third house is the Moon, which is conjunction Venus in the 11th house (being pleasant in associations in the world-at-large). The 11th house, in turn, with Pisces on the cusp is ruled by Neptune, which is in the 6th house of everyday work (using their imaginations to serve and fulfil their duties), which is in opposition to the Sun-Mercury conjunction (imagination serving their core communicative task). The 6 planets in cardinal signs describe the enthusiastic "get-up-and-go" spirit of their relationship. The Descendant (their individual relationship to each other) has Sagittarius on the cusp, which is ruled by Jupiter, which is in the 9th house (of publishing) conjunction Mars, describing the enthusiasm and energy they jointly bring to their work.

He has 3 planets in cardinal signs while she has only 1, which enables him to be the natural leader in their relationship (which is appropriate for a boss to an employee) and her 6 planets in mutable signs compared with his 3 underline her willingness to be led by him.

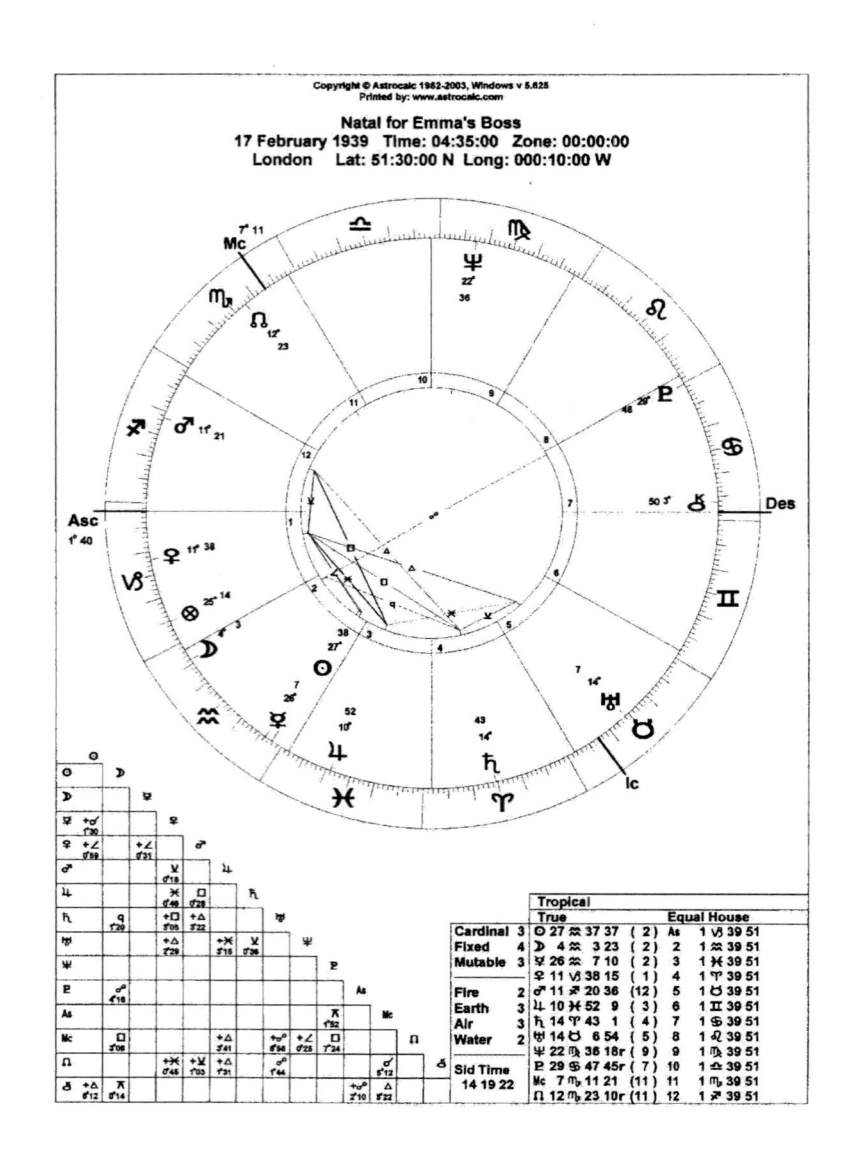

Chart 56

Their Mercurys are trine by degree as well as sign (easy flow of everyday communication) and their Mars's are sextile by sign (compatible ways of asserting themselves).

There are 4 synastry aspects to his Sun (she is significantly connected to his ambitions_ and 3 aspects - all trine - to his Moon (he likes her). There are 2 aspects - both harmonious - to her Sun (their relationship is pleasingly relevant to her ambitions) and 3 aspects to her Moon (she responds to him). His Uranus conjunction her Moon probably adds a frisson of excitement and maybe a pleasant flirtatiousness to their relationship.

The double-whammies in their synastry are: Sun-Sun (trine), Sun-Mercury (trine, trine), and Mercury-Mercury (trine), all of which are excellent for their working relationship.

His Mercury is very closely sextile her Midheaven (he tells her things that promote her career); and his Mars and Saturn both trine her Ascendant, describing her easy ability to respond to his assertive demands of her and the controls he imposes on her.

Emma's 6th house (employment) has Capricorn on the cusp, which is ruled by Saturn, which is in her 10th house (career), so she clearly works very hard in the fulfilment of her everyday work responsibilities in the name of her long-term career goals. Her Moon is also in her 10th house of career, describing her need to be in touch with the public (which her present job gives her) and also to be femininely responsive in her career, which is fulfilled in her happy relationship to her dominant male boss.

Emma's boss's 6th house (employees) has Gemini on the cusp, which is Emma's Sun sign, and is ruled by Mercury in the 2nd house (earning money) conjunction Sun (his overall ambitions), which is exactly trine Emma's own Sun and Mercury. What a great relationship!

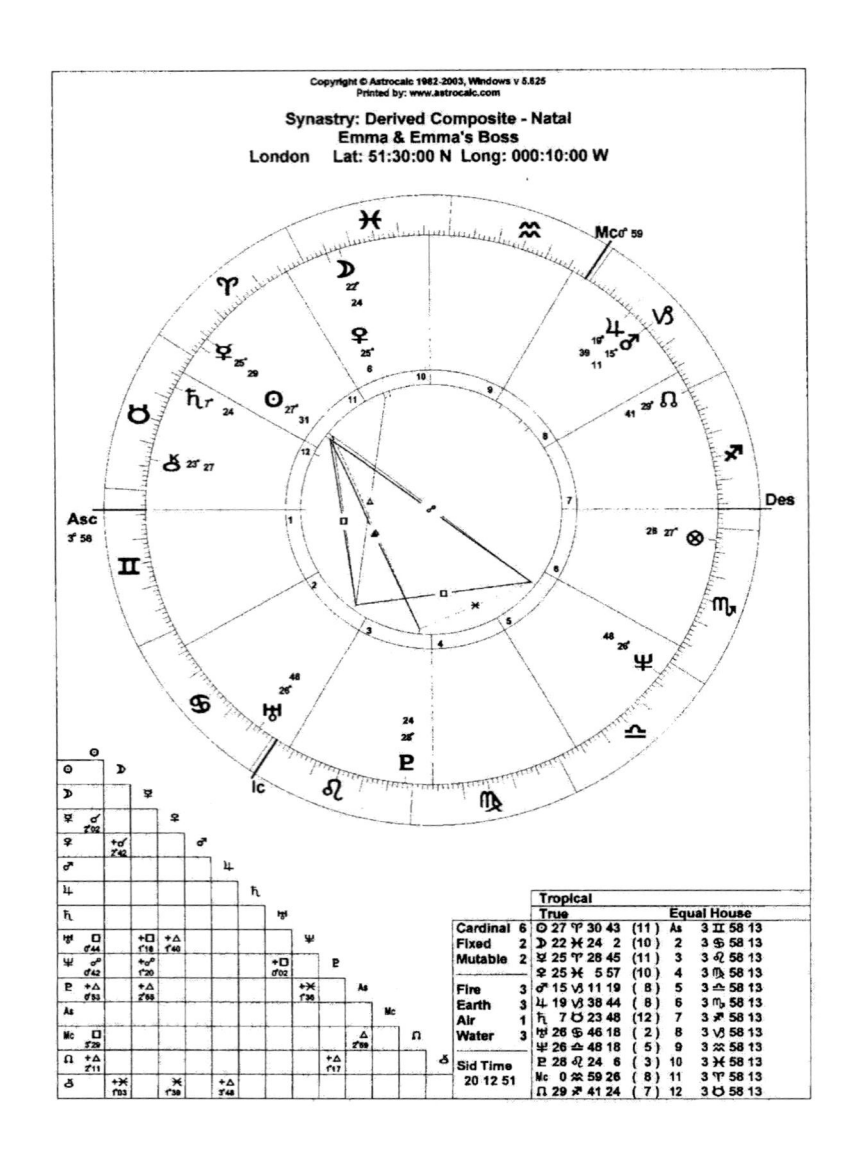

Chart 57

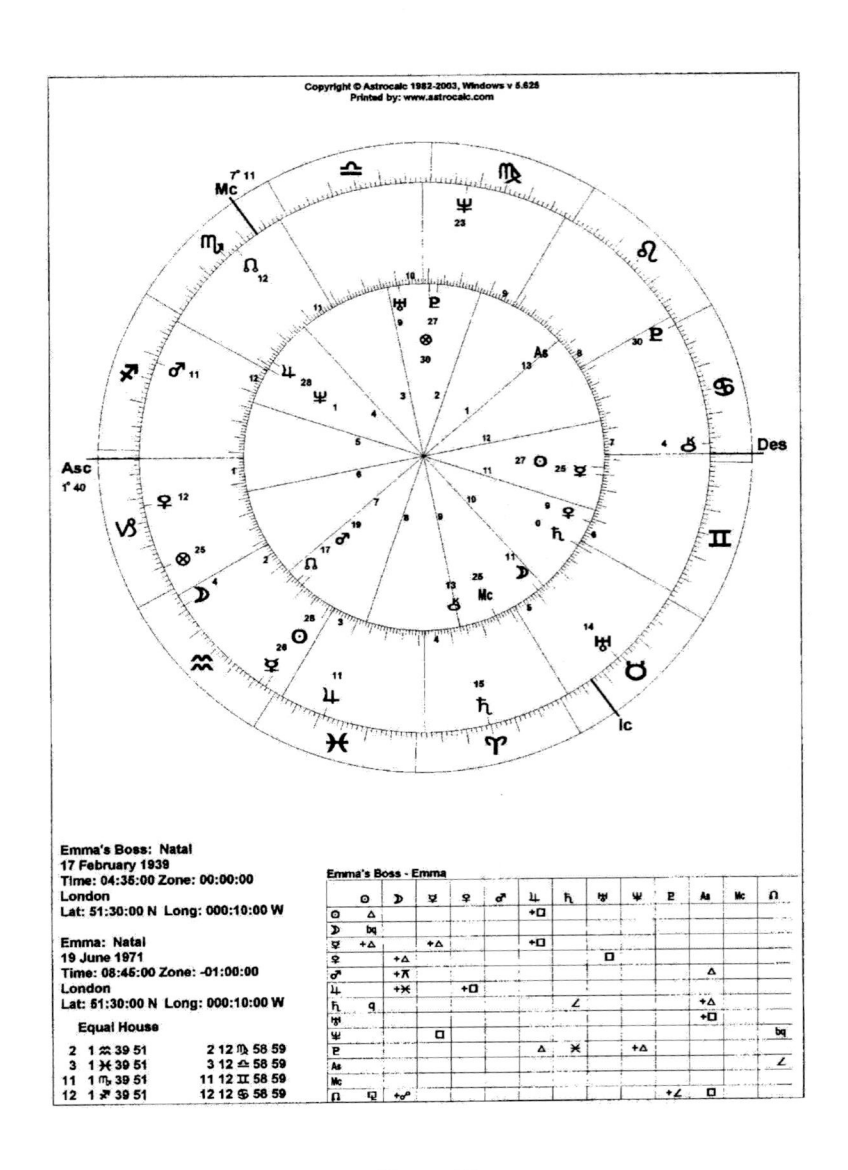

Emma's Boss: Natal
17 February 1939
Time: 04:35:00 Zone: 00:00:00
London
Lat: 51:30:00 N Long: 000:10:00 W

Emma: Natal
19 June 1971
Time: 08:45:00 Zone: -01:00:00
London
Lat: 51:30:00 N Long: 000:10:00 W

Equal House

2   1 ♒ 39 51   2 12 ♍ 58 59
3   1 ♓ 39 51   3 12 ♎ 58 59
11 1 ♏ 39 51   11 12 ♊ 58 59
12 1 ♐ 39 51   12 12 ♋ 58 59

Chart 58

Exercises

1. What is the most important foundation of friendship?

2. Which house rules friendship?

3. What is the most important foundation of working relationships?

4. Which houses are associated with our working lives?

Do be aware that important significators in any relationship will be shown several times, in different aspects and configurations.

Don't lose sight of the wood for the trees.

Chapter 11
Relationships and Life Cycles

Summary: At every moment of our lives our overall response to our situation and to other people is informed by three contexts: the unchanging attributes of our humanity; our present stage of development in life; and our individuality. The relative influence of each of these contexts on a given moment may vary although, broadly speaking, our "stage of development" tends to predominate in childhood, our individuality in our middle years and, ideally, as we grow old, the spirituality associated with our humanity, especially in our coming to terms with aging and death. This chapter outlines the astrological "stages of development" in childhood and adulthood, including the psychology of parenting.

General Considerations
Irrespective of our individuality, we are all the same in being united in our lifelong concerns with pain and death, good versus evil, conflicting quests for excitement and security, and the overall quest for meaning in our lives. These are constant dynamic components of our minds that we need to be implicitly and explicitly aware of in every consideration of a horoscope of a human being.

Between our life-long communalities with all other human beings and the ultimate uniqueness of our individuality represented by our natal horoscopes, there are stages of life that unite us in special ways with our near-contemporaries.

It is often valuable and important to refer to these stages in consideration of the overall meaning of what a person is experiencing at any particular time.

Consider a number women having babies. There are many transits that may describe the particular meaning of the event to each woman. For example, one may have Jupiter transiting her 5th house, another Saturn transiting her Midheaven, and another may have Pluto transiting her Moon ... all of which will reflect the different experiences that these women will have of the same external event. And in addititon to these individualistic factors each of their experiences of childbirth will also be modified by the stage of life that she happens to be living in at that time.

The transits of the inner planets - Sun, Moon, Mercury, Venus, and Mars - have relatively fleeting effects on our lives, although an inner planet transit often triggers an outward manifestation of a long process of change delineated by a major outer planet - Chiron, Uranus, Neptune, or Pluto - transit to our horoscopes.

Jupiter and Saturn are neither wholly personal planets as are the inner planets nor wholly ego-transcending energies as are the outer planets. Rather they are intermediary between inner and outer and operate essentially at the social level of our lives.

The Jupiter cycles in our lives tend to bring optimistic new beginnings and general feelings that all is all right with the world. Being human, we often tend to expect more of Jupiter's transits than they can deliver.

The Saturn cycles in our lives bring us responsibilities and hard work and they remind us of our mortality and the general limitations of our willfulness. Being human, we tend to resent Saturn and fear its effects on our lives although, paradoxically, our submission to its "reality principle" brings us our greatest and most lasting rewards in the form of achievement and wisdom.

The cycle of Jupiter is most obviously manifest in unmitigated joyous expansiveness in the innocence of our childhoods. The cycle of Saturn becomes increasingly conscious to us in maturity.

Following, is a brief outline of the universal astrological stages of life in terms of the experiences of the cycles of the outer planet transits which are experienced universally at approximately the ages given. However, because of its extremely erratic orbit, people experience the transiting cycle of Chiron at widely diverse ages. Only Chiron's return is experienced by everybody at the same age of about 51.

For the stages of childhood, I have included the Jupiter conjunction and opposition to its natal place. I have also described the specific challenges facing all parents at particular stages of their children's development.

Five to Six
Jupiter opposition Jupiter and Saturn sextile Saturn.

The typical five-year old is a charming delight. The exuberance of Jupiter and the self-discipline of Saturn combine and the child seems like a perfectly formed miniature adult. Many children are just starting school at this age, the Jupiter opposition being manifest as great happy enthusiasm for what school teaches, and the Saturn sextile ensures that the child easily accomodates to the new restrictions imposed on him by the rules of school. Now, for the first time, he begins to have to fend for himself, away from the protection of his mother, and this is also a significant and poignant moment for parents as they become fully conscious that healthy parenting means letting go of their dependence on their child's dependence on them. But, by and large, this is a stage of equilibrium and balance and the child moves forward confidently to enlarge his world and achieve his goals without being difficult to control or being aggressively competitive with his peers.

But beneath this delightful surface, in his relationships to his mother and father, the child is in the middle of the most influential experiences of his life. He is learning about sexuality and all the other emotions associated with forming satisfactory relationships to other people. He is becoming emotionally literate, and the parents' insightful handling of these issues will be the basis of the child's happy relationships with other people for the rest of his life.

At five, the child is in the middle of the stage begun at about three and ending at about six, when every little boy tends to fall in love with his mother and every little girl falls in love with her father. The parents' roles at this stage of the child's development demand that they express the best possible compromise between reinforcing the child's sexual self-esteem while denying it the specific gratification it presently seeks. The boy wants to feel that his mother loves him more than she loves his father; the girl wants to feel that her father loves her more than he loves her mother. It is imperative that the child be defeated in these aims. The child experiencing him- or herself to be the victor in this battle is one of the greatest tragedies that can occur with respect to his or her subsequent lifelong ability to form satisfying relationships with the opposite sex and, indeed, to establish and maintain a satisfying self-image and satisfying attitudes to the world and life in general. The parents' effective role at this stage of the child's development is to walk the tightrope of offering a just-right balance of indulgence and control of the child's emotional demands. A girl profoundly needs her father, at this stage, to express admiration for her looks and her clothes and to pay homage to her sweetness and charm; and a boy profoundly needs his mother, at this stage, to express admiration for his attempts to impress her with his strength and bravery and power. Thus, when Daddy comes home from work and his daughter rushes to kiss him before Mummy can, a loving mother understandingly allows this to happen, and a loving father plays with his daughter for a while before firmly telling her that it is time for them to stop playing because he wants to cuddle Mummy now. And when Daddy comes home from work a loving mother insistently pushes her son away from her, telling him she wants to be with Daddy now that he has come home, but that after supper Daddy will play with him.

From this prototypical scenario it is evident that girls' and boys' experiences of this stage of develoment are not symmetrical. Both boys and girls need to be granted some gratification of their possessive attachment to their opposite-sexed parent, while at the same time being somewhat coercively propelled into relinquishing that possessiveness in favour of modelling themselves, by identification, on the attributes of their same-sexed parent. But both boys and girls typically spend much more time with their mothers than their fathers, so a boy's possessive attachment to his mother is likely to be greater than a girl's possessive attachment to her father. In the ordinary course of events, a boy has to struggle harder to free himself from his mother and attain sexual autonomy than a girl has to struggle to free herself from her father and attain her sexual autonomy. (When, for whatever reason, a boy is overwhelmed by his symbiotic attachment to his mother it may be associated with his becoming homosexual. And the generally easier task for a girl of separating from her father may, to some extent, account for the greater prevalence of male over female homosexuality.)

What emerges out of all of this is the child's character which, broadly speaking is his or her morality and ability appropriately both to control and nurture his or her own and others' selfish impulses in the light of recognition of the need to compromise between his or her own and others' desires. The child is now able appropriately sometimes to feel responsible or guilty, and sometimes to blame others. The child is now capable of sharing and caring responses towards other people, and also expressing a considerable degree of self-discipline in maintaining his or her own general well-being. Now he understands the justifications for many of the prohibitions that were imposed on him when he was a toddler which, at that time, he was made non-comprehendingly simply to obey. Now he fears the retribution of his own conscience as much as the withdrawal of the approval of his mother and father.

The child now knows that "giving" as well as "taking" is inevitably demanded of him if he is to receive the affectionate attention he wants from others. From now on, he or she is implicitly aware that tenderness and aggression (Venus and Mars) have to be balanced in the expression of his or her desire for intimacy with others.

Seven
Saturn square Saturn

At this time the child experiences her or his first "identity crisis". Insofar as the Saturn aspect is a square, it is an introverted crisis, more associated with the child's private awareness rather than to do with his relationships to other people. This is the time when the child first becomes aware of death in a realistic way and knows that everybody, including his mother and father and, most terrifyingly, he himself will one day die. The fear of death is defended against by all human beings, and exaggeratedly so in childhood, from about this age onwards. Some children will openly express their terror of death, but for others it will be a closely guarded secret, observable only in the many compulsive rituals and magical rites they surround themselves with in their fearful bids to "stop bad things happening" (the ultimate "bad thing" being death) or in their inchoate fears of "bogey men" or animals or ... any number of things. More defiantly, some children revel in war games, horror stories, and violent films - the more gruesome the better - although girls are more inclined to prefer psychological to physical viciousness. However, these attitudes are only partly successful defences against the fear of death, which is the greatest threat to the child's confidence at this time. Cynicism and depression are more often experienced by a child during this stage of development than is commonly realized. Children are as capable of being depressed as adults, but are not articulate enough to describe the state as adults do. Prolonged quiet withdrawal from activities or from interactions with other people suggest a child may be depressed and in need of being loved back to life with abundant physical and verbal expression of affection. When there is no obvious precipitating cause for a child's depression (such as the death of a loved person or a pet) or justified depression extends into weeks or months, psychotherapeutic help should be sought.

But if parents themselves have a wholesomely positive attitude to life they need not fear that their seven-year-old's transient negativity will be lasting. However unspoken a child's fear of death is, parents need to be sensitive to it. If a child does express explicit fear of his own or others' deaths, in normal circumstances, he should be told something along the lines of, "Yes, everybody dies one day, but not until they are ready. Mummy and Daddy and you probably won't die for a very, very, very long time, until we've done all the things we want to". Do not describe death as "like going to sleep", which readily invokes in a child a fear of going to sleep; nor even "stopping breathing", which may prompt a child to fear that unless she self-consciously breathes she will die. Probably the best verbalization for a child is some form of tautology like, "You just stop being alive".

When a grandparent or other loved old person dies, a child might be told, "She was happy to die because she had had her turn of being alive and had done all the things she wanted to do. Of course it's sad for us that we won't see her again, but she can still make us happy when we remember her and talk about her."

When the death of a loved relative or friend is tragically untimely, there is an added dimension of anger and (irrational) guilt that needs to be expressed by the bereaved survivors. The death of either parent before the child has reached full maturity- which is astrologically not until the first Saturn return at twenty-nine - is probably the greatest tragedy that can befall a child. At the deepest level of the child's being, the untimely death of a parent is experienced as overwhelming abandonment and cannot but have profound and permanent consequences for the child. A secondary consequence of the premature death of a parent is the child's appreciation of the "unfairness" of the fact that his parent was not granted enough life to fulfil his or her potential. This fact may seriously inhibit the child in fulfilling his own potential throughout his life. That is, it is as if the child is unwilling to exploit his "unfair advantage" of more life to live than his parent had. The negativity of these consequences can be minimized by the prompt help of a competent psychotherapist, who can facilitate the child in "working through" the implications of his bereavement before they are unhealthily suppressed or repressed.

Ten
Saturn trine Saturn

This is a period of quiet equilibrium in the child before the storm of puberty. Children of this age have achieved a stable understanding of their own identity. All being well, by this time they have acquired basic numeracy and literacy, have become proficient in forming relationships with their peers, and usually hve a same-sexed "best friend". They also feel pride in their status of being at the "top" of their primary school.

Usually parents feel they have nothing to complain or worry about in their children at this age. The most likely difficulty is the possibility that parents at around this stage in their children's development may find themselves disapproving of a friend their child has made, and are prompted to tell the child this and discourage the continuance of the friendship. However, it is important for parents to realize that no friendships between people - children or adults - are arbitrary. There is always a significant meaning and value in any intimate relationship formed between people, no matter how implausible the relationship may appear to be at a superficial, face-value level. By all means express your disapproval of behaviour you don't like in your child's friend, but also encourage your child to tell you - if she can - what it is she most likes about this particular friend. This may provide you with some deep understanding of your child and her emotional needs that you did not before realize.

If you are nonetheless deeply concerned that your child's friend is a truly bad influence on her, diplomatically tell your child's friend's parents about your concern that both your children are behaving in disturbing ways that you feel sure upset the other parent as much as you. See if you can join forces - parent to parent - to modify the undesirable influence your children have on each other. Better this than forcibly breaking up the friendship, which is a cruel thing to do and should only be considered as a very last resort.

Eleven to Twelve
Jupiter conjunction Jupiter

As the first Jupiter cycle in the life is completed and added to the equilibrium and self-control of the Saturn trine Saturn transit at age ten, at age eleven to twelve the child's calm and confident commonsensical attitude to life reaches its peak, and he looks forward to the excitement of starting secondary school. The new Jupiter cycle is represented in the child beginning a new cycle of growth and progress in his education, and increased freedom through acquired competencies. He or she experiences and enjoys new privileges, like staying up later in the evenings, perhaps being allowed for the first time to ride his bicycle to school, increased pocket money, etc. If this is their first child, parents may feel that their essential task of parenting is accomplished and they are proud of themselves and their child for the disciplined, sensible, considerate young person he or she has become. Little do they know!

Fourteen to Fifteen
Saturn opposition Saturn and Uranus sextile Uranus

Almost overnight the calm, controlled, sensible, considerate child becomes a seething cauldron of hormones, often displaying wild mood swings depicted by all the novel excitement of becoming fully sexually aware (Uranus) and the reality (Saturn) that the world and parents and teachers will not allow them the fulfillment of all their impulses. These Saturn and Uranus transits are amongst the most disturbing combination that most people experience in their lives (although a similar crisis arises at around thirty-eight to forty-two). Whereas the first crisis of confidence accompanying the Saturn square at age seven was an introspective one, demanding new ways of coping with the self in the face of mortality, the Saturn opposition finds expression as an extraverted first poignant awareness that other people exert power and control over us against our own will. Combined with the Uranus sextile, the typical response to the coercion of parents and teachers and the restrictions of the world-in-general is at least protest if not outright rebellion. There is probably only one more disturbing state of being than being a fourteen to fifteen-year-old and that is being the parent of one! However, parents can find comfort in the fact that their moody and difficult pubescent child is perfectly normal. Indeed, in those cases whee parents proudly proclaim that their pubescent children are "no trouble at all" and remain as compliant, polite, and obedient as previously have cause to be concerned that their child is incipiently seriously disturbed, even though the pathology may not become fully apparent until the child is in his or her twenties or thirties. Then it will be, through the breakdwon of adult relationships, the failure of ambition, or just general misery that psychotherapeutic intervention may be required to correct his or her failure to live out the natural tempestuousness of puberty.

Puberty is the challenge for parents to rise to their highest skills in their relationship to their children. All human beings, however healthy, naturally have some neurotic tendencies, and it is these that parents are challenged, as far as is humanly possible, to become aware of and control in relationship to their pubescent and adolescent children. Following is a description of the five broad neurotic components that all people can have in their personalities and the pitfalls that each needs to be aware of and seek to modify. Being human, no parent is going to succeed fully in this task, but doing the best we possibly can for our children is ultimately the most creative and rewarding challenge of our lives.

The Perfectionist Parent
Perfectionist parents demand and get obedience and respect from their children. In return, they care for their children, physically and morally, with unflagging and utterly reliable devotion. No child of a Perfectionist parent ever has cause to doubt that his or her school uniform will be washed and ironed for school tomorrow, or that his or her material and educational needs will be securely provided for until he or she is well and truly grown-up.

Perfectionist parents tend to be extremely critical of their children, which is extremely destructive of the child's healthy self-esteem and should, as far as possible, be avoided. This does not mean that a child (or adult) never deserves correction - which is quite a different thing. There is all the difference in the world between, for example, "The trouble with you is you are selfish" and "That was a selfish thing to do". The former implies an unchanging attribute of the accused, which powerfully influences him or her to diminished self-esteem. The latter implies that the accused chose to behave in an undesirable way, but it is behaviour of this moment only and may be freely changed by anybody at their will.

It is hard enough for adults to disbelieve critical attributions imposed on them. For children, criticism is agonizing because they deeply believe everything they are told about themselves (especially by their parents), and the critical attributions imposed on them are likely to be negative beliefs they hold about themselves for the rest of their lives.

In so far as Perfectionist parents will tolerate no falling short of their moral and other values, they may seriously fail their adolescent children. Unless they transcend the rigidity of their demands for obedience and respect, out of the wisdom that adolescents must be somewhat disrespectful and disobedient to their parents in order to complete their maturation healthily, Perfectionist parents may pay the price of their grown-up children hating them. Their children will never cease to respect them, but for that respect to be compounded with affection rather than fear and hate, they must bend a little and admit to themselves and to their children that they have feet of clay. The extreme consequence for a child of having an excessively Perfectionist parent is a deep feeling of worthlessness and depression.

The Hurrier Parent
Hurrier parents demand that their children love them. Hurrier mothers are usually very happy in the first year of motherhood, interpreting their infant's overwhelming

neediness as an expression of love for them; but as soon as the baby becomes "wilful" they become less and less enamoured of parenthood. Children are usually frightened of the volatile unpredictability of their Hurrier parents, and grow up to have little expectation of any emotional security to be derived from them.

Hurrier parents are glad of every intimation that their children are growing less dependent on them, and they are inclined happily to acquiesce to the first adolescent demands their children make to leave home and live their own lives. The children of Hurrier parents are granted a great deal of licence in their adolescence which, superficially, they want. But deeply they know they are being deprived of the control they need and the feeling of being cared for when appropriate restrictions are firmly imposed on their freedom. Even adolescents know, in a vague way, that the outcome of fulfilling their every immediate desire is not always happy, and they rely on the greater knowledge and conviction of their parents to stop them doing what is not good for them even though, being adolescents, they are likely to protest. Appropriately controlled children feel loved, uncontrolled children feel unloved.

When their children have left home, Hurrier parents expect their children regularly to telephone them to see how they, the parents, are but show little interest in finding out how their children are managing their lives and what help they might be to them. The children may remain tied to a continuing relationship with Hurrier parents by a sense of obligation or pity but they know they have to look elsewhere for any reliable nurturance for themselves. The extreme consequence for child of having a Hurrier parent is a deep sense of loneliness and inability to be a responsible member of society.

The Doormat Parent
The Doormat parent is overwhelmingly concerned that his or her children are well-scrubbed, "nicely" dressed, well-spoken and well-behaved enough to call forth credit to themselves from family, friends, neighbours, and their children's teachers. They value conformity above all other values. They fear being disliked by their children, and so indulge them materially as much as they can possibly afford. They presume that this is a measure of their great affection for their children, for which the children are expected to be duly appreciative and, as they grow up, increasingly to reciprocate their parents' gifts and favours.

Doormat parents are committed to the closely-guarded and insistent presumption that theirs is an unequivocally happy family. They are profoundly hurt nd shocked by their pubescent and adolescent children's defiance, anti-conformity, and general lack of consideration for them, and they loudly bemoan, "After all we've done for you..." Eventually, they are likely to get from their children just what they deserve: respectful consideration in outer action which pays lip service to affection, without any of the authentic feeling that they, the parents, crave. They feel hurt by their children, but never realize that they are getting back from them exactly what they have given. And these parents usually go on, throughout their lives, giving material things to their children in the name of love. The extreme consequence for a child of having a Doormat parent is an inability to express authentic feelings or to form truly intimate relationships with others.

The Try Harder Parent
Try Harder parents are very fond of telling their children how lucky they are to have the material and other privileges and opportunities denied them, the parents, in their childhoods. While, on the surface, the parents insist how glad they are that their children have so many advantages they never had, the children hear the much louder and truer unspoken

message of envious discontent with their lives. In response, the children pity their parents and are unwilling to make them envious, which they know their parents would be if they, the children, dared to achieve the worldly success or happiness they believe their parents were so unfairly denied. Furthermore, if the children do succeed, in whatever way their parents did not, the children feel they are not entitled to take credit for getting what they want in life; it is all due to the "luck" of the advantages they were given by their "unlucky" parents.

The adult children of Try Harder parents continue to pity their parents and defend them to the world at large, but they also bitterly resent their parents for their crippling of them, and this resentment is often expressed as regular outbursts of aggressive and hostile quarrels with them. Try Harder parents need to become aware that the greatest gift we can give our children is our contentment with our own lives. The extreme consequence for a child of having a Try Harder parent is to feel him- or herself a failure in the world and to be hostilely aggressive towards the world in general and authority figures in particular.

The Stiff Upper Lip Parent
Stiff Upper Lip parents enjoy parenthood very much because it legitimizes their felt need to "earn" affection by giving without any expectation of being given to in return. They are wise as parents because, by default, they know the truth that children are not really capable of loving in the mature sense of the word until they have been given love bounteously and without price until their twenty-odd year maturational process is complete. Stiff Upper Lip parents are deeply gratified by the mere glad acceptance by their children of the affection they give them, which acceptance they so doubt in their relationships with their adult peers. Stiff Upper Lip parents often feel the deeply wounded loneliness of their own childhoods to be largely healed by the happiness of their relationships to their children.

The respect in which Stiff Upper Lip parents fail their children is in their unwillingness to allow their children to express emotional pain. In so far as they have found it necessary to protect themselves against their own emotional deprivation as children by rigid self-control of their feelings, they cannot bear any emotional pain experienced by their children. It is as if they say desperately to their children, "Just don't feel pain. I'll do anything you like, so long as you are always happy". But in adolescence children quite natur-ally have to experience large emotional swings consonant with their hormones, and in response to their knowledge of their Stiff Upper Lip parent's inability to cope with their pains, they are forced unnaturally to protect their parent's vulnerability by pretending, as far as possible, that they are constantly optimistic and cheerful. The Stiff Upper Lip parent can learn from his or her children that to feel pain and express it makes people "human" and is not as unmanageable as they falsely presume it to be. To deny people their needed experiences of pain is as selfish as denying them the right to any of their happier experiences. The extreme consequence for a child of having a Stiff Upper Lip parent is a lonely inability to ask for or receive any affection from others.

Seventeen to Nineteen
Jupiter opposition Jupiter and Saturn trine Saturn

These Jupiter and Saturn transits declare that "the worst is over" for the adolescent - and his or her parents! The parents now reclaim, as a young adult, the child who is beginning again to be both exuberantly enthusiastic about life and appropriately self-disciplined and considerate of other people, the child they last saw, fleetingly, at the combined Jupiter and Saturn transits when he or she was between five and six years old. The young adult now has probably achieved some educational qualifications and is preparing, calmly and with control, to look forward to further education and the willing acceptance of adult responsibilities. But the final stage of moral maturity is still to be achieved, and the parents are put through their final major challenge in the rearing of their child.

At this stage the child knows that she still needs her parents to help her consolidate all their moral teachings and, in this respect, she continues to challenge them. With her now well-developed capacity for logical reasoning, she initiates arguments with her parents, launching a two-pronged attack on their reasoning and their values, with consumate debating skill and sophistry. But covertly she is begging them confidently to lay down the law from their own confident value system, so that she may firmly internalize their values and achieve confidence in herself. The last thing she really wants is for them to crumple under her attacks, although manifestly this seems to be her aim.

At first, most parents are inclined to fall into the adolescent's trap by resonding to her logical attacks on their beliefs and principles with their own logical reasoning, and the child often "wins" the argument. But, in due course, wise and loving parents realize what is going on and accept this final essential responsibility of child-rearing, which is insistently to assert the validity of their own beliefs and discount the relevance of any "facts" or logic to the contrary. Internally, the child is profoundly grateful, but is unlikely to show it or express thanks to her parents until she is confidently established in adult life herself and has probably become a good and affectionate parent herself. Then the mutual stable affection between parents and child, last experienced fully when the child was an infant, is finally restored.

Twenty-one to Twenty-two
Saturn square Saturn and Uranus square Uranus

Now the young adult steps out into grown-up life and makes his or her first autonomous choice: to "do his thing", sow his wild oats and live for present impulse; or to work hard to establish himself securely within the conventional structures of society. While the choice may not be a complete either-or, by and large one of these alternatives is chosen and the other put aside.

Twenty-two to Twenty-five
Jupiter conjunction Jupiter and Saturn sextile Saturn

Another combination of Jupiter and Saturn transits mark a further development of the now young adult's sensible, controlled, and enthusiastic embarkation on a new cycle of learning and assumption of adult responsibilities.

This is the time when, in most developed cultures, the child completes the gradual process of leaving his parents' home. The emotional process of making the radical detachment from parents associated with no longer living with them usually takes a few years to complete. In many societies, at about age eighteen children begin their tertiary education in places other than their home-town, which is a useful external structure students are granted that enables them to have left home during term-time and yet to return home during vacations, in a natural way that avoids any loss of face for them. Then by about age twenty-two the child should be capable of making the final severance of his attachment to his parents' home and creating his own domestic environment. Parents can know their child has attained psychological adulthood when he or she calls his own, rather than his parents' address "home". This is a poignant time for parents, especially mothers, who are bound to find new structures in their lives to replace the past twenty years devotion to the task of child-rearing. The child is deeply missed, but wise parents have been beginning the necessary adjustment to their own lives for some years.

Healthily, a child leaving home is continuing the natural process of separation from her parents that began when she was born. If the overall development of the child has been seriously hampered by any abnormality of events or circumstances in previous years, the impact of these may be felt in a young adult's inability willingly to leave his or her parents' home. He or she is likely to find justifiable excuses, such as the high cost of rented accommodation, unemployment, or whatever, but he is actually deeply demanding - albeit often unconsciously - to finish his "unfinished business" with his parents before he can become the self-sufficient adult they now expect him to be. In such cases parents need to accept the responsibility for the underlying difficulties in the child, whose symptom is his clinging to living with them. Parents who collude with or passively accept unhealthy clinging of their adult child out of their own unwillingness to face "the empty nest" and move forward to a new stage in their own lives, will pay the price of an ever-increasing resentfully hostile relationships with their child who, when he finally breaks free, may feel impelled to cut himself off from them completely.

Parents and children who healthily face the poignancy of the children leaving home in early adult life are typically surprised and happily rewarded a few years later with a new close intimacy that develops between them, especially when the children make their parents grandparents.

Twenty-eight to Thirty
Saturn conjunction Saturn, Uranus trine Uranus, and Neptune sextile Neptune

This is a time of reckoning and one of the most significant turning points in life. True adulthood begins now as the individual realizes the world is not his oyster, but rather that his life is severely circumscribed by his abilities, his childhood conditioning, and the consequences of the choices he has already made. Depression is common at this time, accompanied by a feeling of, "My life is nearly half over and I've accomplished nothing!" In truth, the life of the autonomous self is just beginning. Those who rebelled against staid conventionality at twenty-one now urgently want to "settle down"; those who created conventional structures in their lives may feel desperate to escape from the prisons they feel they have locked themselves in. Childhood is over; adulthood begins with the realization that only we can make our dreams come true by what we are willing to do for ourselves.

Thirty-four
Saturn sextile Saturn

As at twenty-four to twenty-five, a time of equilibrium and balance as conscious goals are pursued.

Thirty-five to Thirty-six
Saturn square Saturn

Between the crucial awareness associated with the first Saturn return at twenty-eight to thirty and the mid-thirties most young adults are progressively and diligently pursuing their personal goals. But at thirty-five to thirty-six stumbling blocks are encountered and/or a sense of boredom and stagnation sets in. Early ambitions for affluence and prestige may be well on their way to fulfillment, but the price now seems high. Life seems full of duty and responsibility.

Thirty-eight to Forty-four
Saturn opposition Saturn, Uranus opposition Uranus, Neptune square Neptune, and (for recent generations) Pluto square Pluto

Between thirty-eight and forty-four life crises crowd in on one another and the individual may wonder if he will ever again be free of depression, self-doubt, onerous burdens and obligations, nervous instability, confusion about anything and everything, painful confrontations, and forced catharses of his deepest hang-ups. This is a time of reckoning for choices made, and past personal goals are now seen as illusory in terms of their hoped for satisfactions. But concurrently there is excitement, albeit unstable and somewhat frightening, for this is also a time of revelation, when the mind is opened to new possibilities and, for the first time, the "other side" of some coin we have been trading with all our lives is seen. Long-buried ambitions, often dating back to the dreams of glory we had for ourselves at our first Saturn opposition when we were fourteen or fifteen, may re-surface and seek fulfillment. At first, in response to the excitement of this time, the individual may kick over the traces in whatever area of life his new awareness pertains to, and the "opposite" values of the past may be totally discarded. However, gradually, the new and the old are recognized as two sides of one coin and they become integrated at a higher level where they are no longer incompatible.

Forty-seven
Saturn trine Saturn

A period of steady and responsible work within the established structures of the individual's life, giving satisfaction and a sense of security.

Forty-nine to Fifty-one
Saturn square Saturn and Chiron conjunction Chiron (Previous significant Chiron to Chiron transits will have occurred at various times for different individuals because of Chiron's erratic speed in its orbit, but it returns to its natal place for everybody at fifty to fifty-one.)

The individual has no option now but to admit he or she is middle-aged, and there is a last surge of ambitious energy directed to the fulfillment of personal ambitions "before it is too late". Concurrently, especially for those people who are conscious of bearing deep scars from their childhood wounds, there is a dissolution of fears lived with up until now, and a serene self-acceptance begins to emerge.

Fifty-four
Saturn sextile Saturn

Personal challenges that were met at forty-nine to fifty-one are now integrated as achieved structures in life, and opportunities open up for new patterns of living. For many people this is associated with the last of their children leaving home.

Fifty-six to Sixty
Saturn conjunction Saturn, Uranus trine Uranus, and Neptune trine Neptune

This time is in many ways a recapitulation of the "identity crisis" of twenty-eight to thirty. We are again forced to face our limitations and we again feel that "time is running out".

As twenty-eight to thirty brought awareness of the limitations of our abilities and our childhood conditioning as a preliminary to autonomously pursuing our self-development, fifty-six to sixty brings awareness of how far we have fulfilled our worldly ambitions and recognition that the era of achievement in the wider world is essentially over. Now we should have, and appropriately want, more time to enjoy contemplative pursuits, general relaxation, and the enjoyment of life for its own sake. While we may not be able from now on to gain much more power in the external world, this is compensated for by our realization that we now care more for self-approval than for the world's evaluation of us. We are looking forward to progressive changes in our lives arising from our diminished need for striving, and we are becoming more idealistic and serene.

Sixty-three
Saturn square Saturn and Uranus square Uranus, a mature recapitulation of Twenty-one to Twenty-two.

As at age twenty-one when we had these same transits, we are again required to choose and, if possible, find a balance between freedom and structure in our lives. We are nearly old and, especially for men, there is a mixture of excitement and fear at the prospect of retirement. New and absorbing activities must be found to stucture the post-retirment years.

Seventy
Saturn opposition Saturn and Uranus sextile Uranus, a mature recapitulation of Fourteen to Fifteen

At seventy, everybody is aware that their "three-score-years-and ten" are up, and continued life is a bonus. Now is the time when we need to put our worldly affairs in order in readiness for death. But at the same time there is also a sense that our duties are finished and, with whatever life is left to us, we are entitled to "do our own thing", out of which a seventy-year old may develop a new enthusiasm or activity or new friendships, untrammelled by any "oughts".

Eighty-four to Eighty-eight
Saturn conjunction Saturn, Uranus conjunction Uranus, and Neptune opposition Neptune

Now the whole of our lives can be surveyed with wisdom and detachment. Ideally, with a total sense of selfhood, we withdraw from mundane concerns into a serene, mystical transcendance of the self and all its fears and strivings. Now is a good time to die.

Exercises

1. What are the 3 contexts that constantly inform our responses to life?

2. Which transits occur to everybody at age twenty to twenty-one?

3. Which transits constitute the "mid-life crisis"?

4. At approximately what ages do people experience a "Saturn return"?

5. At approximately what ages do people experience Saturn, by transit opposing its natal place?

6. What is the core conflict that all people experience at about the age of twenty-one?

7. What planetary energies best represent our conflicting quests for security and excitement?

8. Which planetary cycle neatly divides our lives into 3 phases of youth, vigorous adulthood, and spiritual maturity?

9. Which planet mediates between the conflicting impulses of Saturn and Uranus in our nature?

10. Which planetary energies best represent our conflicting desires for self-assertion and peaceful cooperation with others?

11. Which planetary energies best represent our conflicting needs to be realistic and also have dreams?

12. Which planetary energies best represent the difference between orthodox religion and mysticism?

13. Which planetary energies best represent the combination of lust and tenderness in the act of making love?

14. Which planetary energies best express our conflicting desires to compete with others and to be sensitively responsive to others' needs?

15. When you were twenty-one, did you respond more to the Saturn square Saturn or Uranus square Uranus transit that you experienced at that time? If you have passed your first Saturn return, how did you, at the time of your Saturn return, compensate for the choice you didn't make at twenty-one?

Do take into account the current life-stage of any person whose horoscope you are interpreting.

Don't mistake external events (or even obvious personality traits) as meanings in themselves. The meaning of anything pertaining to any human being can only be confidently known by asking the person (although some good "educated guesses" can be made from analysis of the horoscope).

Answers to Questions

Chapter 1
2(i) Saturn
 (ii) Neptune
 (iii) Uranus
 (iv) Pluto
 (v) Mercury
 (vi) Sun
 (vii) Moon
 (viii) Mars
 (ix) Jupiter
 (x) Venus
 (xii) Mars
 (xiii) Saturn
 (xiv) Jupiter
 (xv) Sun
 (xvi) Saturn
 (xvii) Mercury
 (xviii) Uranus
 (xix) Venus
 (xx) Sun
 (xx1) Jupiter
 (xxii) Venus
 (xxiii) Neptune
 (xxiv) Moon
 (xxv) Uranus
 (xxvi) Mercury
 (xxvii) Mars
 (xxviii) Pluto
 (xxix) Pluto
 (xxx) Neptune

Chapter 2
1a Earth
 b Air
 c Fire
 d Water
2a Fixed
 b Mutable
 c Cardinal

3a Uranus
 b Mercury
 c Neptune
 d Pluto
 e Venus
 f Saturn
 g Moon
 h Sun
 i Mars
 j Chiron
 k Jupiter
4a Sun
 b Mars
 c Venus
 d Pluto
 e Neptune
 f Jupiter
 g Saturn
 h Uranus
 i Chiron
 j Moon
 k Mercury

5a South
 b North

Chapter 3
1a Venus in Leo
 b Venus in Gemini
 c Neptune in Pisces
 d Mercury in Libra
 e Moon in Scorpio
 f Mars in Virgo
 g Sun in Aries
 h Saturn in Cancer
 i Saturn in Sagittarius
 k Chiron in Leo
 l Jupiter in Virgo

2a 1st
b 2nd
c 10th
d 6th
e 7th
f 12th
g 11th

3a Capricorn MC, Saturn in 7th house
 b Gemini on 2nd house cusp, Mercury in 9th house
 c Pisces Ascendant, Neptune in 7th

Chapter 4
1a conjunction
b opposition
c sextile
d inconjunct
e trine
f square

2a Moon inconjunct Venus
b Mars square Venus
c Mercury conjunct Neptune
d Sun opposition Saturn
e Saturn square Neptune
f Mercury trine Neptune
g Moon conjunct Mercury
h Mars trine Jupiter
i Moon conjunct Uranus
j Moon trine Uranus
k Moon opposition Uranus
l Sun conjunction Mars
m Sun conjunction Jupiter
n Sun conjunction Saturn

Chapter 5
Chart 4 is the horoscope of Mahatma Gandhi

Chart 5 is the horoscope of Shinichi Suzuki
Chart 6 is the horoscope of Princess Diana
Chart 7 is the horoscope of Muhammed Ali
Chart 8 is the horoscope of Bill Gates
Chart 9 is the horoscope of Uri Geller
Chart 10 is the horoscope of when Louis and August Lumi re recorded the first movie (which was of the men and women leaving their father's factory for their Noontime break).

2a 4th and 10th
b 5th
c 7th
d 11th
e 7th
f 12th
g 5th
h 3rd and 9th
i 3rd
j 3rd
k 8th
l 8th
m 9th

3 To reassure them
4 No
5 trine and Grand Trine
6 square and T-square

Chapter 6
1 righteousness
2 the need for certainty
3 denial and projection
4 their outer planets in aspect to our inner planets

293

5 Saturn
6 Venus and Mars
7 Chiron
8 Chiron
9a tense
 b harmonious
 c harmonious
 d tense
10 a composite chart
11 1st, 5th, 7th, and 11th
12 2nd, 6th, 7th, 8th, and 10th
13 double whammie
14 Uranus
15 Pluto
16 Neptune
17 bi-wheel
18 b and c (opposite Sun signs)
19 Moon and Mercury
20 Venus and Mars
21 Sun and Moon

Chapter 7
1 synastry
2a 5th
2b 11th
 c 9th
 d 12th
3a 2nd
 b 10th
4a 2nd
 b 6th
 c 12th
 d 3rd
5a 2nd
 b 9th
 c 4th
 d 5th
6a 1st
 b 3rd
 c 9th
 d 11th
7a 9th

b 10th
c 2nd
d 1st
8a 3rd
 b 6th
 c 7th

Chapter 8
1 trine and sextile
2 square, opposition, and inconjunct
3 conjunction
4 Venus and Mars
5 Sun and Moon
6 Ascendant
7 Saturn
8 Venus
9 Saturn (old) and Uranus (new)
10. Mars (old) and Pluto (new)
11 Jupiter (old) and Neptune (new)
12 5th
13 3rd and 6th
14 2nd and 7th
15 1st and 8th
16 4th
17 Sun and Mars
18 Moon and Venus
19 Uranus
20 Saturn
21 Pluto
22 Sun
23 Moon
24 Neptune
25 Mars

Chapter 9
1 Jupiter and Saturn
2 Moon
3 Sun
4 Moon
5 Mercury

6 Jupiter
7 at the Saturn return at age twenty-nine to thirty
8 Saturn
9 Jupiter
10 4th and 10th
11 first-born
12 Uranus
13 Jupiter and Saturn
14 Pluto
15 Mars
16 Jupiter
17 Neptune
18 Uranus
19 Saturn
20 Pluto
21 3rd

8 Saturn
9 Chiron
10 Mars and Venus
11 Saturn and Neptune
12 Jupiter and Neptune
13 Mars and Venus
14 Sun and Moon

Chapter 10
1 perceived sameness to ourselves
2 11th
3 mutual benefit
4 2nd (money, 6th (everyday work), 10th (career)

Chapter 11
1 our humanity, our age, and our individuality
2 Saturn square Saturn and Uranus square Uranus
3 Saturn opposition Saturn, Uranus opposition Uranus, Neptune
square Neptune, and Pluto square Pluto
4 twenty-nine to thirty, fifty-eight to sixty, eighty-eight to ninety
5 fourteen, forty-two, seventy
6 freedom versus responsibility
7 Saturn and Uranus

Index

anxiety (of clients) see professional practice
Ascendant-Descendant axis 38, 74 see also houses
aspects, in general, 46-70
  'hard' and 'soft' 48,70, 104-5, 164, 137-8
  closeness of 141-2
  orbs 122, 142
  outer to inner planets 104, 122-3, 141
astrologer, task of see professional practice
astrology
  and genetics 2,13,18,207-10
  and prophecy 11-14
  and religion 2-4,9-10
  and science 2
  and spirituality 4
  as algebra 1,11-13,71
  as empirical truth 2
  as language 13
  as magnetic fields 2
  as potential 1-2,18,72
  basic assumptions 1-2
  uses 13

bi-wheel 123
birth times (unknown) 42-3
blame and responsibility 4-5, 103-6,272 see also parenthood
Burton, Richard 143-55
business relationships 121,252

categorizing 107-8
certainty, need for 11,102-3
Charles, Prince 181-93
chart shapes 39-40,45
Clinton, Bill 127-136
composite charts 117-121
  and synastry 143

death 3,7,267
  fear of 6,11,272-4
  prediction of 11,88 see also astrologer, task of
Descendant see Ascendant-Descendant axis
destiny see fate and free-will
Diana, Princess 181-193

elements 19-22

family relationships
  child-parent 12,204
  cousins 237

family tree, biographical information 225-233
grandparent-granchildren 206-211, 237-9
parenthood 196-202, 235, 269-85
siblings 211-21, 237
twins 163-4, 212
fate and free-will 7-10, 15-16
fear of death 5, 11, 272-4
femininity and masculinity 142, 164-5 ,270-1
Final Cause see God
Freud, Lucien 207-11
Freud, Sigmund 207-11, 252-9
friendship 121,141-2, 163, 240-1

gender 13, 71, 107, 206
Genesis 3
genetic inheritance 2, 6, 13, 196, 206
genetics 13, 18, 207-10
God 2-3, 9-10, 15, 99, 105, 164
'good' and 'evil' 1, 2-4, 9-10, 13-14, 267

happiness and unhappiness 9-10
homosexual relationships 163
horoscopes, in general 1-2, 13, 18
house systems 37

houses 38, 40-2, 44-5, 72-4, 120-1
angular, succedent, and cadent 38
in synastry 142-3,165
rulers 40-42
human nature 13-14,71-2, 102-6, 267-9

IC-MC axis 38 see also houses
interpretation of horoscopes
general principles 71-4
quick and easy 107-27
interpretations in text:
Anita and Julie (friends) 243-51
Anita and Stella (sisters) 213-21
Bill Clinton and Monica Lewinsky 127-137
Daniel 75-81
Dr. Harold Shipman 84-87
Elizabeth Taylor and Richard Burton 143-155
Emma and her boss (work) 261-5
Esther and Mark (marriage) 165-170
Mark and Miriam (father and daughter) 202-6
Michael 81-84
Michael and Ruth (marriage) 123-7
Miriam and Tony (marriage) 170-81

297

Prince Charles and
Princess Diana 181-193
Sigmund Freud and Carl
Jung (work and friend-
ship) 252-9
Sigmund Freud and
Lucien Freud (grandfather
and grandson)
Susan and Helen (twins)
intimacy 16,101-6

Jung, Carl 252-9

Lewi, Grant 12
Lewinsky, Monica 127-37
Life:
  as game of cards 14-16
  as game of chess 12
  meaning of 4-10, 267-9
life cycles (astrological and
  psychological) see stages of
  life
love
  and lovingness 14-16
  and marriage relation-
  ships 121,163-5
luck 5

masculinity and femininity
  142, 164-5, 270-1
meaning of life 4-10, 267-9
Midheaven see IC-MC axis
modes 22-4
Moon's nodes 29-30
mysticism 5

orbs see aspects

pain 4, 7-8, 10
  in relationships 102-6
  and death 267
  avoidance of 13
paranoia 9
parenthood see family
  relationships
parents, personality types of
  Perfectionist 277-8
  Doormat 280
  Stiff-Upper-Lipper 281-2
  Hurrier 278-9
  Try Harder 280-1
planets 24-9
planetary inter-aspects see
  aspects
planetary rulers 24-9
prediction 11-14
  of death 11
professional practice
prophecy 11-14

quadruplicities see modes

relationship analysis, quick
  and easy 121-3
relationships
  astrologer and client 87-9,
  98
  between near contemp-
  oraries 104, 247
  domestic 165
  family see family relationships

friendship see friendship relationships
homosexual see homosexual relationships
love and marriage see love and marriage relationships
purpose of 163-4, 195, 275
twins see family relationships
work see work relationships
religion 9-10 see also God
responsibility
  and blame 103-6, 271-2 see also parenthood
  of astrologer see professional practice
reward and punishment 7-10
righteousness, quest for 102-4

samenesses and differences between people 14-15, 163-4
self-esteem 5-7, 103-4
sexuality 270-1
Shakespeare, William 88
shape of chart see chart shapes
Shipman, Dr. Harold 84-7
signs (of the zodiac) 33-7
spirituality 4
stages of life (astrological and psychological)
  five to six 269-72
  seven 272-4
  ten 274-5
  eleven to twelve 275-6
  fourteen to fifteen 276-7
  seventeen to nineteen 282-3
  twenty-one to twenty-two 283-4
  twenty-two to twenty-five 284-5
  twenty-eight to thirty 285-6
  thirty-four 286
  thirty-five to thirty-six 286
  thirty-eight to forty-four 286-7
  forty-seven 287
  forty-nine to fifty-one 287-8
  fifty-four 288
  fifty-six to sixty 288
  sixty-three 289
  seventy 289
  eighty-four to eighty-eight 289
sun-sign interactions (144) 108-17
synastry 140-56
  between composite and natal charts 143
  double-whammies 122, 141
  elements and modes 121
  gender significance 142
  houses 142-3, 165

in friendship 240-1
in love and marriage 164-5
in work relationships 252
inner planets and Ascendants by sign 121
like permanent transits 141
orbs 122, 141
outer to inner planet 122-3, 140-1
planets in houses 142-3
sameness and comple-mentarity 163-4
sun-signs 108-17

Taylor, Elizabeth 143-55
theology 10
transits 2, 141 see also stages of life
triplicities see elements

unknown birth times 42-3

work relationships 121, 252

Other astrology titles from Capall Bann

Interpreting Solar and Lunar Returns Janey Stubbs & Babs Kirby
The Solar Return Chart is a unique forecasting tool. It gives a broad overview of the year ahead as well as shading in the subtler nuances of experience which may not show up in other forms of predictive astrology. This is the first book to offer a psychological and growth orientation to forecasting using Solar and Lunar Returns. The reader is taken through a step-by-step procedure of how to interpret Solar returns, and clear explanations are given of calculation and timing methods. As well as an examination of Lunar Returns, information on Returns for Mercury, Venus and Mars is also included; while detailed case studies demonstrate how a synthesis of the various techniques can be achieved. An important book for the beginner and the advanced astrologer alike, Interpreting Solar and Lunar Returns presents a new approach to a traditional predictive technique and gives guidance on its use in humanistic astrology.   ISBN 1 86163 119 7   £13.95

Sun Moon and Stars   Sheena McGrath
It's amazing how many stories there are about those little lights in the sky. Even fairly obscure stars often had an interesting or quirky tale attached to them. Ancient peoples had a much better view of the sky than most of us do today, which probably spurred them on. While the Classical myths of the constellations had to be included, if for no other reason than that the Latin names are based on those myths, there are also a great many of other, less well-known, myths and names for the constellations, planets, stars and comets. This book will give you a whole new way to see the stars and planets, as well as the history of mythology and science with ancient peoples' explanations of our universe.   ISBN 1 86163 210X   £12.95

A selection of other titles from Capall Bann

Healing With Astrology   Sue Lilly
This book is intended to act as a guide for a complete beginner, in both astrology and healing, and to act as food for thought for a more seasoned practitioner in both. Sue Lilly has developed a cunning way of combining kinesiology and astrology to give a very powerful, but simple, healing tool. Healers now have access to astrological charts through the many computer programs and chart services available and can use the practical advice in this book to take advantage of astrological information to augment their skills and knowledge. This book broadens and enhances healing skills in beginners and those already practising alike. ISBN 186163 184 7   £9.95

Everything You Always Wanted To Know About Your Body, But, So Far, Nobody's Been Able To Tell You   Chris Thomas & Diane Baker
"...easy to understand...insight into how you can heal yourself...comprehensive guide" Here's Health Have you ever wondered why some people become ill and others do not? Why some people recover from illness and others do not? Do you know how your body really works? Why do diets rarely work? Is there an alternative approach to treating symptoms of illness instead of using prescriptive drugs? This book leads you through the body, organ by organ, system by system, and explains in clear language how illness arises and what to do about it. It explains the workings of the human body in simple language and clear illustrations; which elements are connected together and why they can influence each other. It also relates each region and organ to its associated chakra and how our day-to-day lives have an influence on our health and well-being. This book also takes a look at how some illnesses are brought about by past life traumas and looks at ways of healing the symptoms of illness without the need for prescriptive drugs: Bach Flower Remedies, Reflexology, Herbalism, Biochemic Tissue Salts and Homeopathy are the main approaches used, with a further twenty seven therapies fully described. An extensive, comprehensive look at the body and illness. ISBN 186163 0980 17.95

Creative Astrology - Experiential Understanding of the Horoscope   ed. Prudence Jones
Creative Astrology allows us to take interpretation into our own hands, answering simultaneously 'What is happening?' and 'What can I do about it?'. Through experiencing astrological placements directly, by means of the symbolic imagination, group dynamics, music, dance, ritual, role playing and modelling, we are able to take control of the way we embody these seemingly external 'influences' in our lives. Creative Astrology helps heal the split between 'external' and 'internal' reality and restores the sense of power over our own destiny that can sometimes be undermined by a detailed knowledge of astrological trends. Several of the original exponents of Creative Astrology share their experiences and their understanding. Prudence Jones describes the history of Creative Astrology and suggests some reasons for its emergence. ISBN 186163 0808   £11.95

FREE DETAILED CATALOGUE

Capall Bann is owned and run by people actively involved in many of the areas in which we publish. A detailed illustrated catalogue is available on request, SAE or International Postal Coupon appreciated. **Titles can be ordered direct from Capall Bann, post free in the UK** (cheque or PO with order) or from good bookshops and specialist outlets.

A Breath Behind Time, Terri Hector
A Soul is Born by Eleyna Williamson
Angels and Goddesses - Celtic Christianity & Paganism, M. Howard
The Art of Conversation With the Genius Loci, Barry Patterson
Arthur - The Legend Unveiled, C Johnson & E Lung
Astrology The Inner Eye - A Guide in Everyday Language, E Smith
Auguries and Omens - The Magical Lore of Birds, Yvonne Aburrow
Asyniur - Womens Mysteries in the Northern Tradition, S McGrath
Beginnings - Geomancy, Builder's Rites & Electional Astrology in the
    European Tradition, Nigel Pennick
Between Earth and Sky, Julia Day
Book of the Veil , Peter Paddon
The Book of Seidr, Runic John
Caer Sidhe - Celtic Astrology and Astronomy, Michael Bayley
Call of the Horned Piper, Nigel Jackson
Can't Sleep, Won't Sleep, Linda Louisa Dell
Carnival of the Animals, Gregor Lamb
Cat's Company, Ann Walker
Celtic Faery Shamanism, Catrin James
Celtic Faery Shamanism - The Wisdom of the Otherworld, Catrin James
Celtic Lore & Druidic Ritual, Rhiannon Ryall
Celtic Sacrifice - Pre Christian Ritual & Religion, Marion Pearce
Celtic Saints and the Glastonbury Zodiac, Mary Caine
Circle and the Square, Jack Gale
Come Back To Life, Jenny Smedley
Compleat Vampyre - The Vampyre Shaman, Nigel Jackson
Creating Form From the Mist - The Wisdom of Women in Celtic Myth and
    Culture, Lynne Sinclair-Wood
Crystal Clear - A Guide to Quartz Crystal, Jennifer Dent
Crystal Doorways, Simon & Sue Lilly
Crossing the Borderlines - Guising, Masking & Ritual Animal Disguise in the
    European Tradition, Nigel Pennick
Dragons of the West, Nigel Pennick

Earth Dance - A Year of Pagan Rituals, Jan Brodie
Earth Harmony - Places of Power, Holiness & Healing, Nigel Pennick
Earth Magic, Margaret McArthur
Egyptian Animals - Guardians & Gateways of the Gods, Akkadia Ford
Eildon Tree (The) Romany Language & Lore, Michael Hoadley
Enchanted Forest - The Magical Lore of Trees, Yvonne Aburrow
Eternal Priestess, Sage Weston
Eternally Yours Faithfully, Roy Radford & Evelyn Gregory
Everything You Always Wanted To Know About Your Body, But So Far Nobody's Been Able To Tell You, Chris Thomas & D Baker
Experiencing the Green Man, Rob Hardy & Teresa Moorey
Face of the Deep - Healing Body & Soul, Penny Allen
Fairies and Nature Spirits, Teresa Moorey
Fairies in the Irish Tradition, Molly Gowen
Familiars - Animal Powers of Britain, Anna Franklin
Flower Wisdom, Katherine Kear
Fool's First Steps, (The) Chris Thomas
Forest Paths - Tree Divination, Brian Harrison, Ill. S. Rouse
From Past to Future Life, Dr Roger Webber
From Stagecraft To Witchcraft, , Patricia Crowther
Gardening For Wildlife Ron Wilson
God Year, The, Nigel Pennick & Helen Field
Goddess on the Cross, Dr George Young
Goddess Year, The, Nigel Pennick & Helen Field
Goddesses, Guardians & Groves, Jack Gale
Handbook For Pagan Healers, Liz Joan
Handbook of Fairies, Ronan Coghlan
Healing Book, The, Chris Thomas and Diane Baker
Healing Homes, Jennifer Dent
Healing Journeys, Paul Williamson
Healing Stones, Sue Philips
Herb Craft - Shamanic & Ritual Use of Herbs, Lavender & Franklin
Hidden Heritage - Exploring Ancient Essex, Terry Johnson
Hub of the Wheel, Skytoucher
In and Out the Windows, Dilys Gator
In Search of Herne the Hunter, Eric Fitch
In Search of the Green Man, Peter Hill
Inner Celtia, Alan Richardson & David Annwn
Inner Mysteries of the Goths, Nigel Pennick
Inner Space Workbook - Develop Through Tarot, Cat Summers & Julian Vayne
In Search of Pagan Gods, Teresa Moorey
Intuitive Journey, Ann Walker Isis - African Queen, Akkadia Ford
Journey Home, The, Chris Thomas
Kecks, Keddles & Kesh - Celtic Lang & The Cog Almanac, Bayley
Language of the Psycards, Berenice
Legend of Robin Hood, The, Richard Rutherford-Moore

Lid Off the Cauldron, Patricia Crowther
Light From the Shadows - Modern Traditional Witchcraft, Gwyn
Living Tarot, Ann Walker
Lore of the Sacred Horse, Marion Davies
Lost Lands & Sunken Cities (2nd ed.), Nigel Pennick
The Magic and Mystery of Trees, Teresa Moorey
Magic For the Next 1,000 Years, Jack Gale
Magic of Herbs - A Complete Home Herbal, Rhiannon Ryall
Magical Guardians - Exploring the Spirit and Nature of Trees, Philip Heselton
Magical History of the Horse, Janet Farrar & Virginia Russell
Magical Lore of Animals, Yvonne Aburrow
Magical Lore of Cats, Marion Davies
Magical Lore of Herbs, Marion Davies
Magick Without Peers, Ariadne Rainbird & David Rankine
Masks of Misrule - Horned God & His Cult in Europe, Nigel Jackson
Medicine For The Coming Age, Lisa Sand MD
Medium Rare - Reminiscences of a Clairvoyant, Muriel Renard
Menopausal Woman on the Run, Jaki da Costa
Mind Massage - 60 Creative Visualisations, Marlene Maundrill
Mirrors of Magic - Evoking the Spirit of the Dewponds, P Heselton
The Moon and You, Teresa Moorey
Moon Mysteries, Jan Brodie
Mysteries of the Runes, Michael Howard
Mystic Life of Animals, Ann Walker
New Celtic Oracle The, Nigel Pennick & Nigel Jackson
Oracle of Geomancy, Nigel Pennick
Pagan Feasts - Seasonal Food for the 8 Festivals, Franklin & Phillips
Patchwork of Magic - Living in a Pagan World, Julia Day
Pathworking - A Practical Book of Guided Meditations, Pete Jennings
Personal Power, Anna Franklin
Pickingill Papers - The Origins of Gardnerian Wicca, Bill Liddell
Pillars of Tubal Cain, Nigel Jackson
Places of Pilgrimage and Healing, Adrian Cooper
Planet Earth - The Universe's Experiment, Chris Thomas
Practical Divining, Richard Foord
Practical Meditation, Steve Hounsome
Practical Spirituality, Steve Hounsome
Psychic Self Defence - Real Solutions, Jan Brodie
Real Fairies, David Tame
Reality - How It Works & Why It Mostly Doesn't, Rik Dent
Romany Tapestry, Michael Houghton
Runic Astrology, Nigel Pennick
Sacred Animals, Gordon MacLellan
Sacred Celtic Animals, Marion Davies, Ill. Simon Rouse
Sacred Dorset - On the Path of the Dragon, Peter Knight
Sacred Grove - The Mysteries of the Forest, Yvonne Aburrow

Sacred Geometry, Nigel Pennick
Sacred Nature, Ancient Wisdom & Modern Meanings, A Cooper
Sacred Ring - Pagan Origins of British Folk Festivals, M. Howard
Season of Sorcery - On Becoming a Wisewoman, Poppy Palin
Seasonal Magic - Diary of a Village Witch, Paddy Slade
Secret Places of the Goddess, Philip Heselton
Secret Signs & Sigils, Nigel Pennick
The Secrets of East Anglian Magic, Nigel Pennick
A Seeker's Guide To Past Lives, Paul Williamson
Seeking Pagan Gods, Teresa Moorey
A Seer's Guide To Crystal Divination, Gale Halloran
Self Enlightenment, Mayan O'Brien
Spirits of the Air, Jaq D Hawkins
Spirits of the Water, Jaq D Hawkins
Spirits of the Fire, Jaq D Hawkins
Spirits of the Aether, Jaq D Hawkins
Spirits of the Earth, Jaq D Hawkins
Stony Gaze, Investigating Celtic Heads John Billingsley
Stumbling Through the Undergrowth, Mark Kirwan-Heyhoe
Subterranean Kingdom, The, revised 2nd ed, Nigel Pennick
Symbols of Ancient Gods, Rhiannon Ryall
Talking to the Earth, Gordon MacLellan
Talking With Nature, Julie Hood
Taming the Wolf - Full Moon Meditations, Steve Hounsome
Teachings of the Wisewomen, Rhiannon Ryall
The Other Kingdoms Speak, Helena Hawley
Transformation of Housework, Ben Bushill
Tree: Essence of Healing, Simon & Sue Lilly
Tree: Essence, Spirit & Teacher, Simon & Sue Lilly
Tree Seer, Simon & Sue Lilly
Through the Veil, Peter Paddon
Torch and the Spear, Patrick Regan
Understanding Chaos Magic, Jaq D Hawkins
Understanding Past Lives, Dilys Gater
Understanding Second Sight, Dilys Gater
Understanding Spirit Guides, Dilys Gater
Understanding Star Children, Dilys Gater
The Urban Shaman, Dilys Gater
Vortex - The End of History, Mary Russell
Warp and Weft - In Search of the I-Ching, William de Fancourt
Warriors at the Edge of Time, Jan Fry
Water Witches, Tony Steele
Way of the Magus, Michael Howard
Weaving a Web of Magic, Rhiannon Ryall
West Country Wicca, Rhiannon Ryall
What's Your Poison? vol 1, Tina Tarrant

Wheel of the Year, Teresa Moorey & Jane Brideson
Wildwitch - The Craft of the Natural Psychic, Poppy Palin
Wildwood King, Philip Kane
A Wisewoman's Book of Tea Leaf Reading, Pat Barki
The Witching Path, Moira Stirland
The Witch's Kitchen, Val Thomas
The Witches' Heart, Eileen Smith
Witches of Oz, Matthew & Julia Philips
Wondrous Land - The Faery Faith of Ireland by Dr Kay Mullin
Working With Crystals, Shirley o'Donoghue
Working With Natural Energy, Shirley o'Donoghue
Working With the Merlin, Geoff Hughes
Your Talking Pet, Ann Walker
The Zodiac Experience, Patricia Crowther

FREE detailed catalogue and FREE 'Inspiration' magazine
Contact: Capall Bann Publishing, Auton Farm, Milverton, Somerset, TA4 1NE